I am full of a sense of promise, like I often have,
the feeling of always being at the beginning.

DIANE ARBUS   JULY 1957

Windblown headline on a dark pavement, N.Y.C. 1956

in the beginning

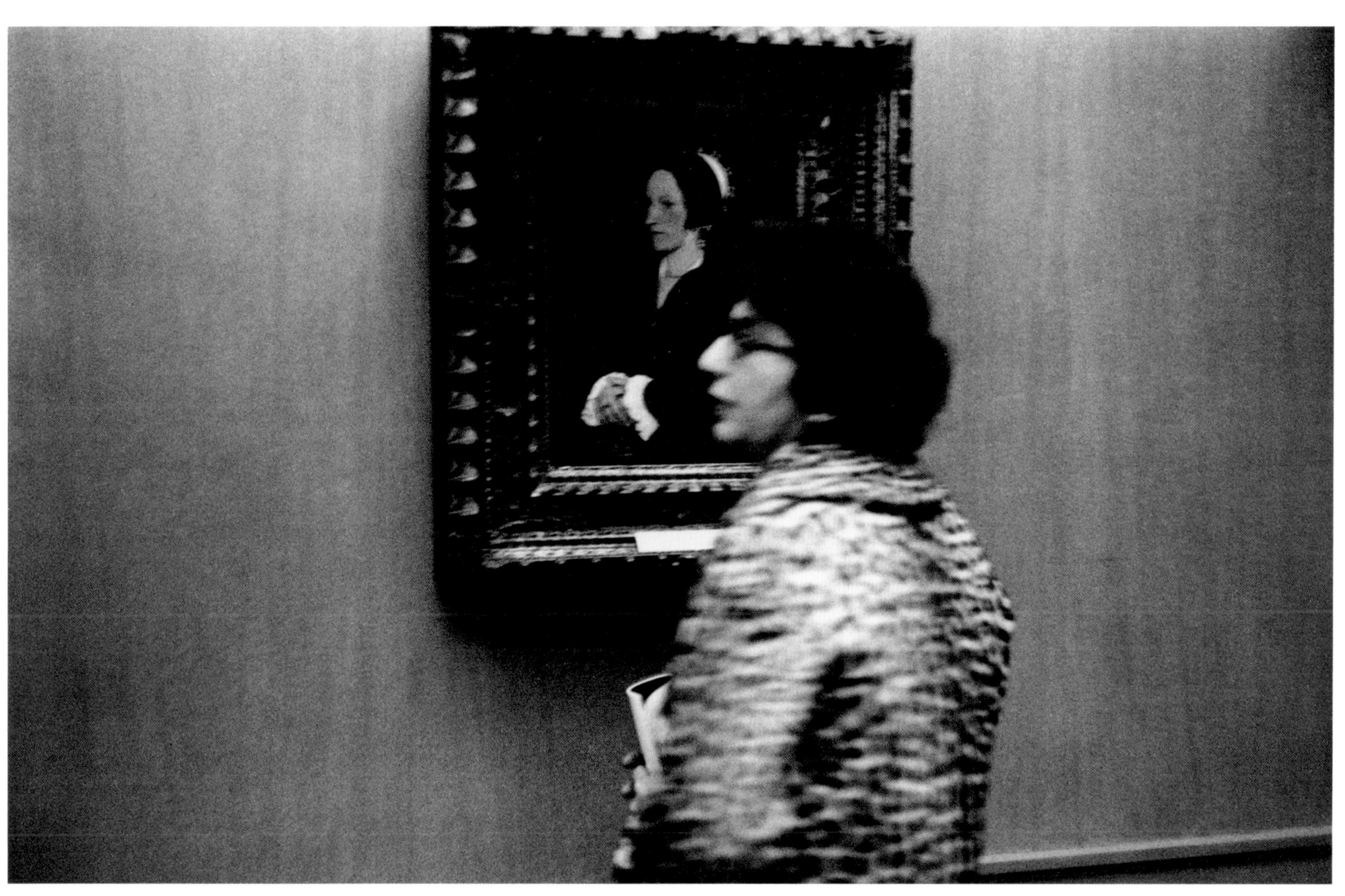

Lady in front of a portrait, N.Y.C. 1956

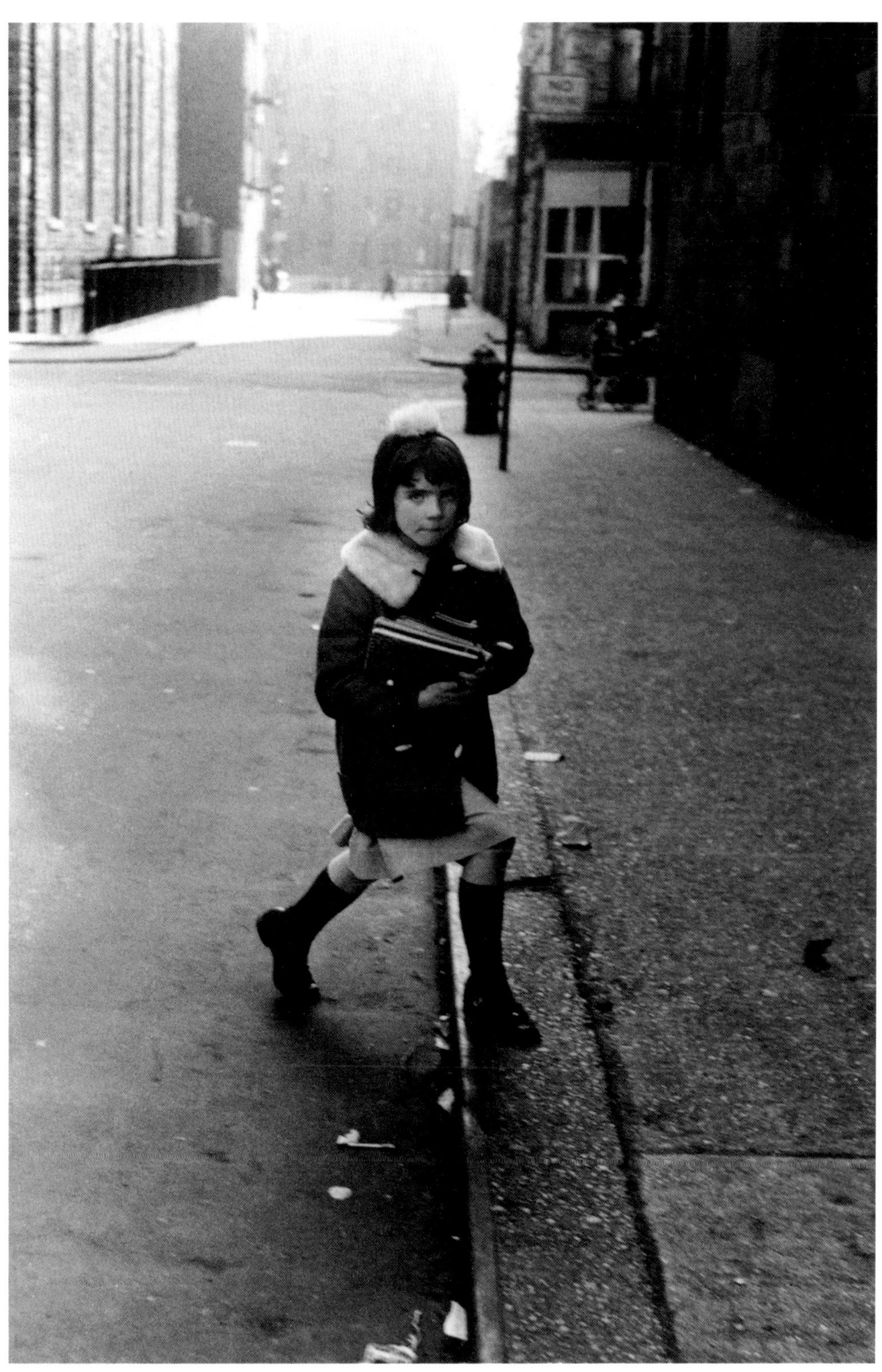

Girl with schoolbooks stepping onto the curb, N.Y.C. 1957

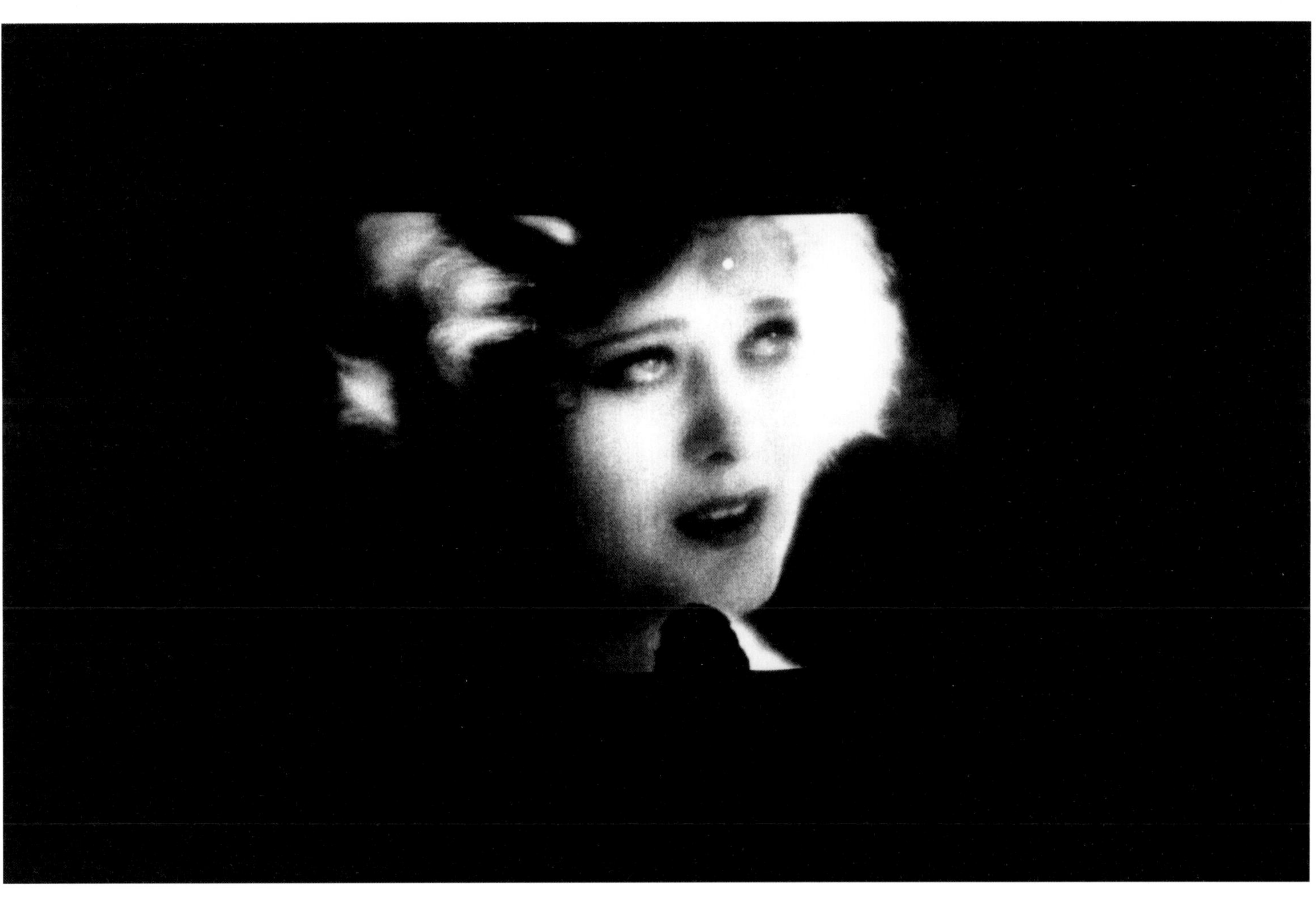

Blonde on screen about to be kissed 1958

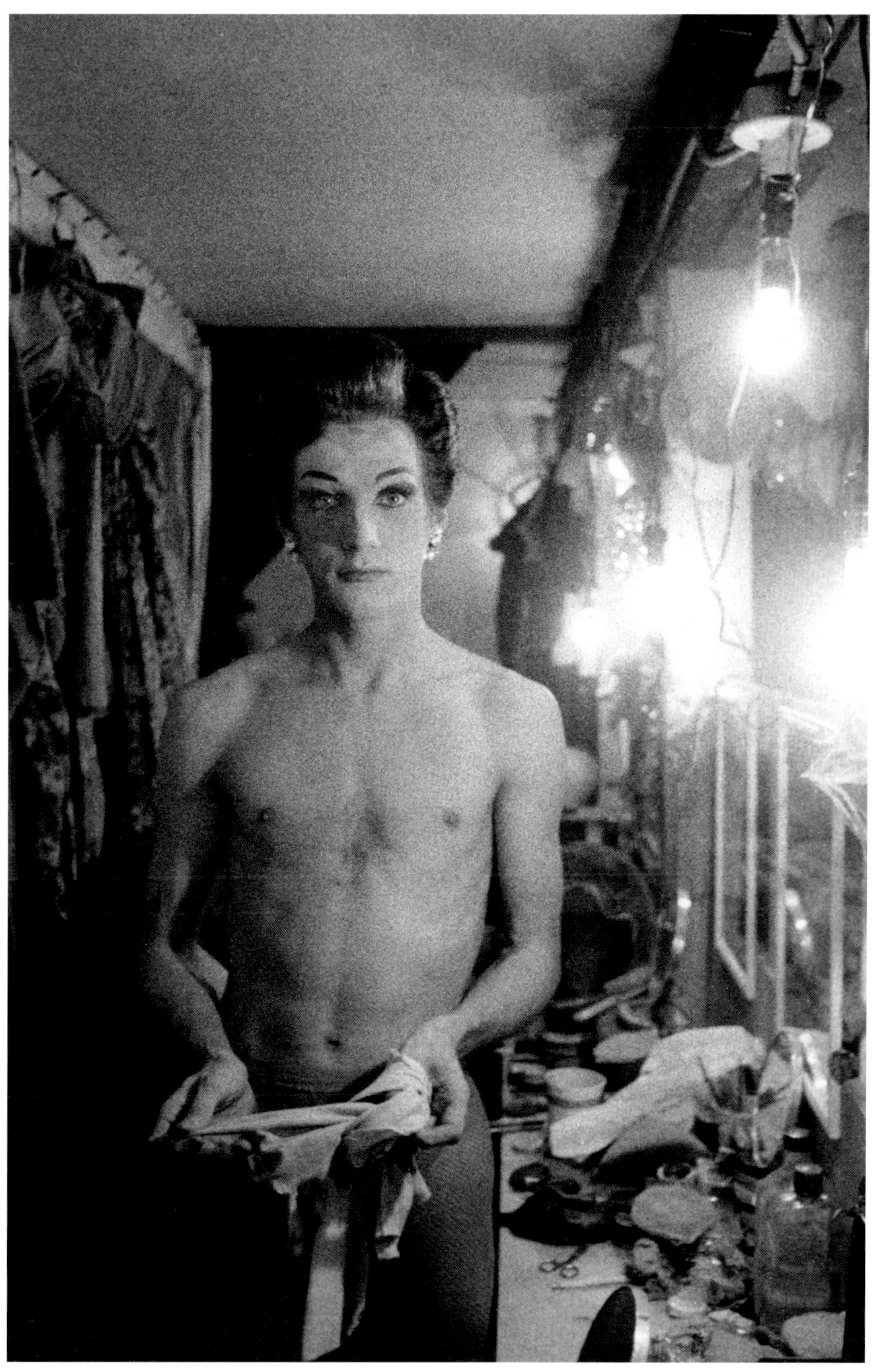

Female impersonator holding long gloves, Hempstead, L.I. 1959

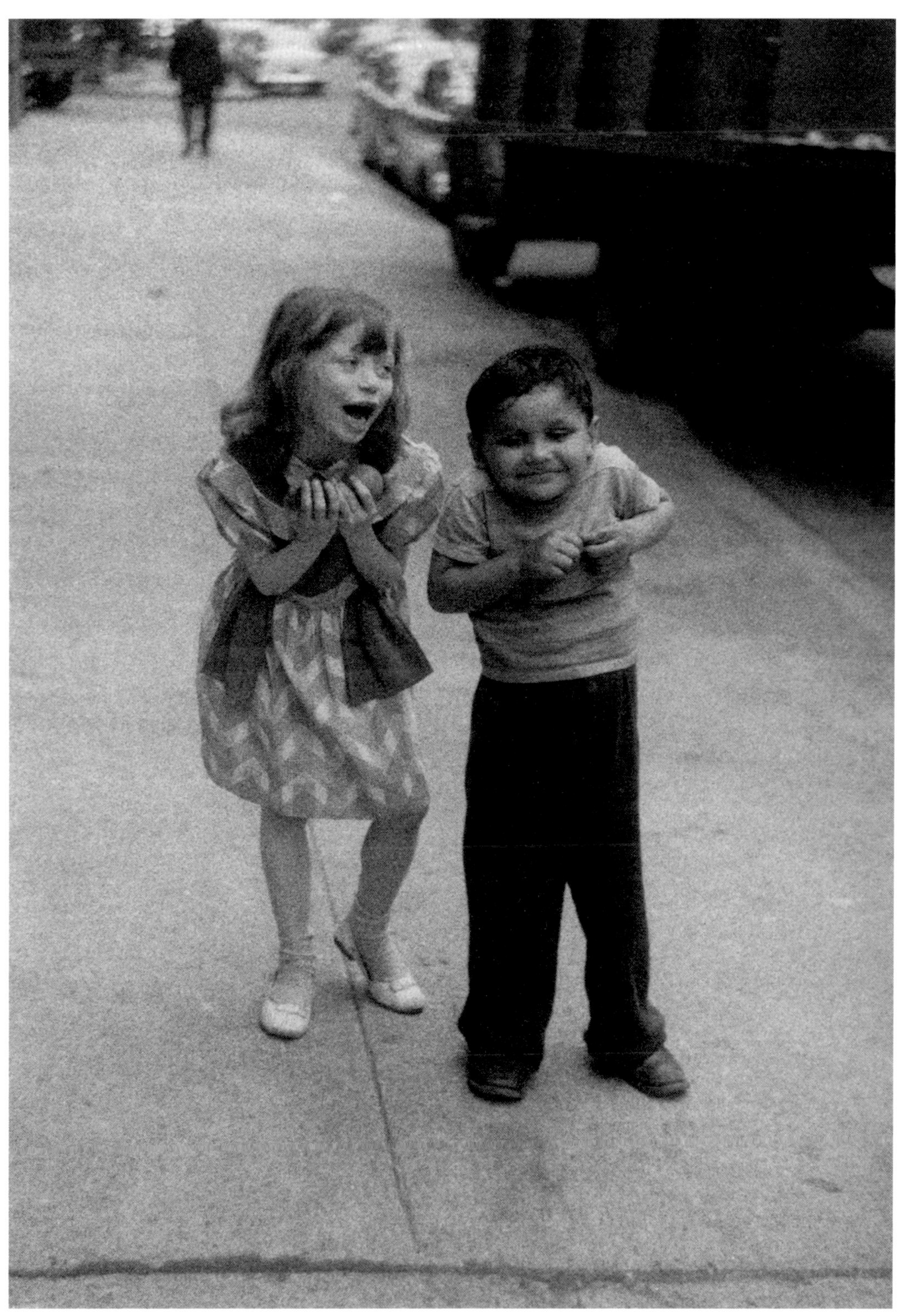

Child teasing another, N.Y.C. 1960

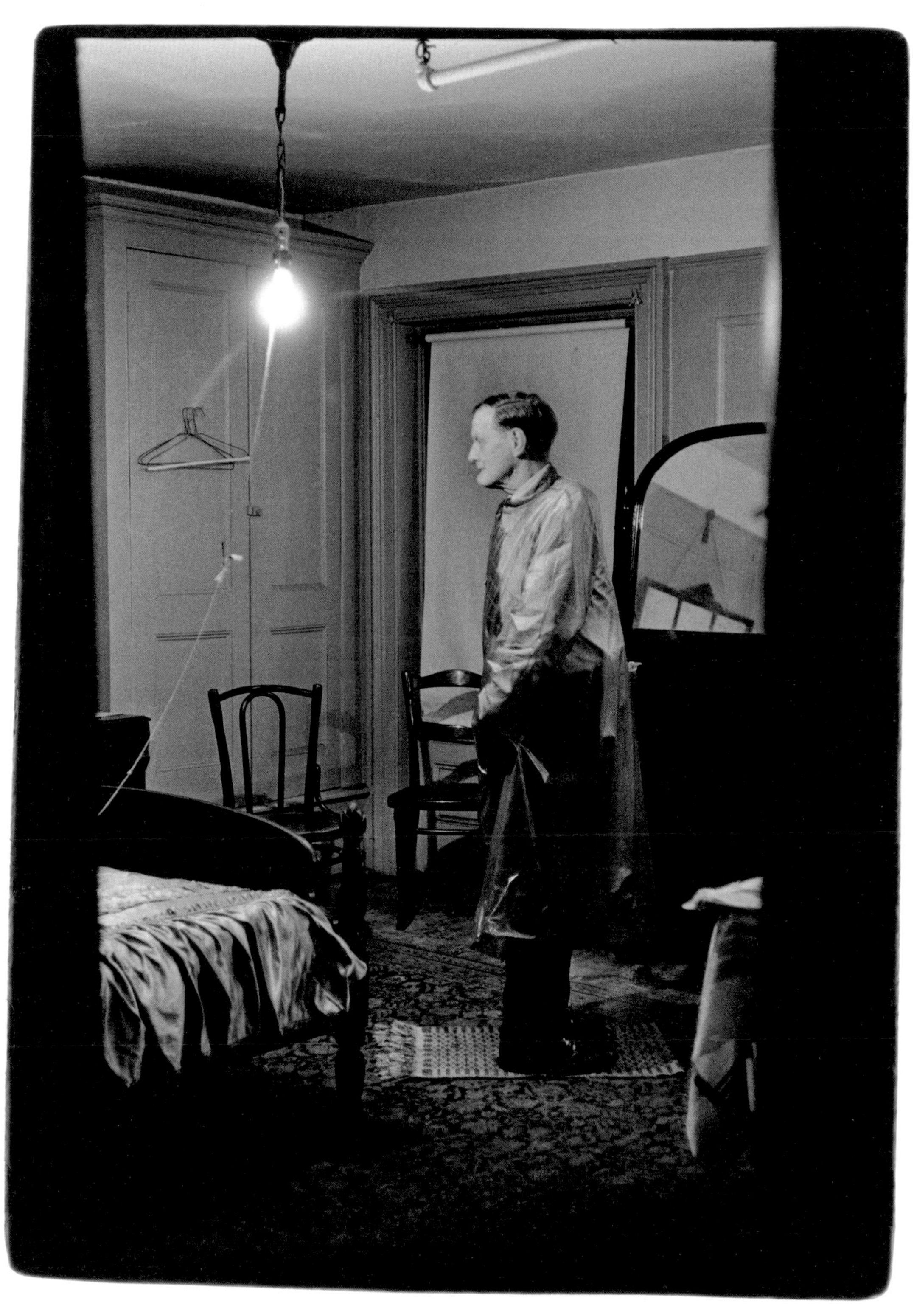

The Backwards Man in his hotel room, N.Y.C. 1961

diane arbus
in the beginning

1956–1962

JEFF L. ROSENHEIM

notes from the archive
KARAN RINALDO

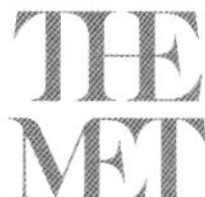

The Metropolitan Museum of Art, New York

Distributed by Yale University Press, New Haven

contents

22

director's foreword
THOMAS P. CAMPBELL

23

introduction
JEFF L. ROSENHEIM

203

in the beginning
JEFF L. ROSENHEIM

219

notes from the archive
KARAN RINALDO

240

list of works

258

acknowledgments

261

selected readings

264

index

267

credits

director's foreword

Few artists of the modern era are as renowned as Diane Arbus. Most of us can effortlessly visualize her photographs from their titles alone: *Child with a toy hand grenade in Central Park*; *Identical twins*; *A Jewish giant at home with his parents in the Bronx*. Her iconic images have been shown in museums worldwide and the subject of generations of critical commentary about the role of the camera in contemporary society. While Arbus did not live long enough to become internationally revered in her lifetime, she is today, and her photographs are among the masterpieces in the collection of The Metropolitan Museum of Art.

diane arbus: in the beginning focuses exclusively on the first seven years that she worked as an artist (1956–62) and is the initial publication to be drawn from The Met's Diane Arbus Archive. A gift from her daughters Doon Arbus and Amy Arbus in 2007, the archive is a treasury of photographs, negatives, notebooks, and correspondence. The Museum recognizes the profound degree to which the stewardship of the archive by The Estate of Diane Arbus has enhanced the understanding of the photographer and her legacy. We are deeply honored to be the permanent caretaker of these invaluable materials, the complex record of the creative process of one of the most provocative artists of the twentieth century.

For the last eight years the archive has been catalogued, housed, and studied by a team of museum curators and conservators led by Jeff L. Rosenheim, Karan Rinaldo, and Nora Kennedy. Their ongoing research forms the foundation of this volume and the exhibition it accompanies. It will be an eye-opener even for those already passionate about Arbus, as more than two-thirds of the photographs here have never before been published. The exhibition is made possible in part by the Alfred Stieglitz Society, whose members provide annual support for the Department of Photographs, and by the Art Mentor Foundation Lucerne.

Arbus's achievement is already the stuff of legend; now for the first time we can examine its origins.

THOMAS P. CAMPBELL
Director
The Metropolitan Museum of Art

introduction

The monograph *Diane Arbus*, with its eighty bold, square-format photographs — published in conjunction with the posthumous 1972 retrospective at the Museum of Modern Art, New York — continues to be regarded as the definitive embodiment of the photographer's art. Although the MoMA show and several subsequent exhibitions and publications have featured examples of Arbus's earlier 35mm work dating from 1956 to 1962, these photographs have always been presented in a supporting role, as antecedents of what was to follow rather than achievements in themselves.

The majority of this work — which comprises approximately half of the photographs Arbus printed during her lifetime — was at the time of her death stored in boxes in an inaccessible corner of her basement darkroom at 29 Charles Street in New York's Greenwich Village. These prints remained undiscovered for several years thereafter and were not inventoried until a decade later. It was only when the Diane Arbus Archive came to The Metropolitan Museum of Art in 2007 that this body of work began to be fully explored. What the research reveals is that the 1972 Aperture monograph was, in fact, chapter two; *diane arbus: in the beginning* is the essential chapter one. The book explores the genesis of Arbus's work and how she developed her evocative and often haunting imagery, honing her subject matter and in full possession of the many gifts for which she is now recognized the world over.

Arbus was fascinated by photography even before she received a camera in 1941 at the age of eighteen as a present from her husband, Allan. She made photographs intermittently for the next fifteen years, but in 1956 she numbered a roll of 35mm film #1, as if to tell herself that this moment would be her beginning. And it was.

JEFF L. ROSENHEIM
Curator in Charge
Department of Photographs

the mistake is to think people are
sealed and absolute. They are just
instruments of life and it flows
through them to the point where their
edges are invisible.

How often people act on each
other in imitation of the way
they are acted upon.

old woman + pig.
            to break this precedent
of the negative action
like changing gaits and the
long pause was the pain of it.

we spent such a long time
limited by sweetness and negation
like comfort in a walnut shell

instead of going into life we
presumed on what we had of it

It matters nothing if one is born
in a duck yard, if one has only
lain in a swans egg.
                    ugly duckling   A.

   A photograph flattens time at the
same instant and in the same way
as it flattens space. contains past
and future . . . . is its own
memory, its own oracle.

that which endures the earth
without being swayed by it.   I ching.

   2. anything that discloses or opens
something to the understanding
as to a subject, puzzle or problem.

selfless as melting ice

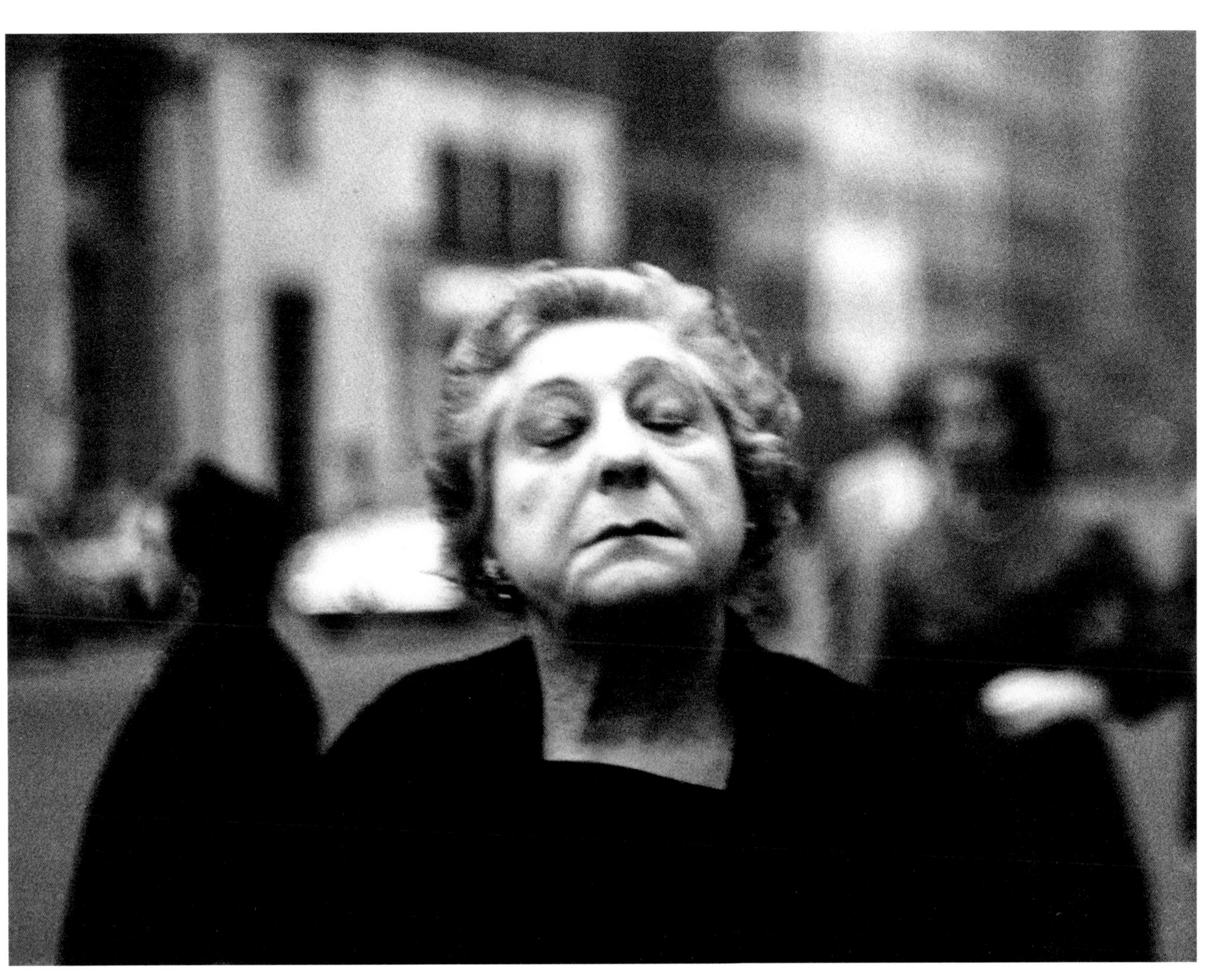

Woman on the street with her eyes closed, N.Y.C. 1956

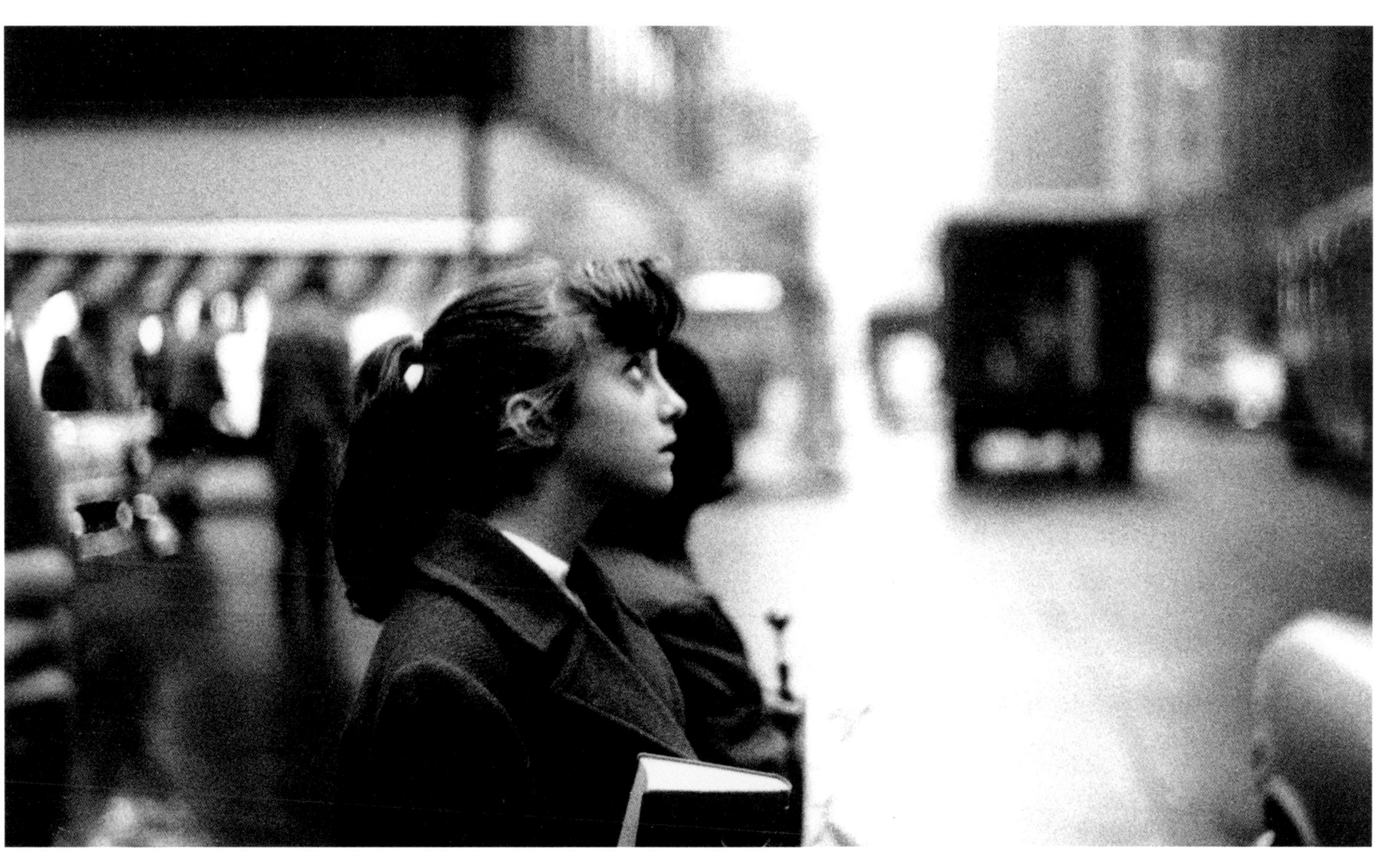

Girl in profile looking up, N.Y.C. 1956

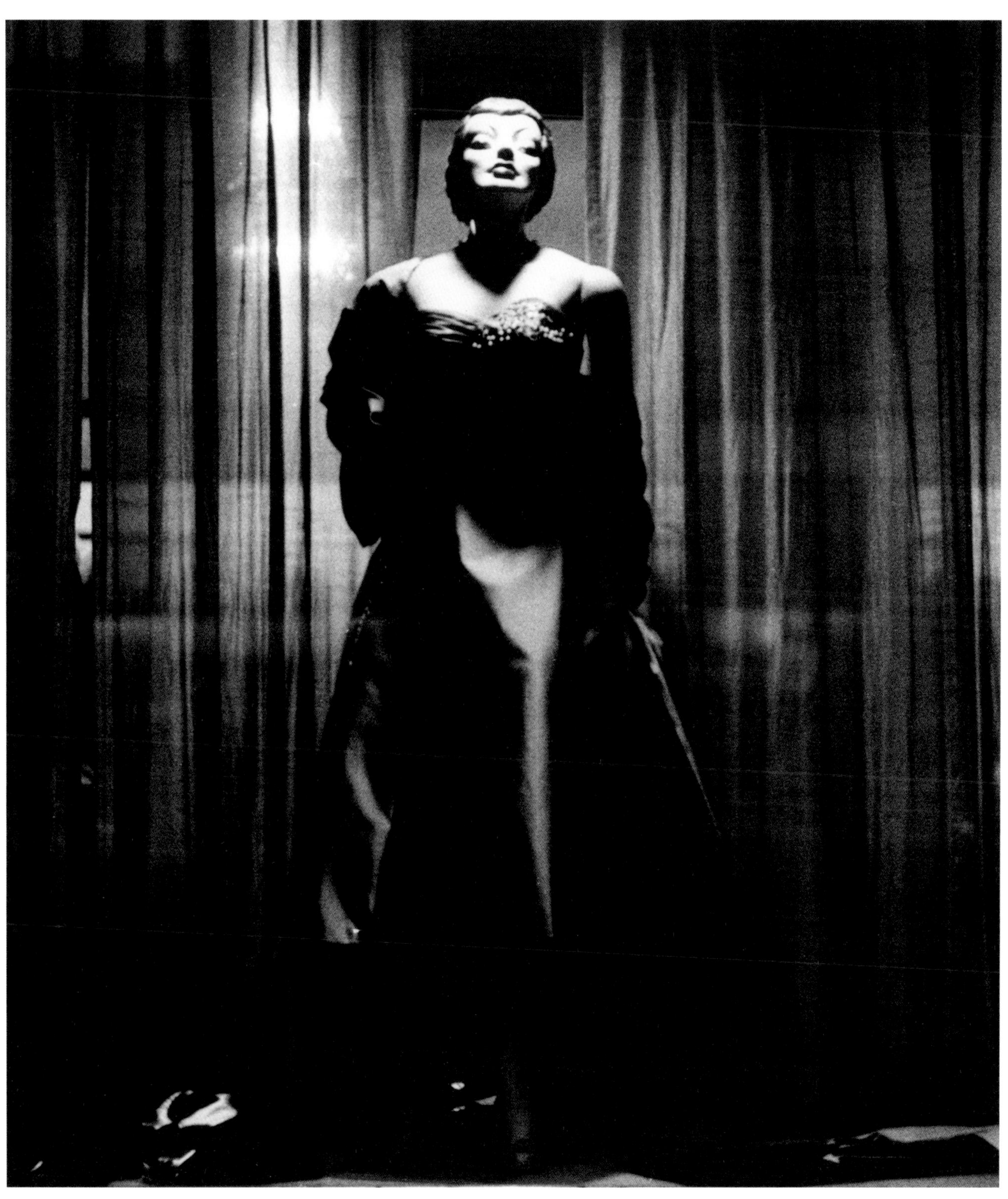

Mannequin in evening gown, N.Y.C. 1956

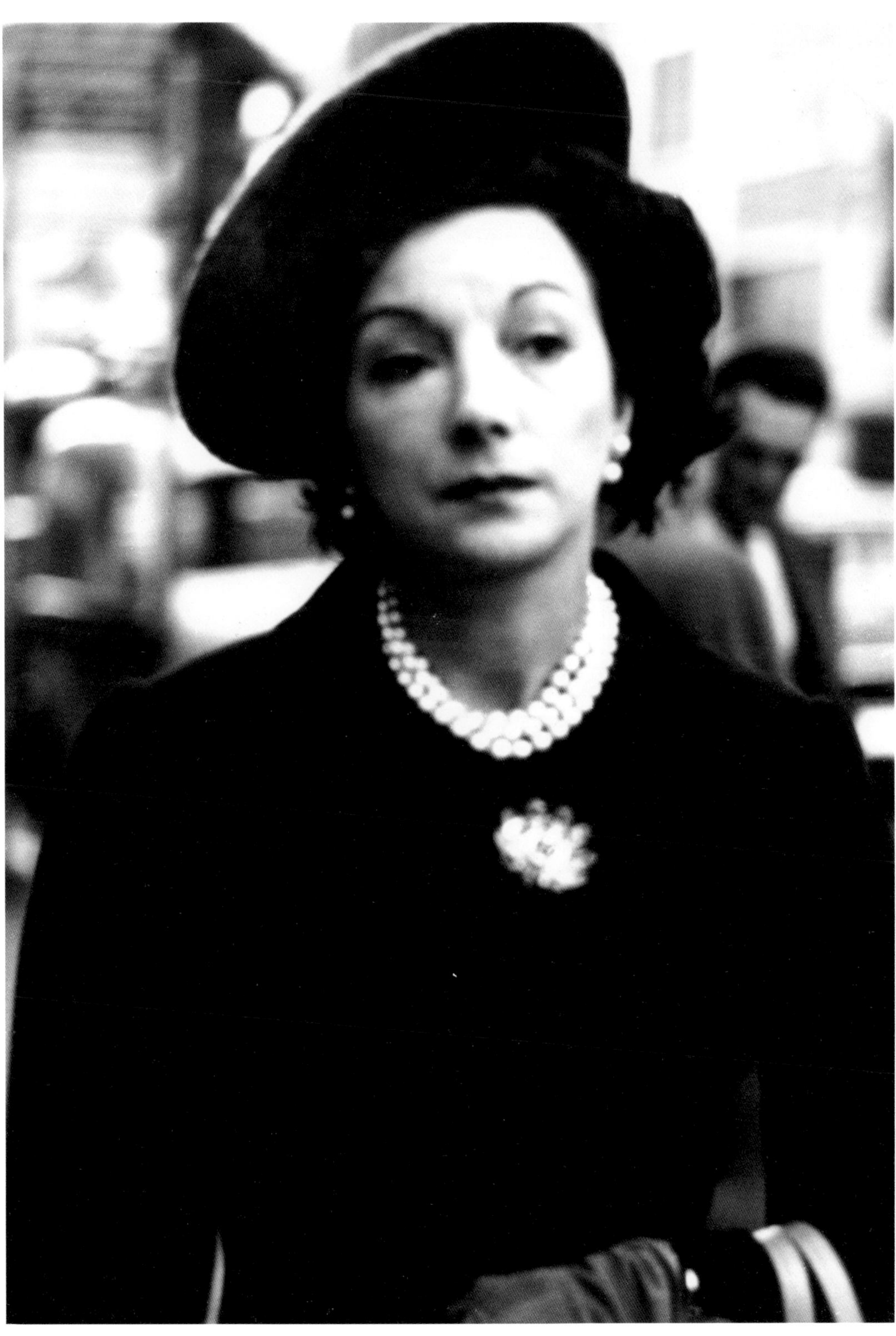

Woman in a black hat with a pearl choker, N.Y.C. 1956

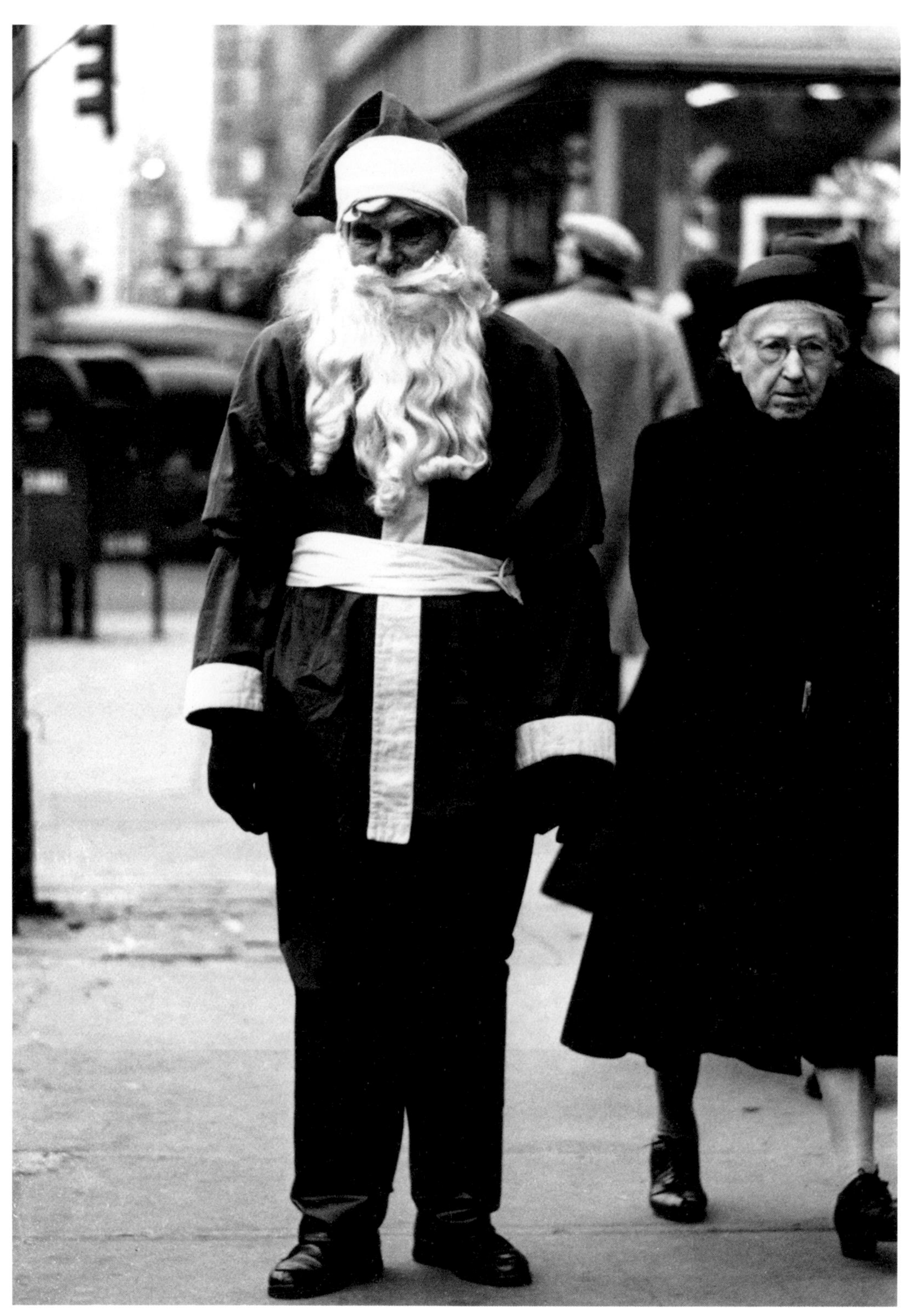

 Santa Claus on the street with a lady passing, N.Y.C. 1956

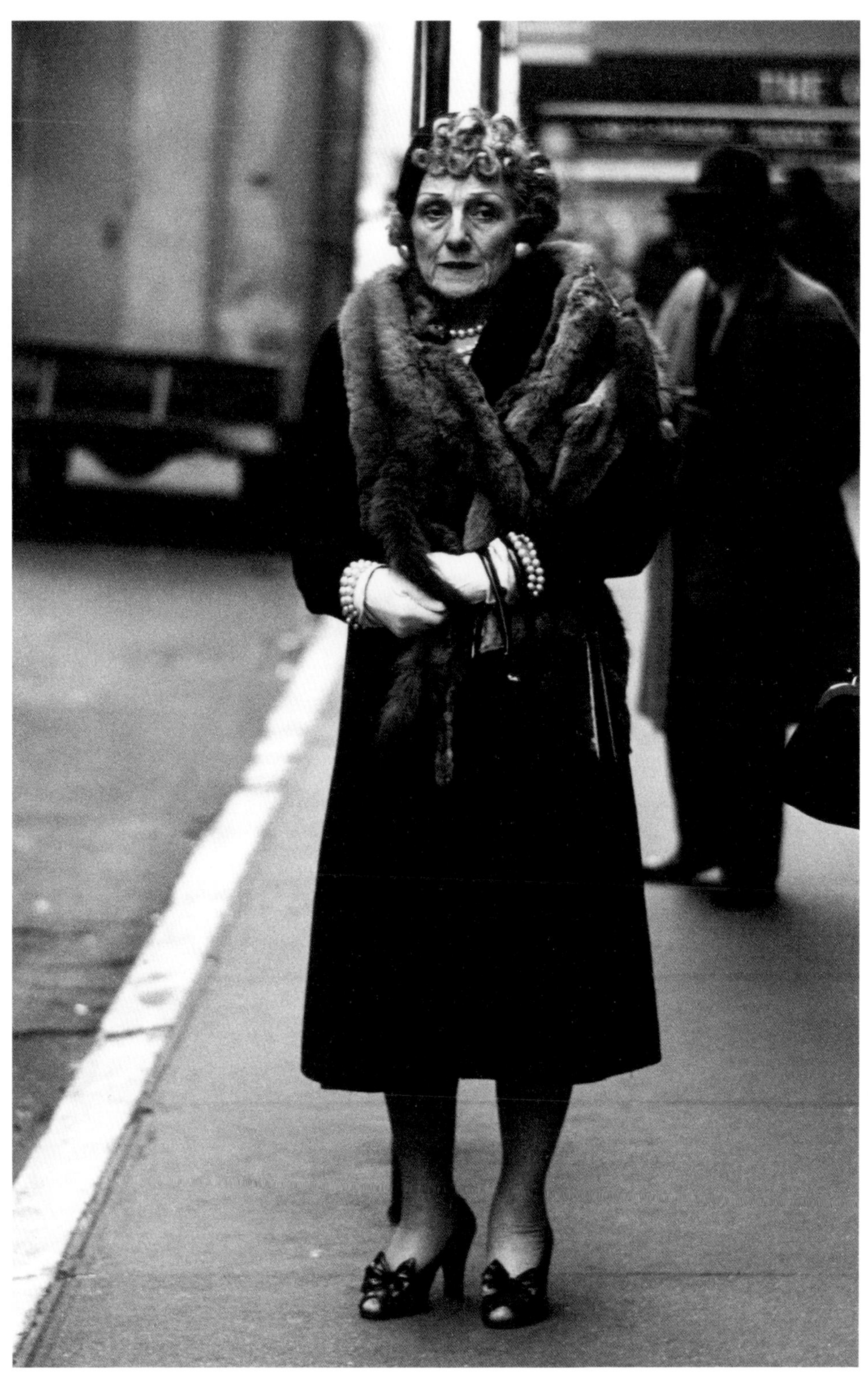

Woman in a mink stole and bow shoes, N.Y.C. 1956

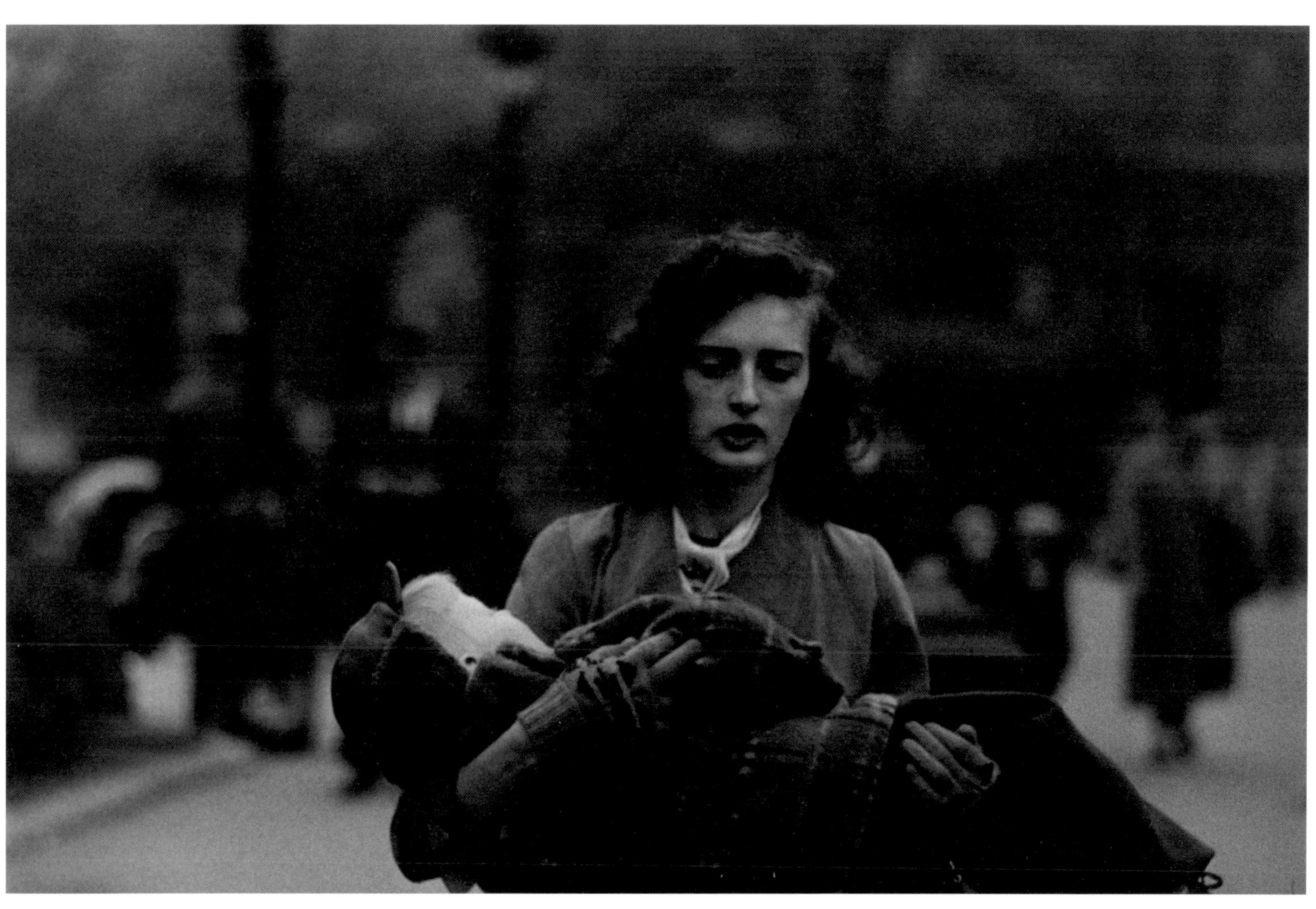

Woman carrying a child in Central Park, N.Y.C. 1956

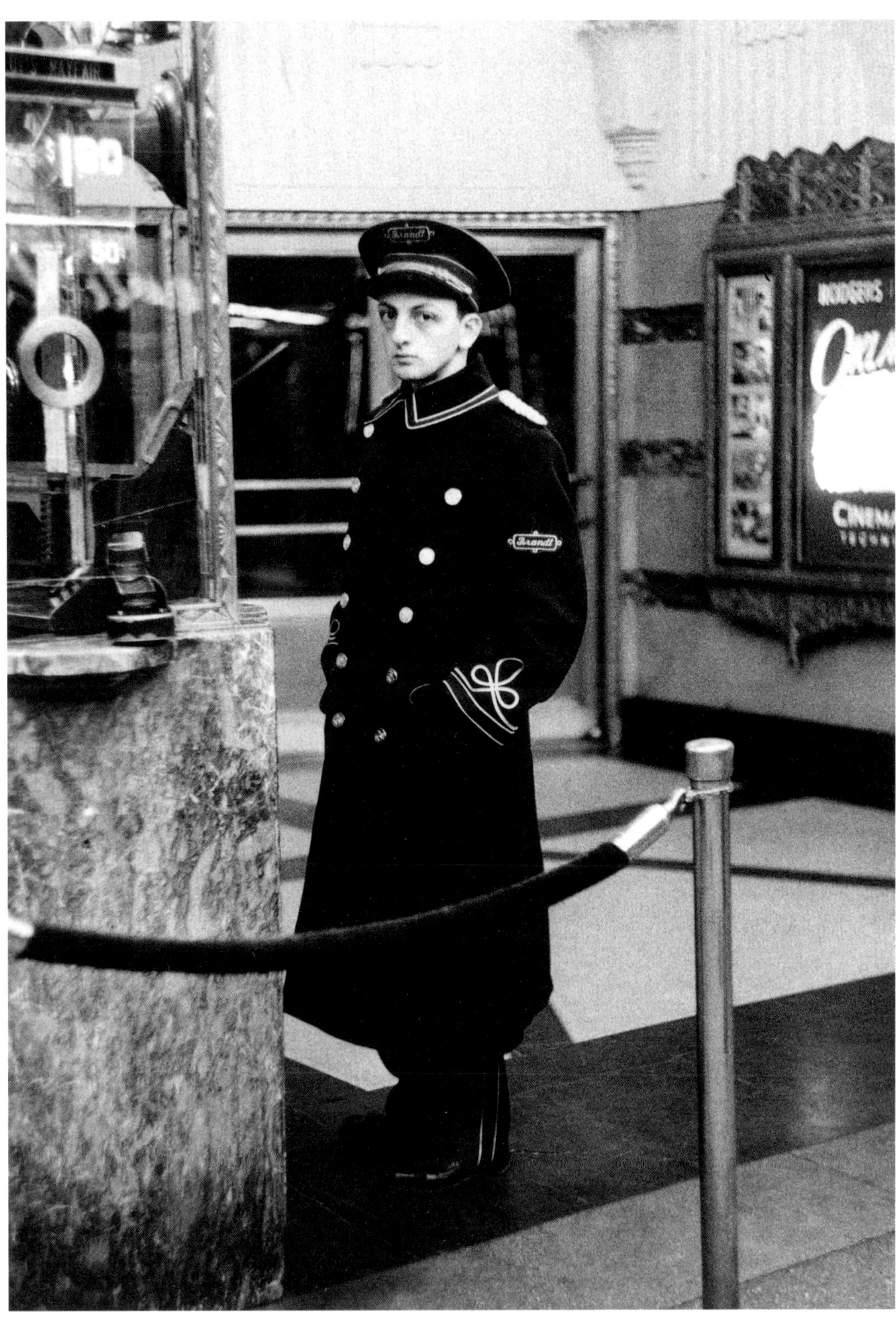

Movie theater usher standing by the box office, N.Y.C. 1956

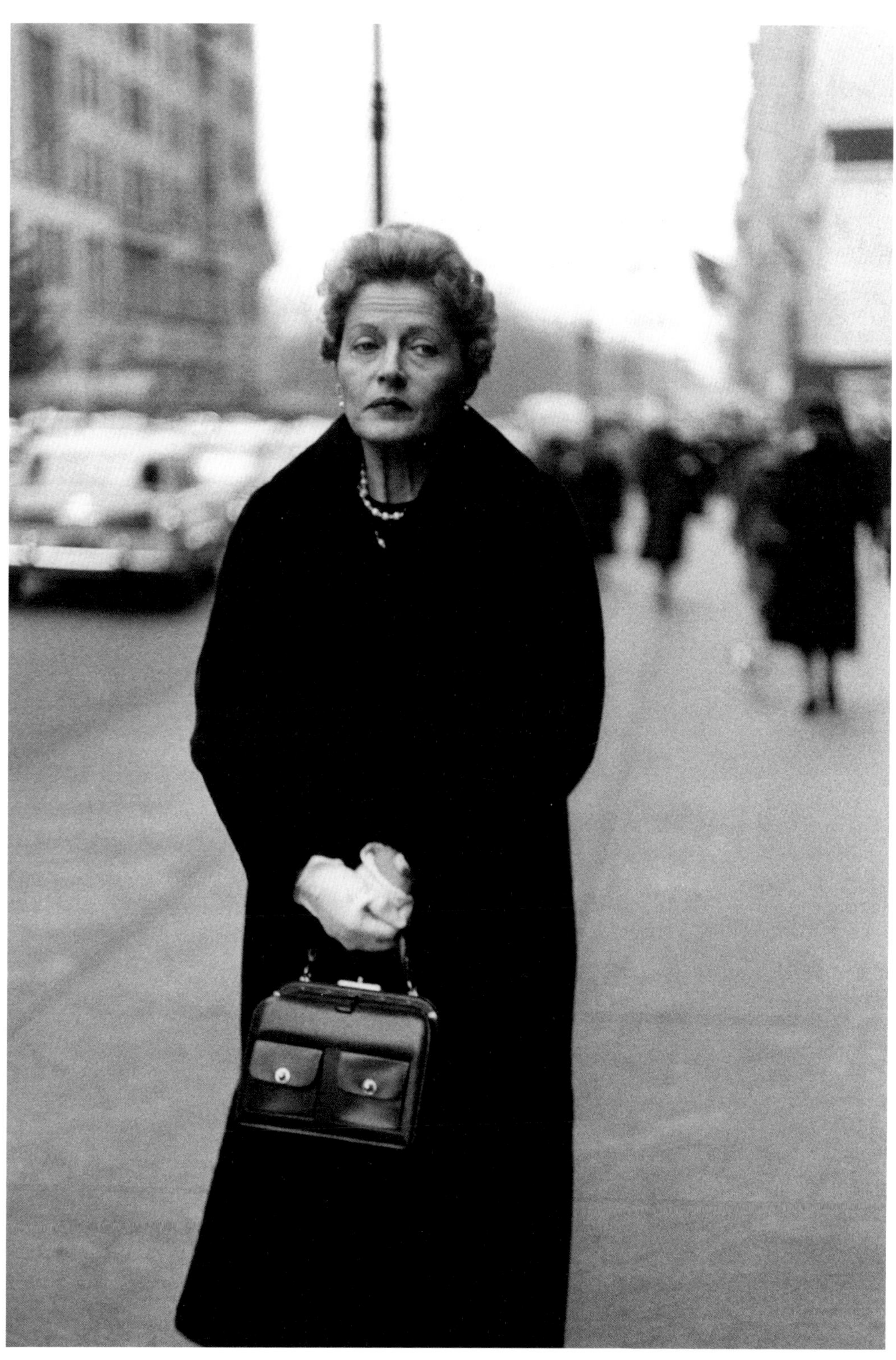

Woman with white gloves and a pocket book, N.Y.C. 1956

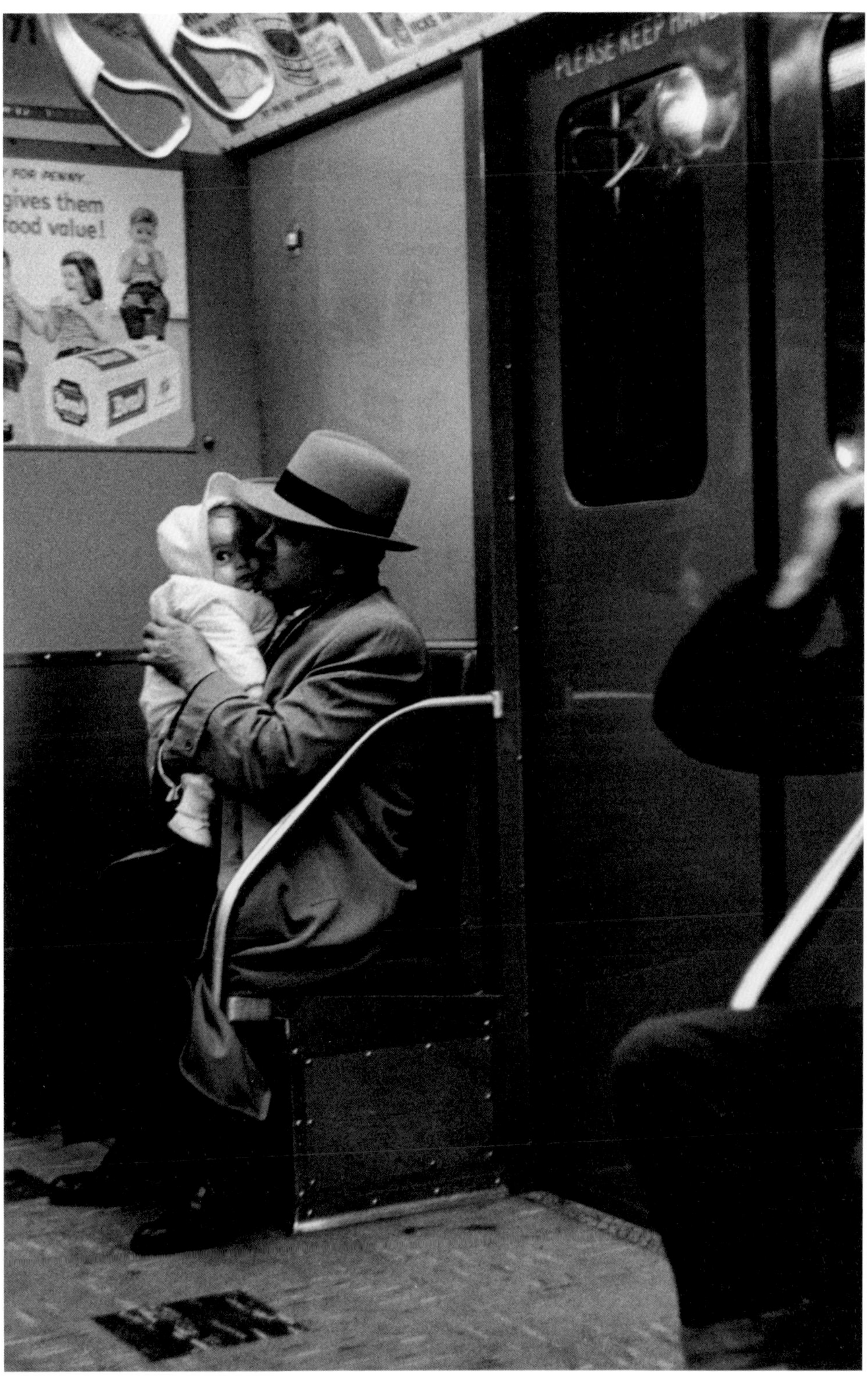

Man with a curious baby on the subway, N.Y.C. 1956

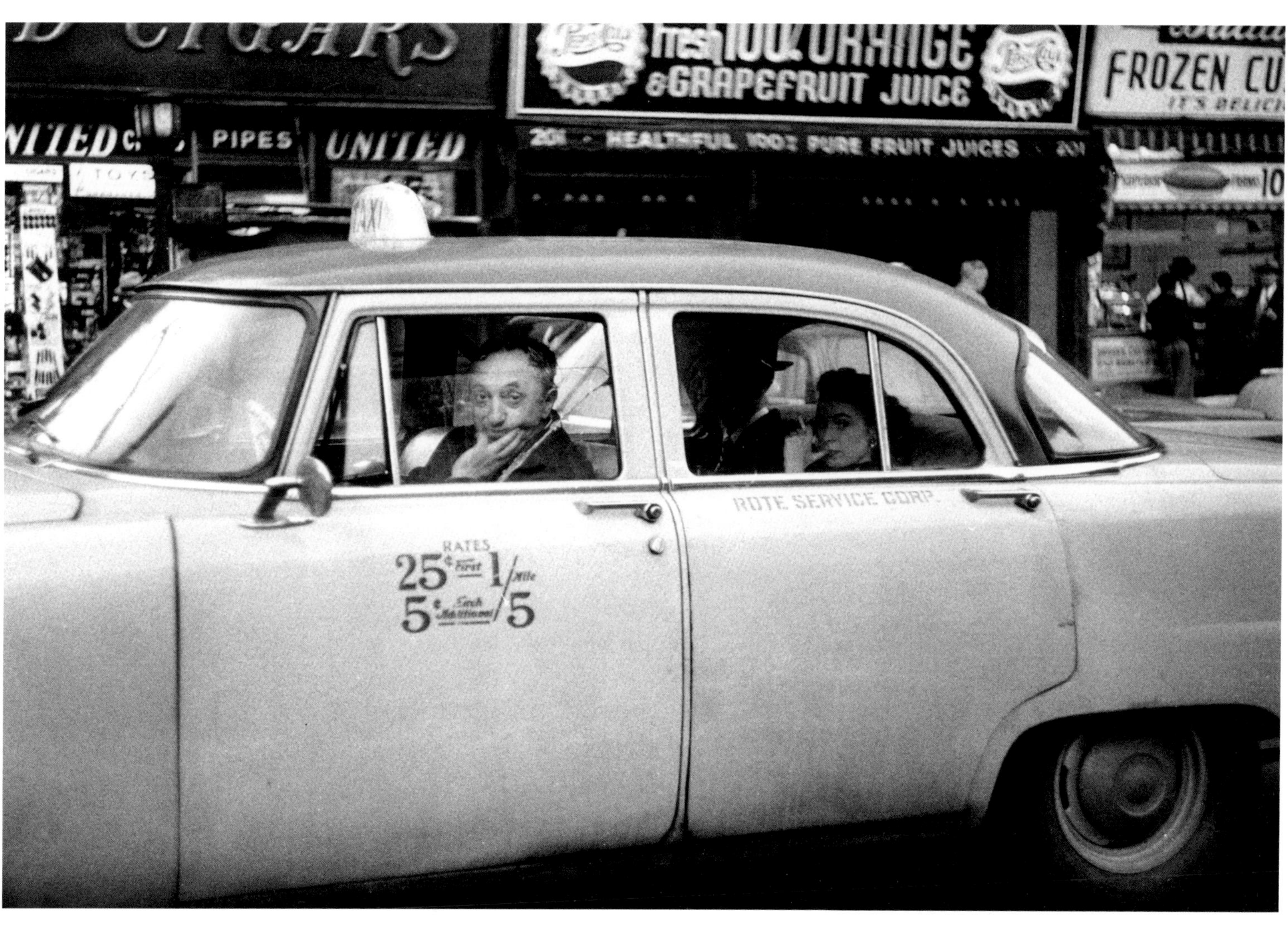

Taxicab driver at the wheel with two passengers, N.Y.C. 1956

Kiss from "Baby Doll," N.Y.C. 1956

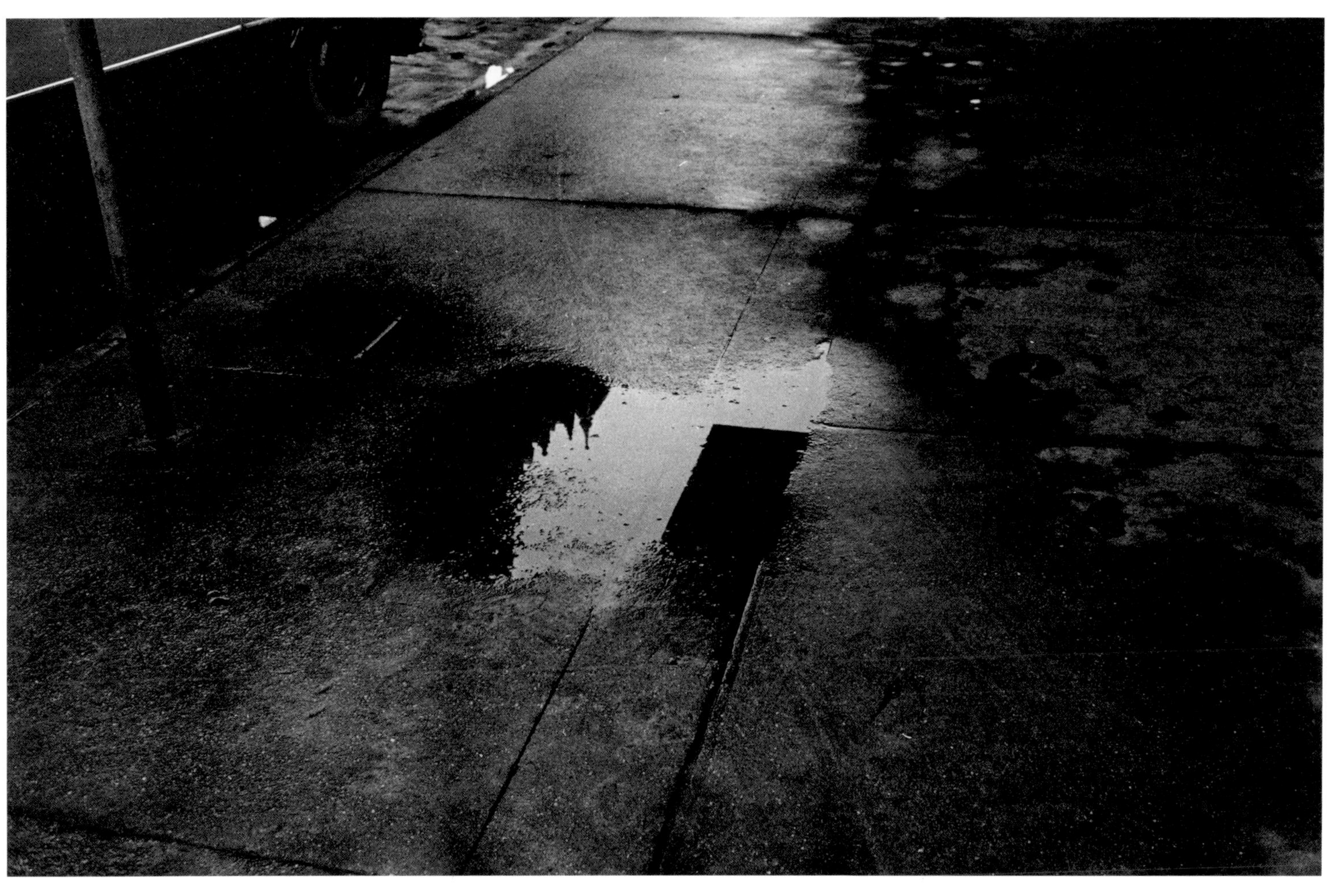

Puddle on the sidewalk, N.Y.C. 1957

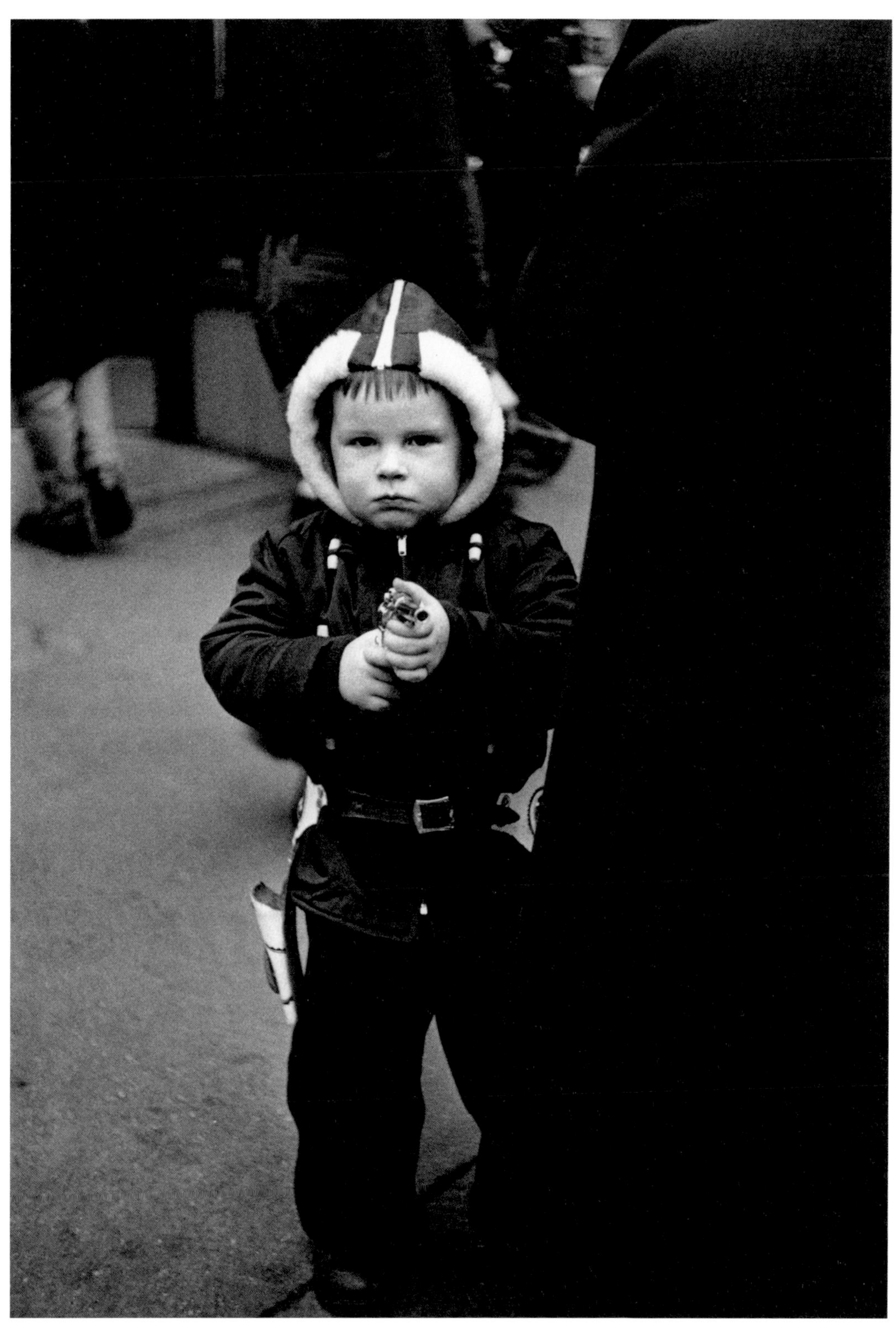

Kid in a hooded jacket aiming a gun, N.Y.C. 1957

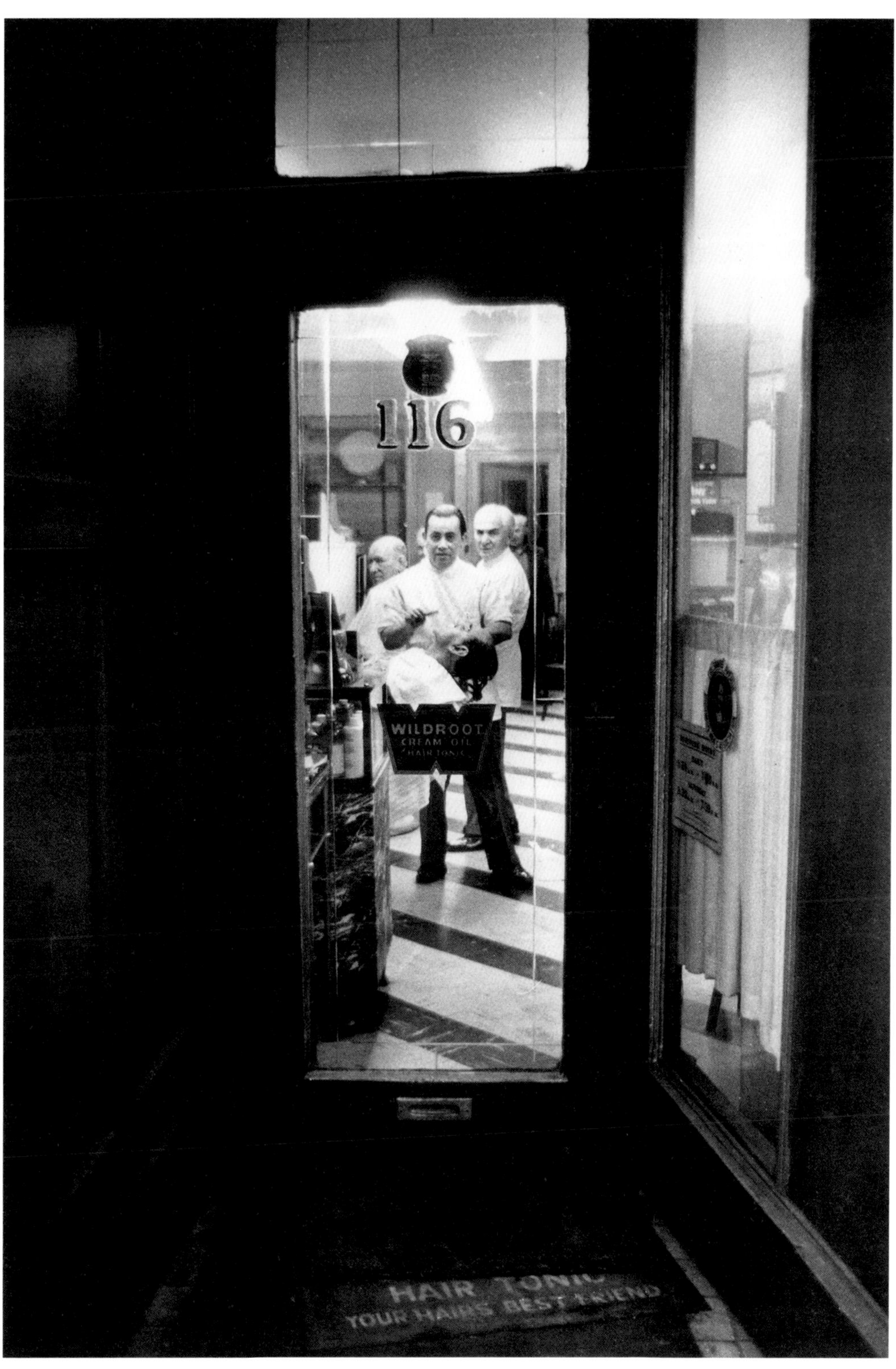

Barbershop interior through a glass door, N.Y.C. 1957

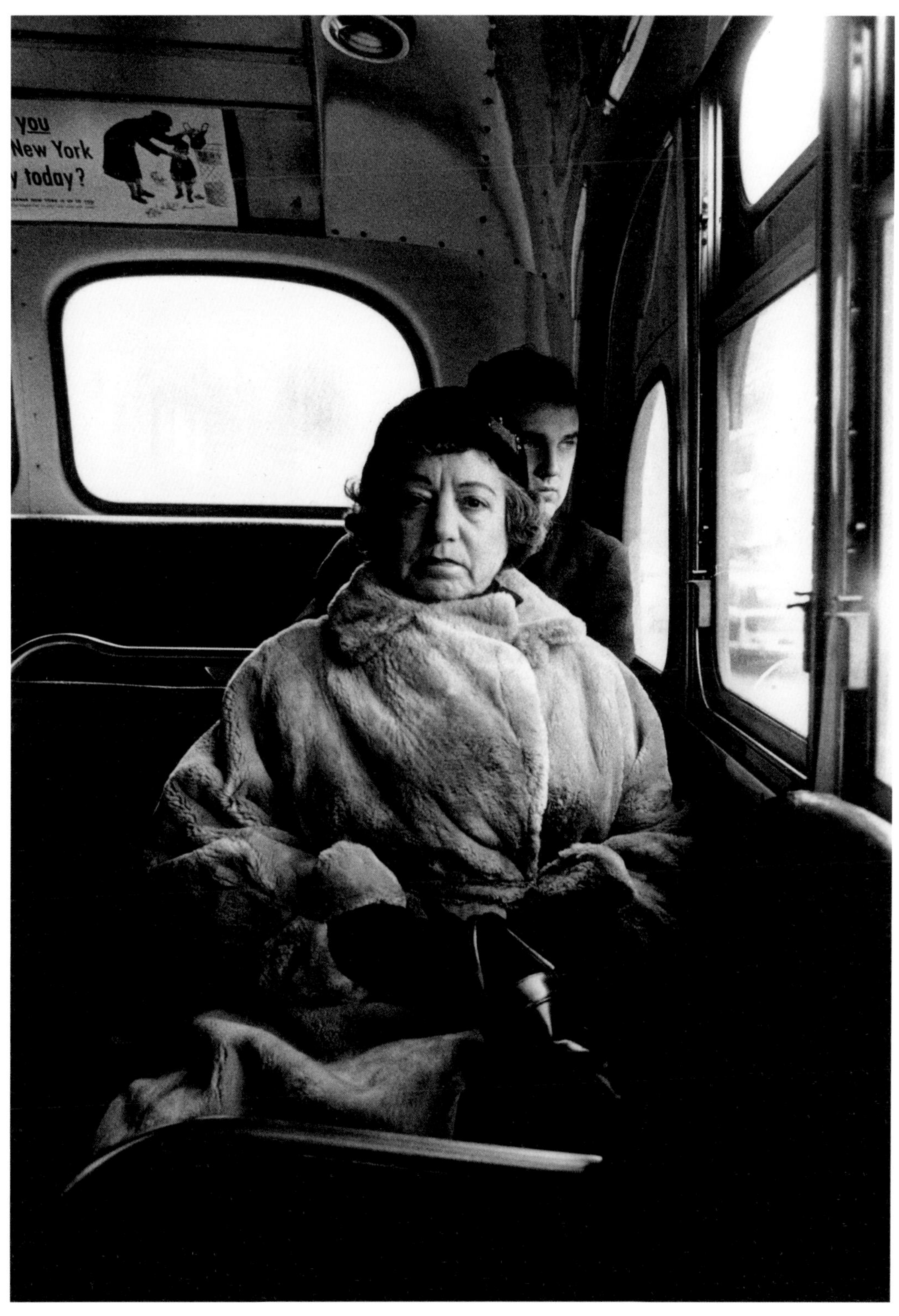

Lady on a bus, N.Y.C. 1957

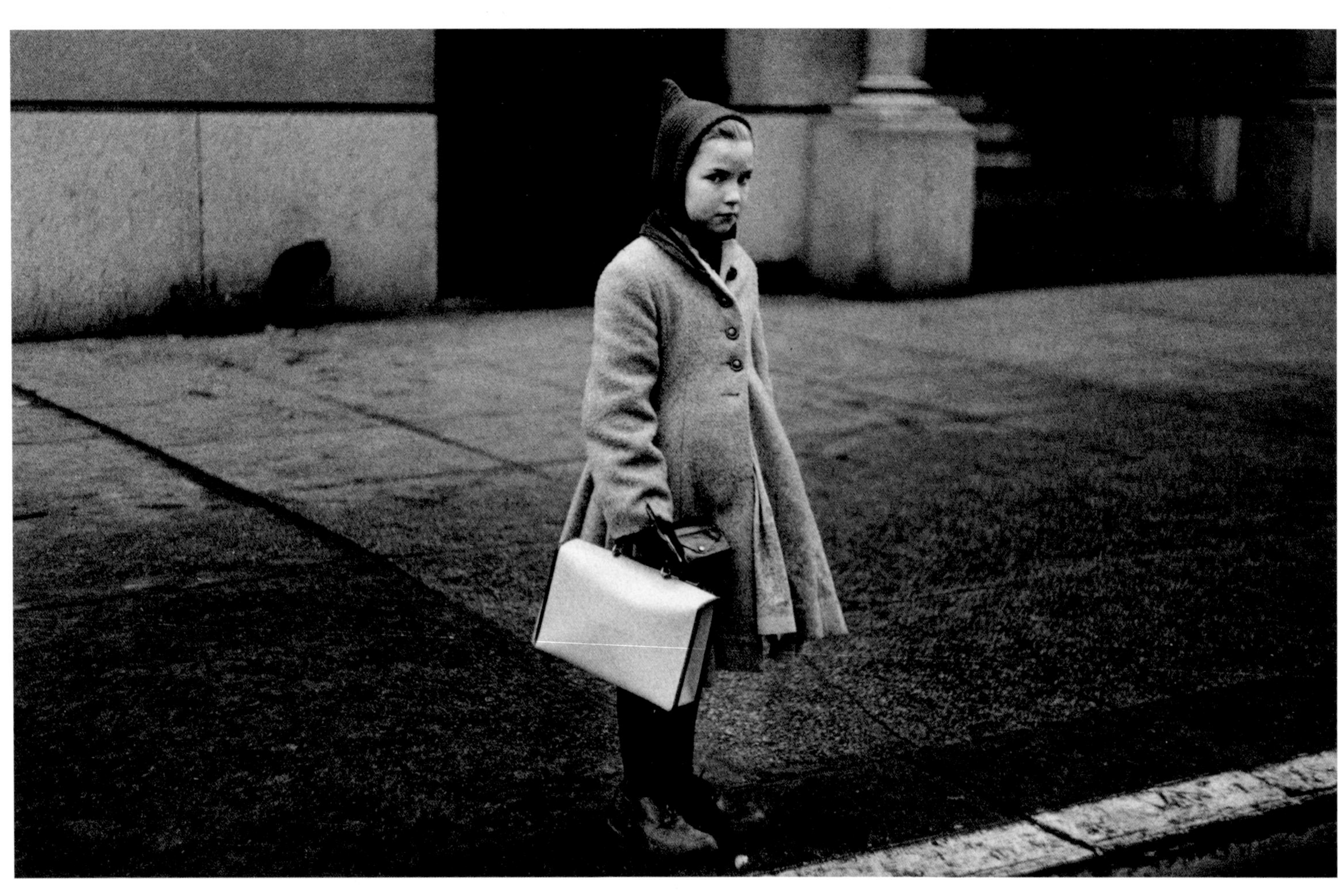

Girl with a pointy hood and white schoolbag at the curb, N.Y.C. 1957

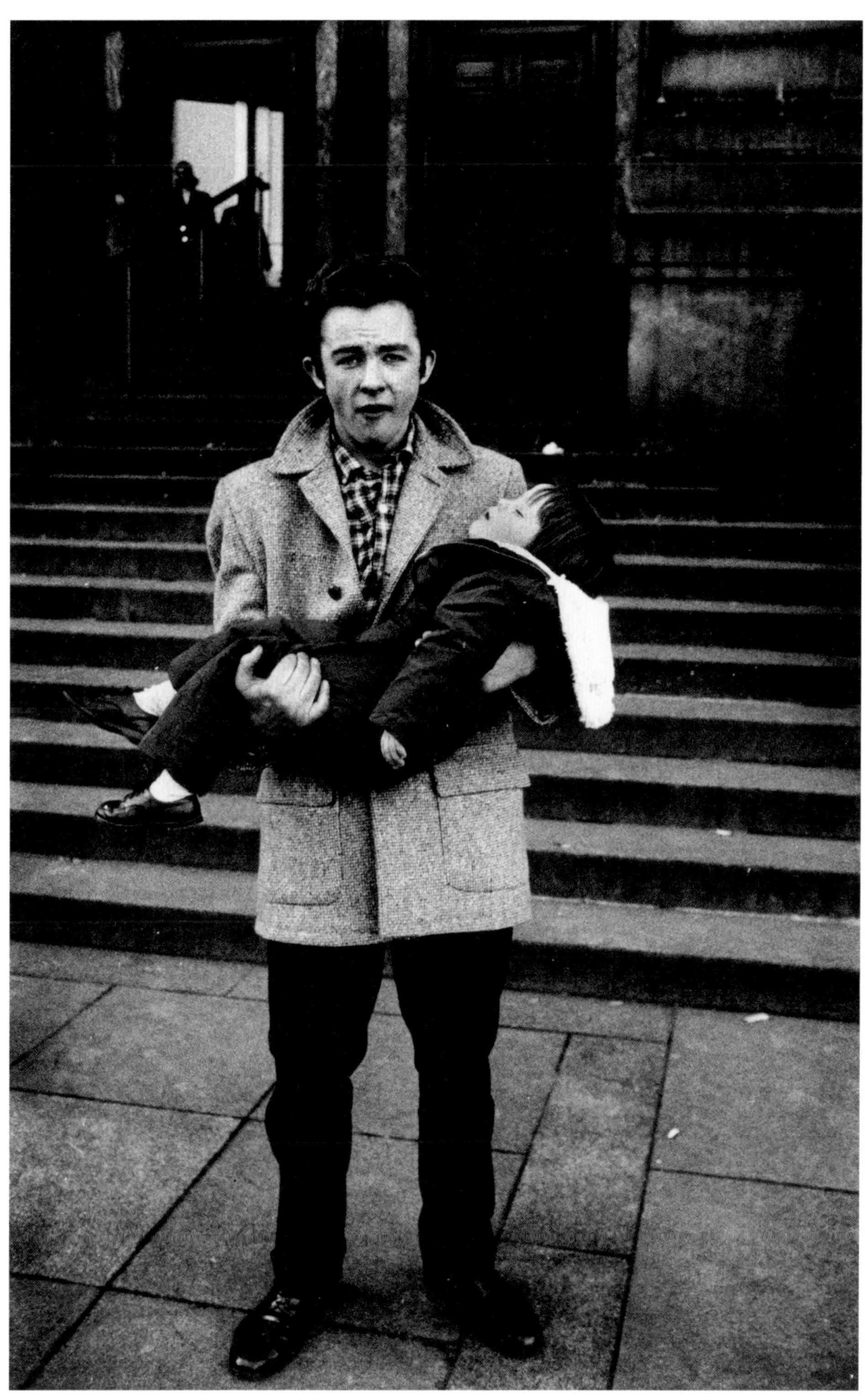

Man holding a sleeping child, N.Y.C. 1957

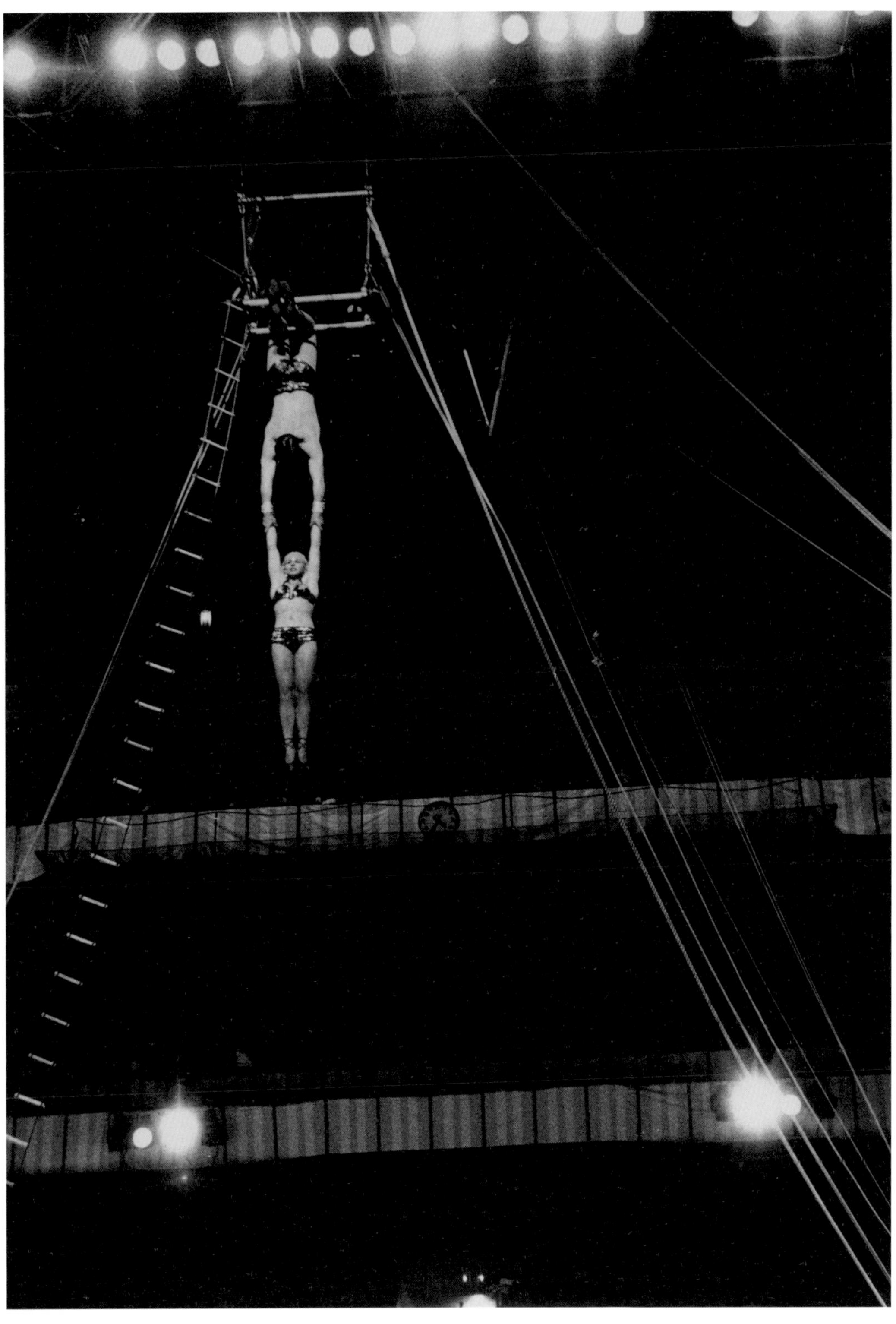

Trapeze act, N.Y.C. 1957

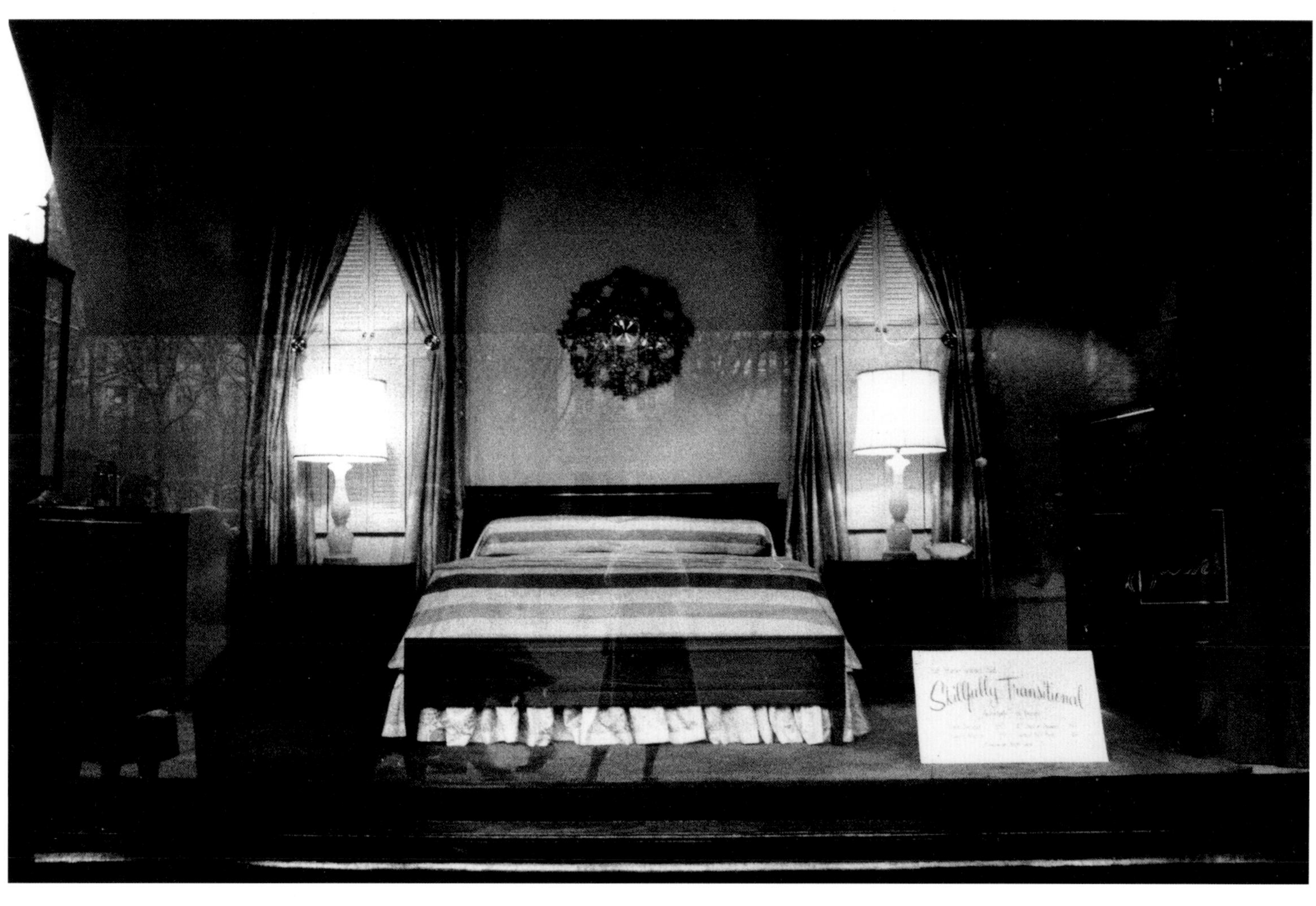

Bedroom in a store window, N.Y.C. 1957

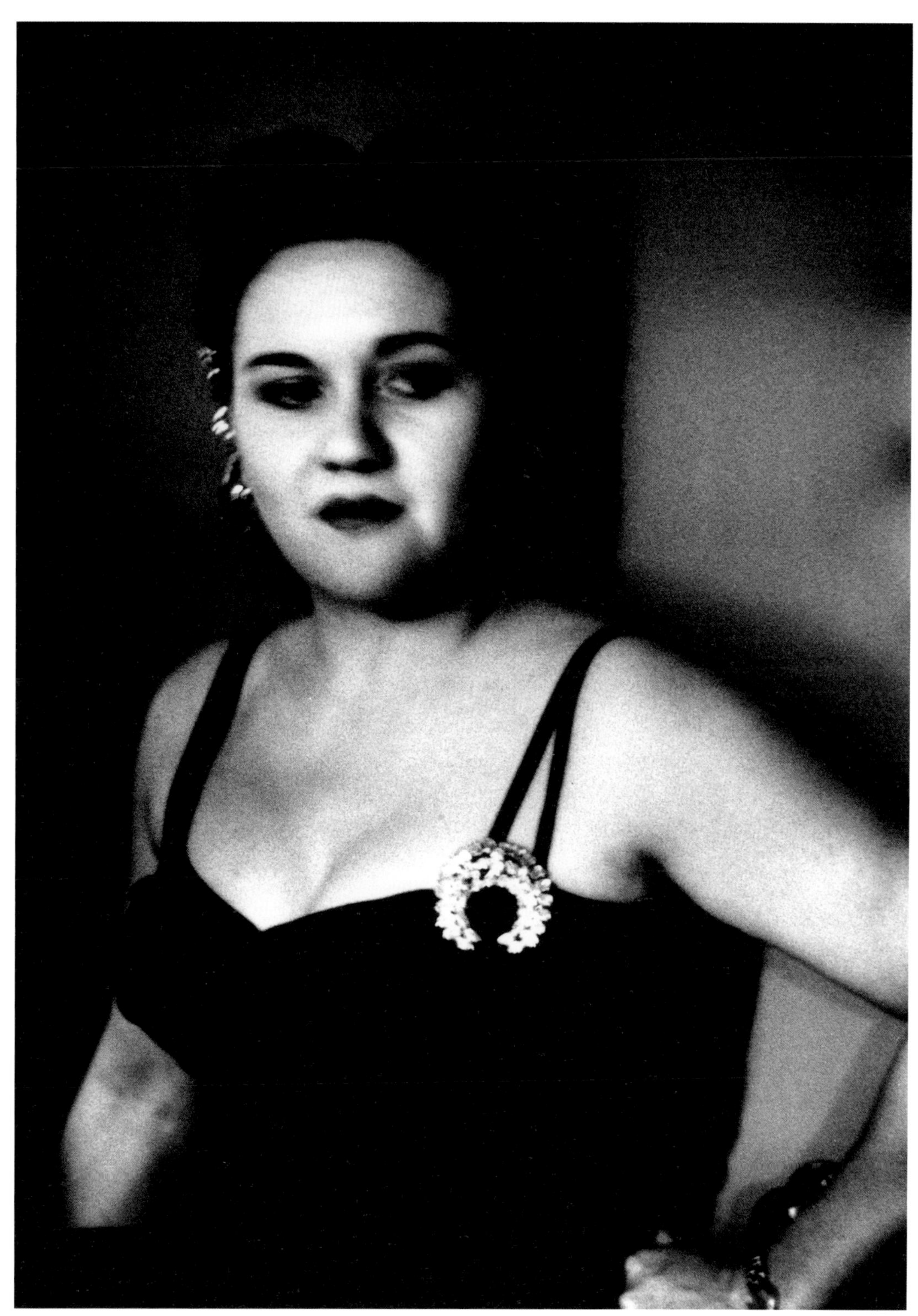

Woman with a crescent rhinestone brooch, N.Y.C. 1957

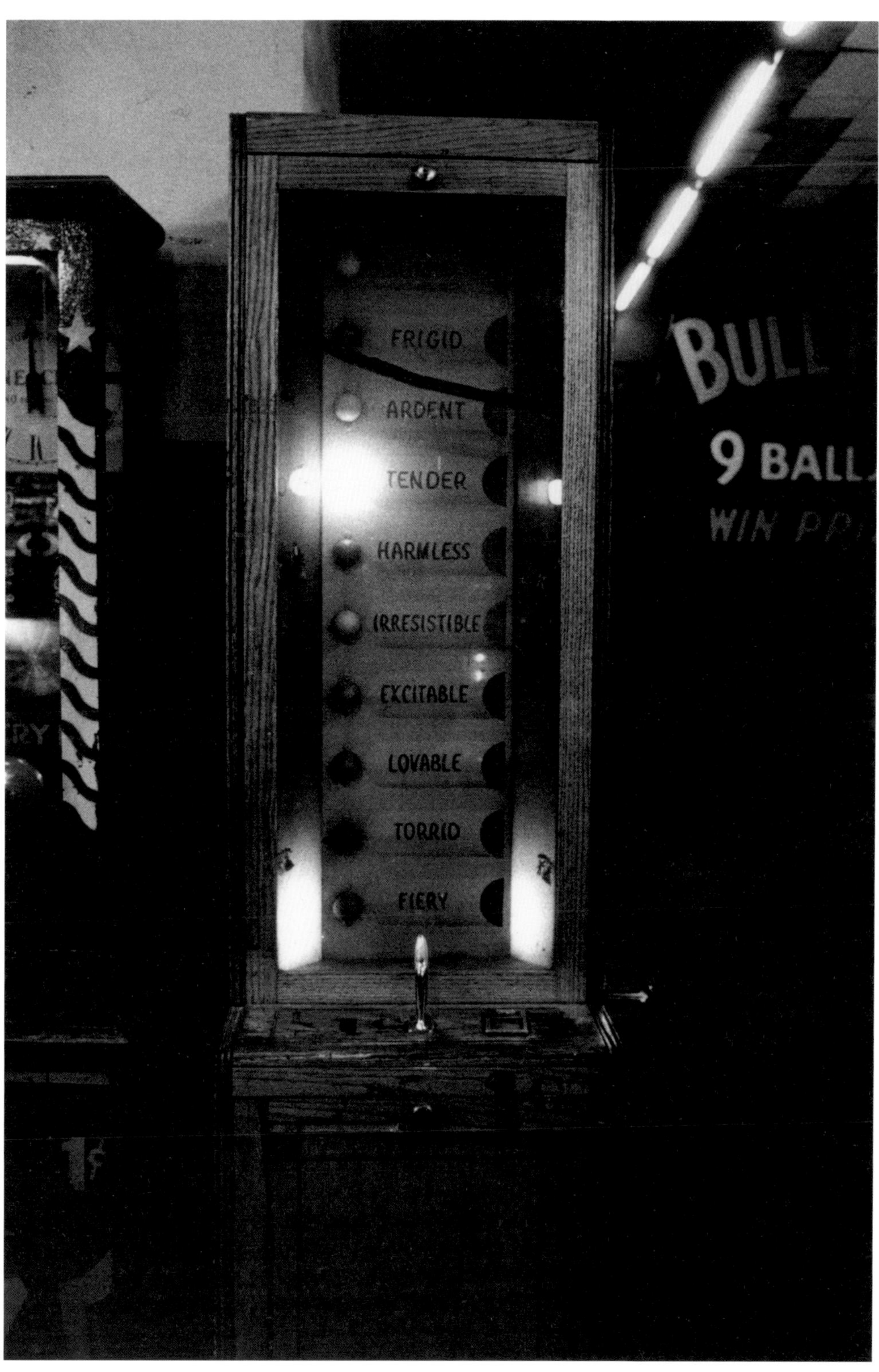

Mood meter machine, N.Y.C. 1957

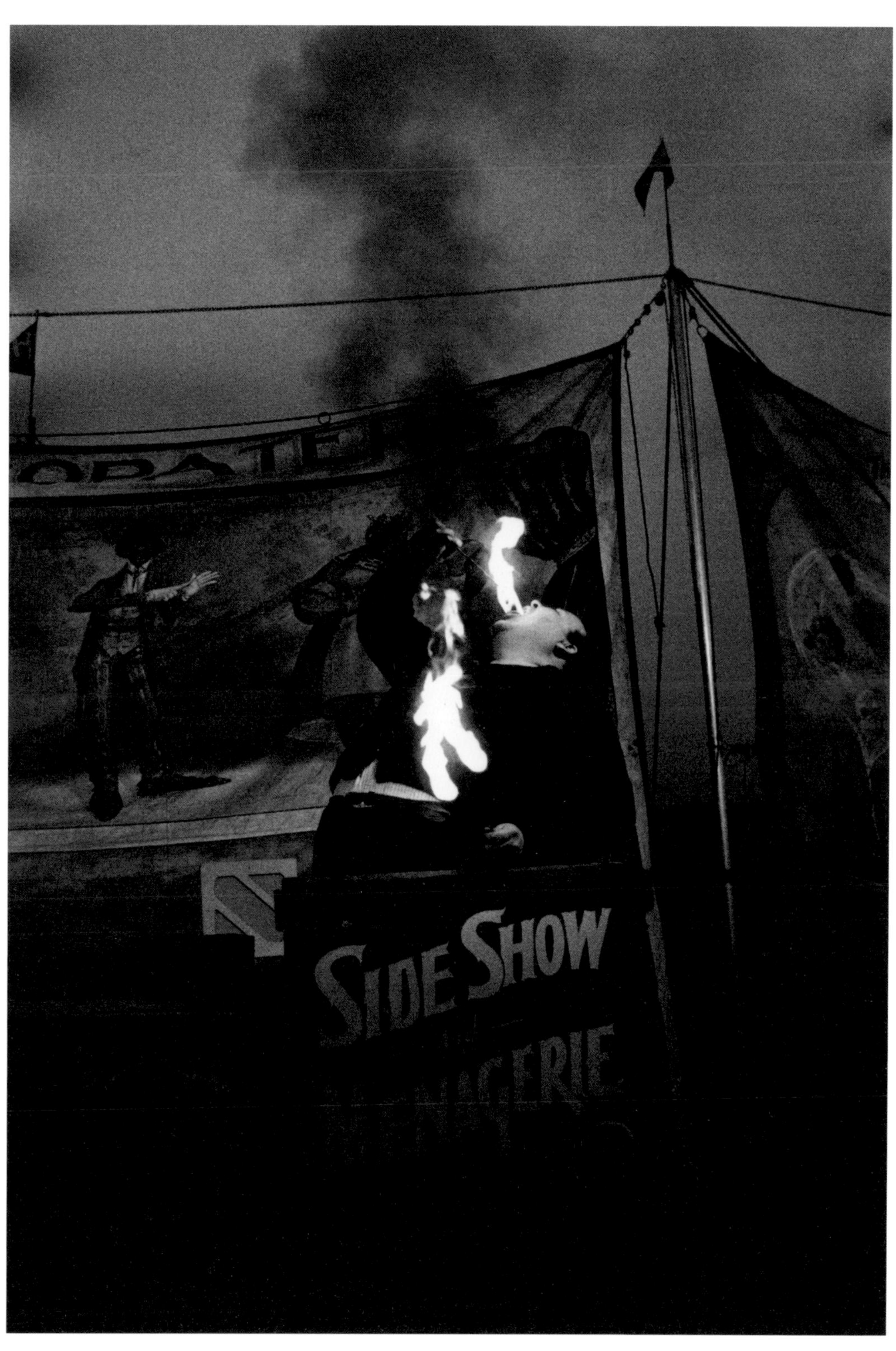

Fire Eater at a carnival, Palisades Park, N.J. 1957

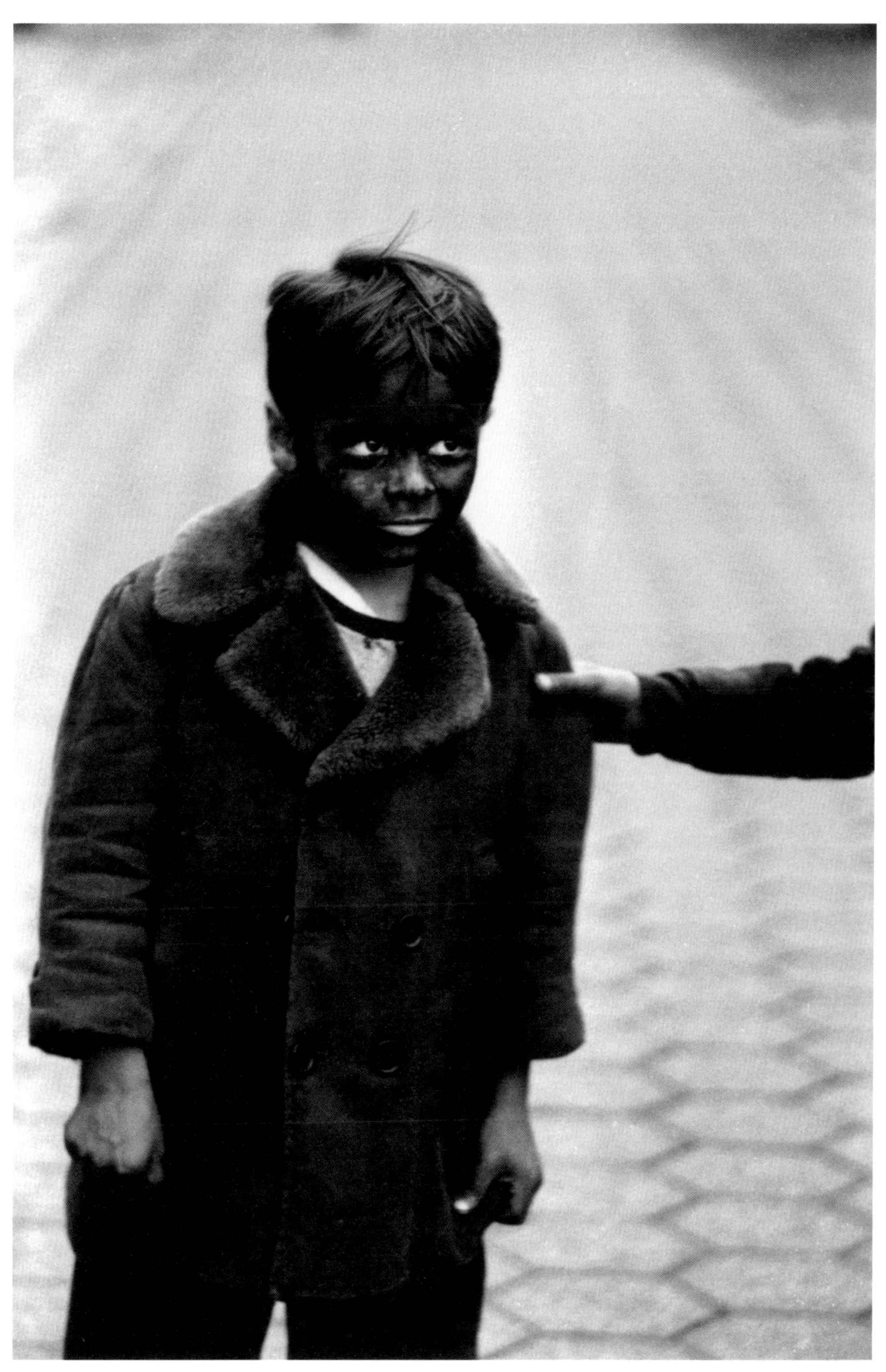

Kid in black face, N.Y.C. 1957

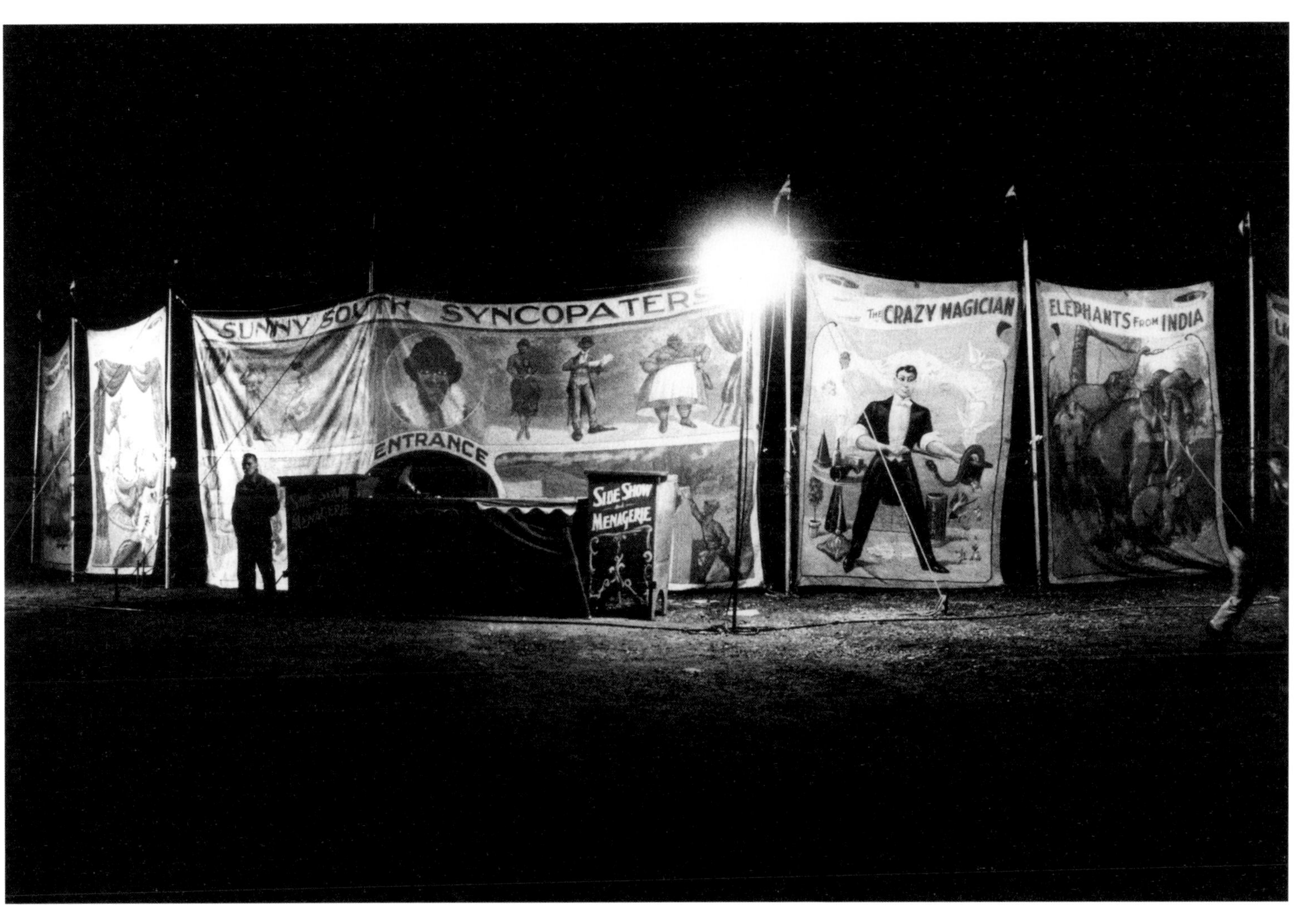

Sunny South Syncopaters and other sideshow banners at night, Palisades Park, N.J. 1957

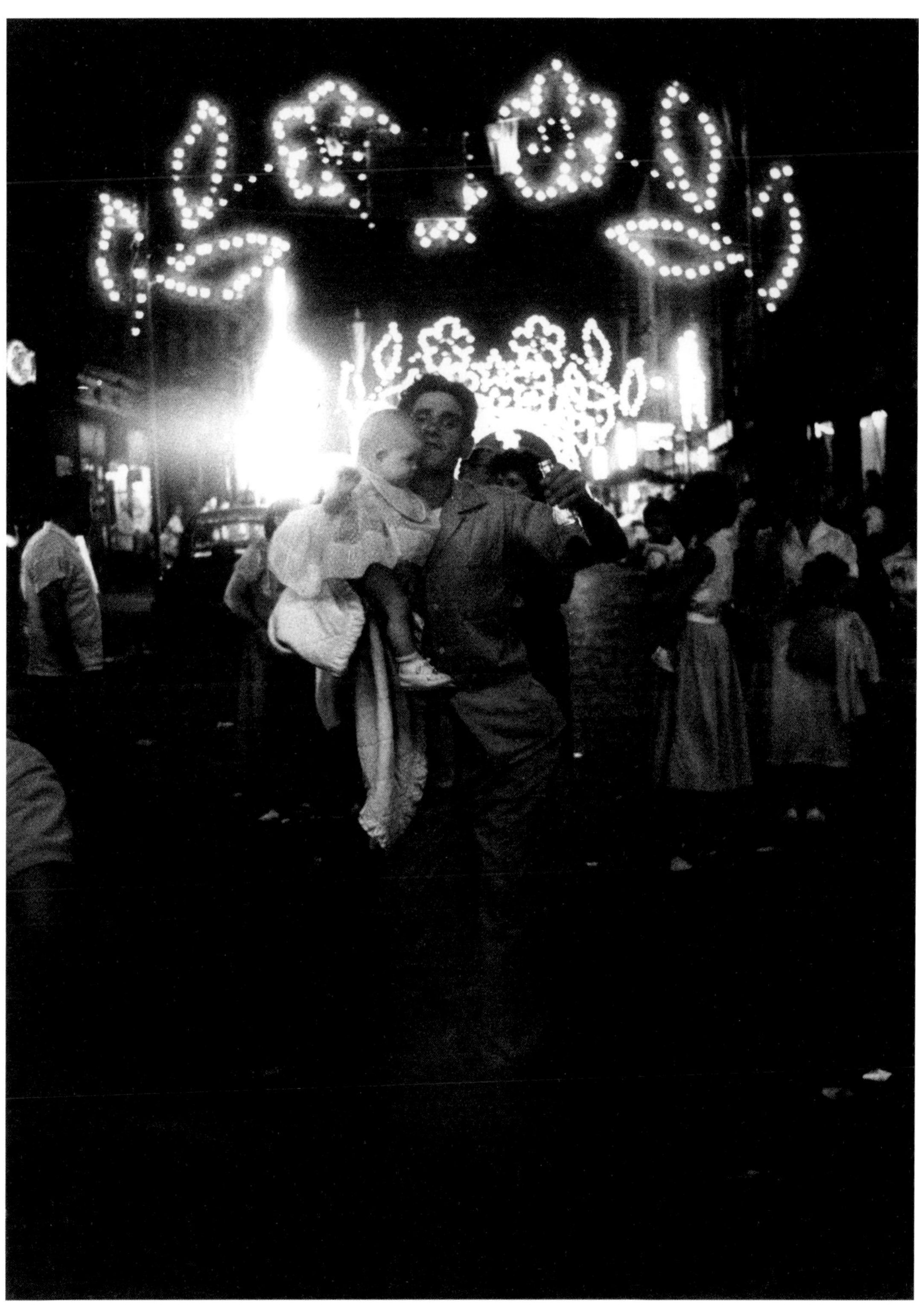

Father and child at Italian Street Festival, N.Y.C. 1957

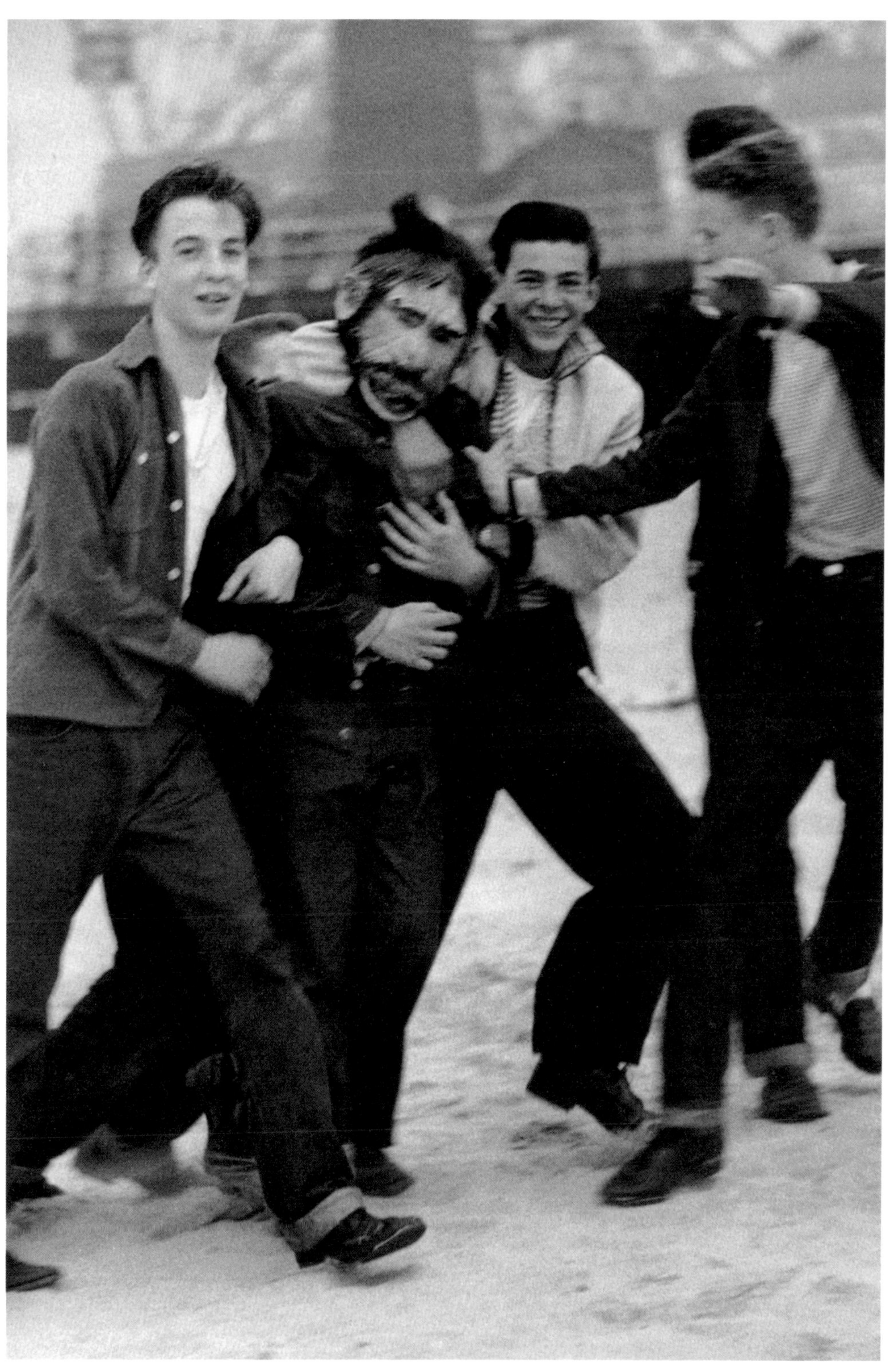

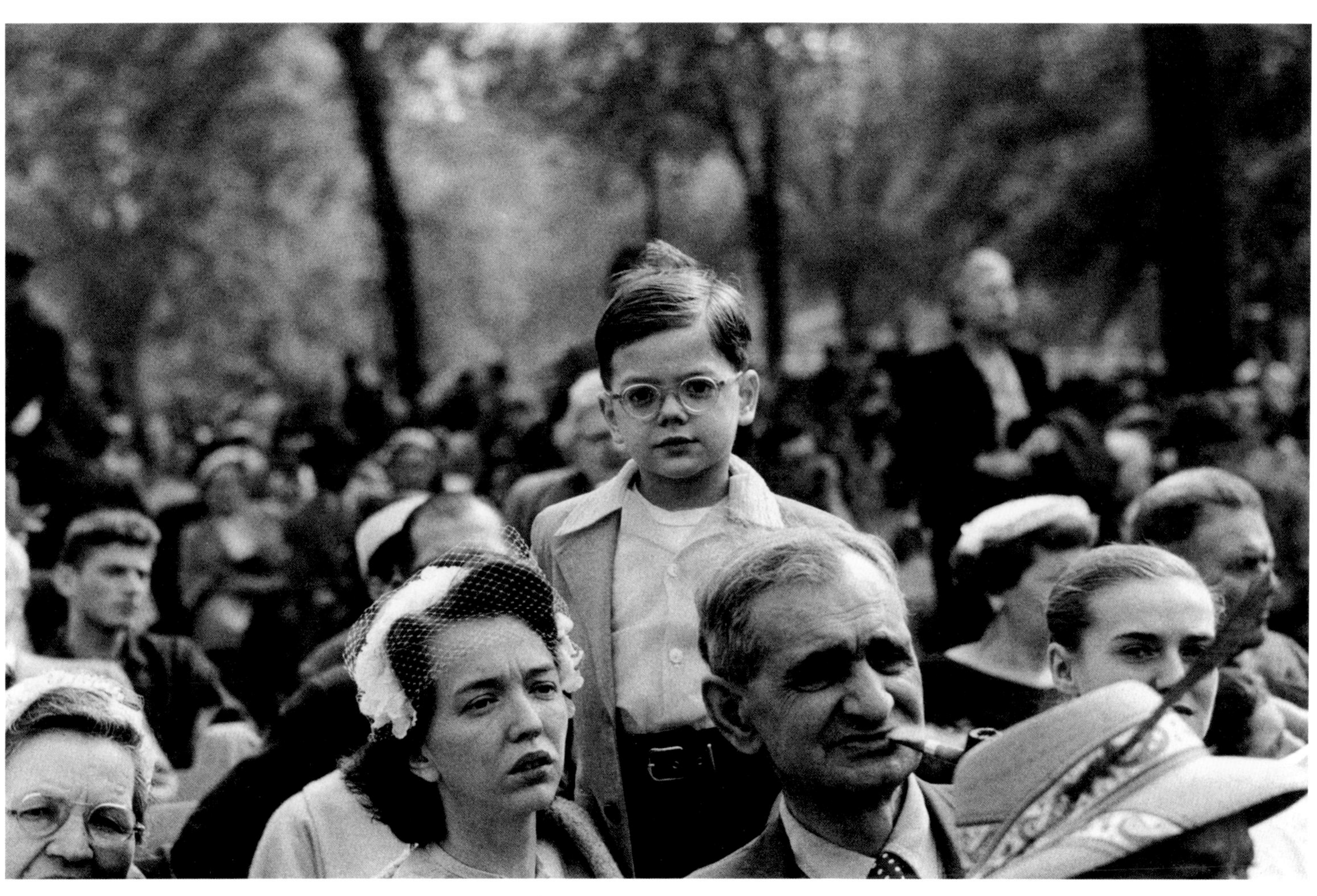

Boy above a crowd, N.Y.C. 1957

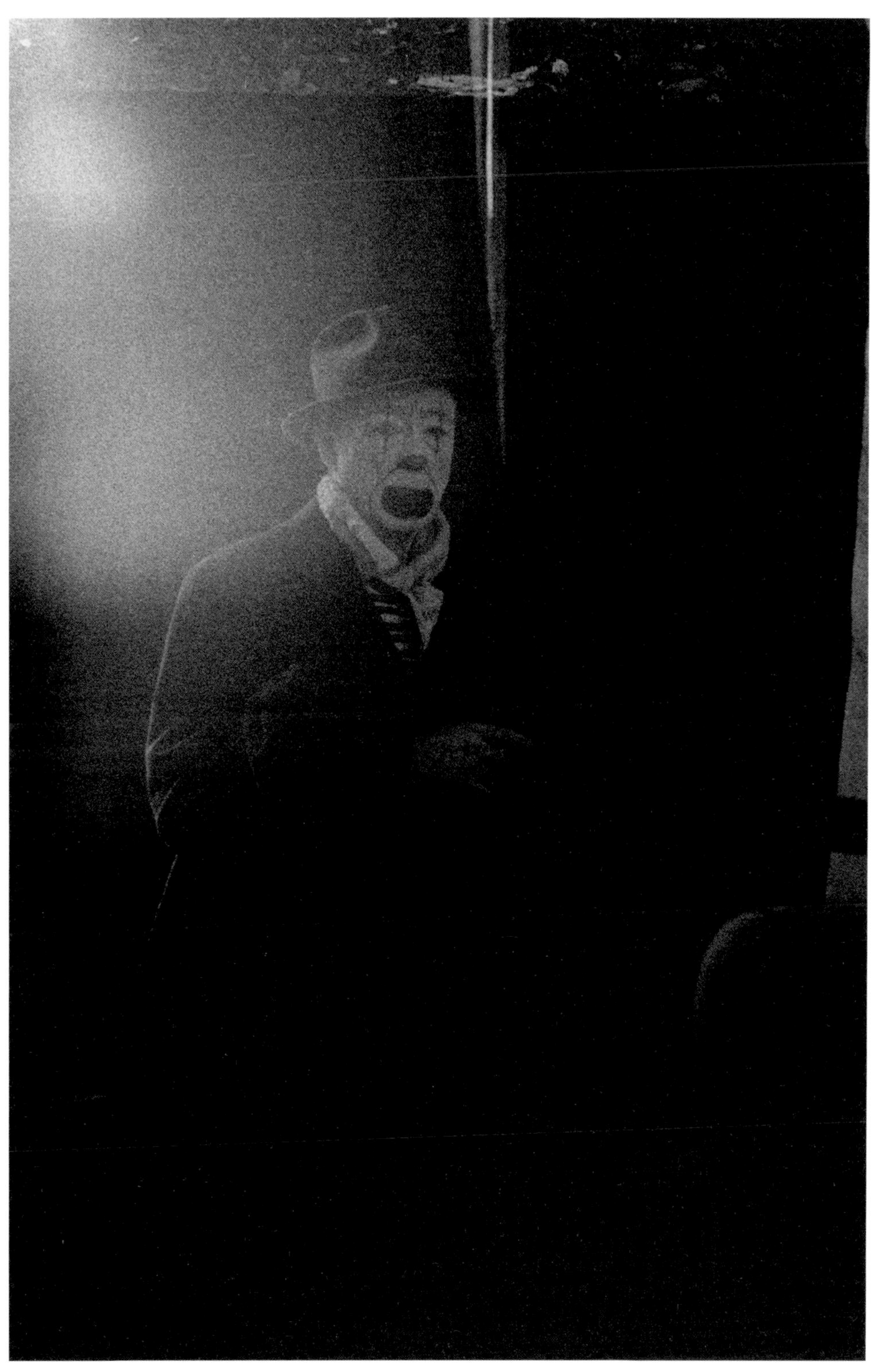

Clown in a fedora, Palisades Park, N.J. 1957

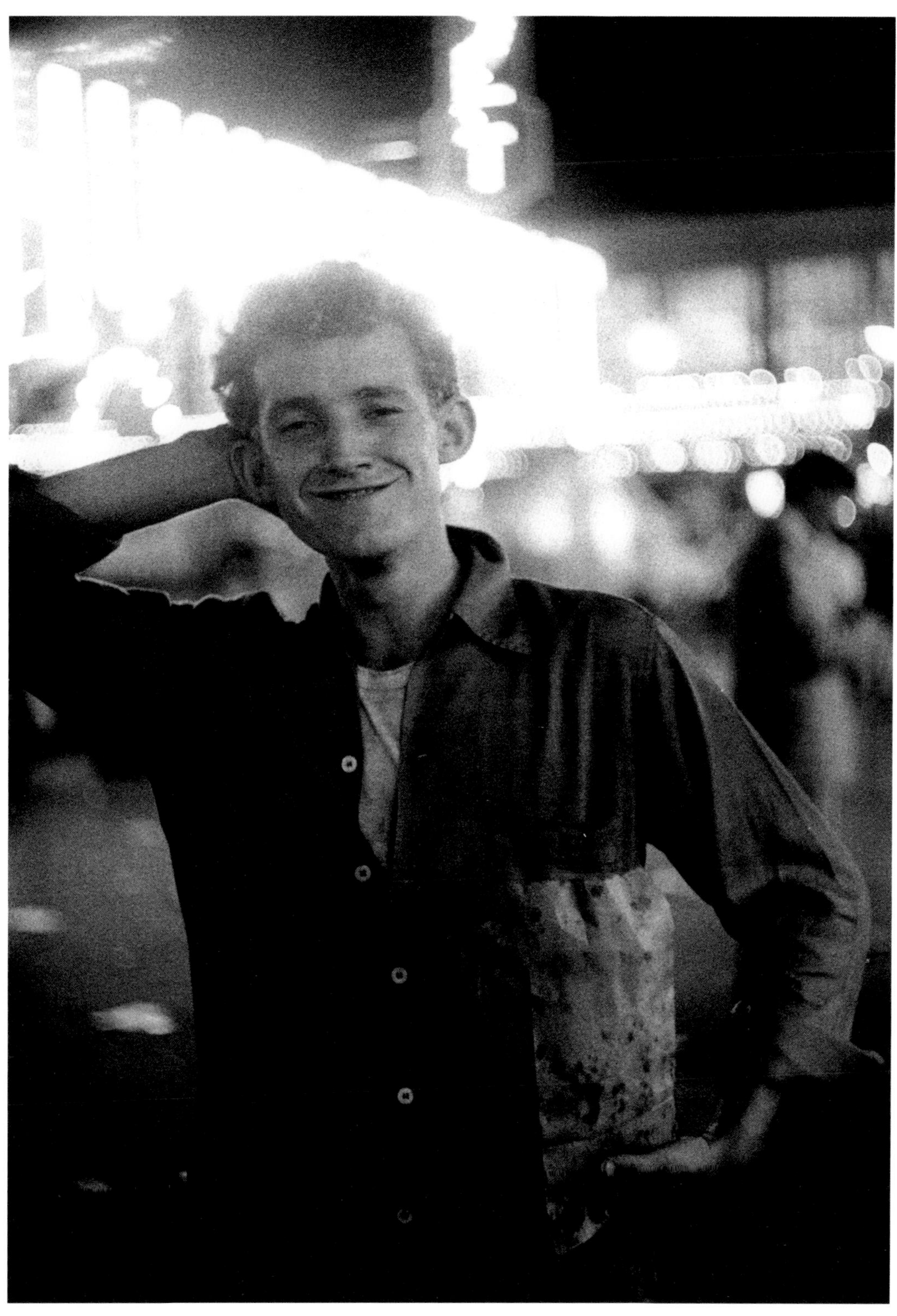

Young man with a paper bag at night, Coney Island, N.Y. 1957

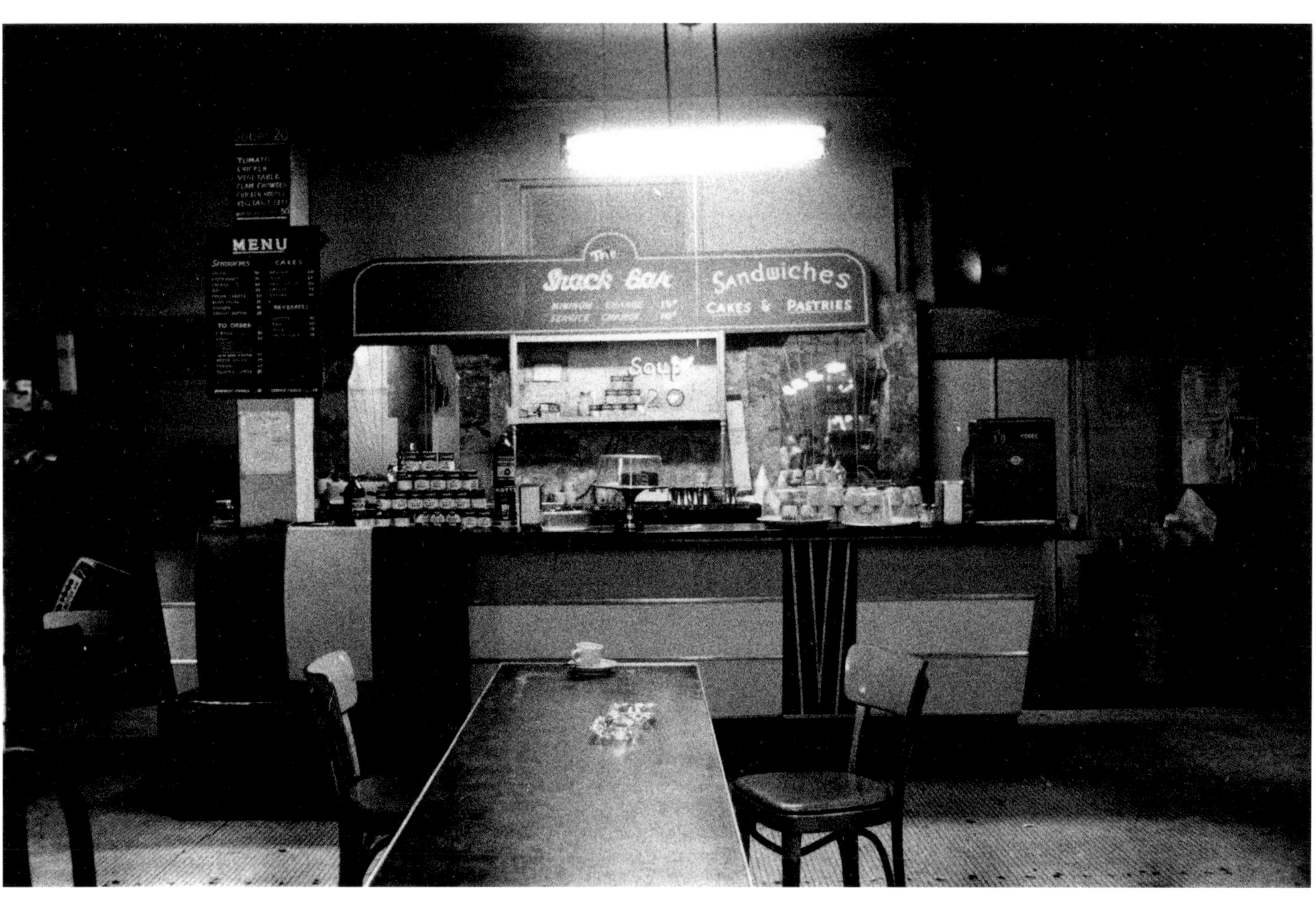

Empty snack bar, N.Y.C. 1957

scare
rump
gate
shower
charlotte
gymny ?
free on head
grandpa four
Rice 59
gypsy   nado
Lefty only
woman of four
Japanese
christ

peak
window
chalk a
monkey
Baby doll
Amy twin
Amy fall
3 girls
Amy road
Amy water
murder
aerialist
freealer
private property
shooting gallery
Amy cat
Boy horn

barber shop
girl CI
girl profile
street face
straight Am
sword swall
Ellie
Nancy's
nambang

TO Esq. 10³⁰ dentist
44 prints

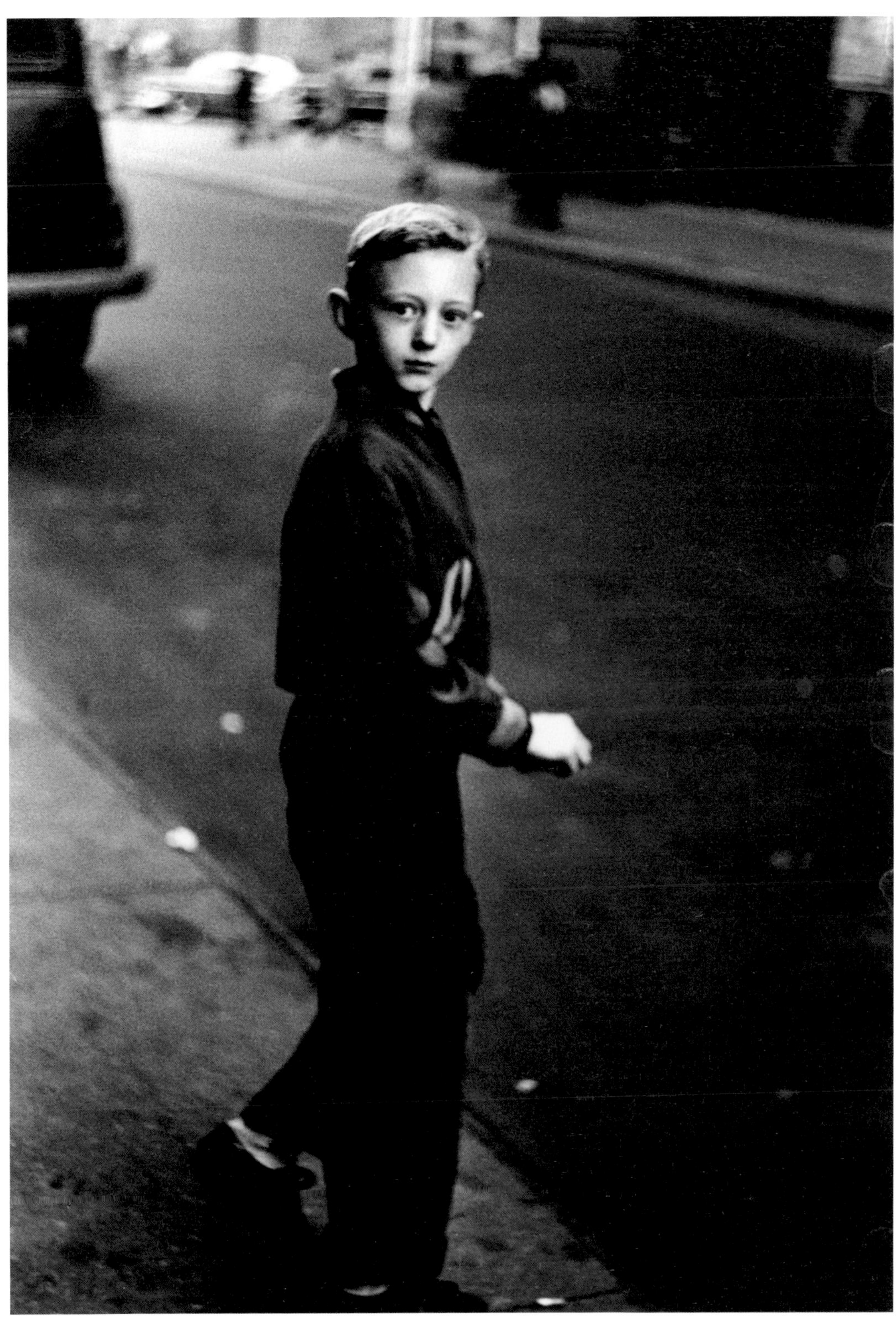

Boy stepping off the curb, N.Y.C. 1957–58

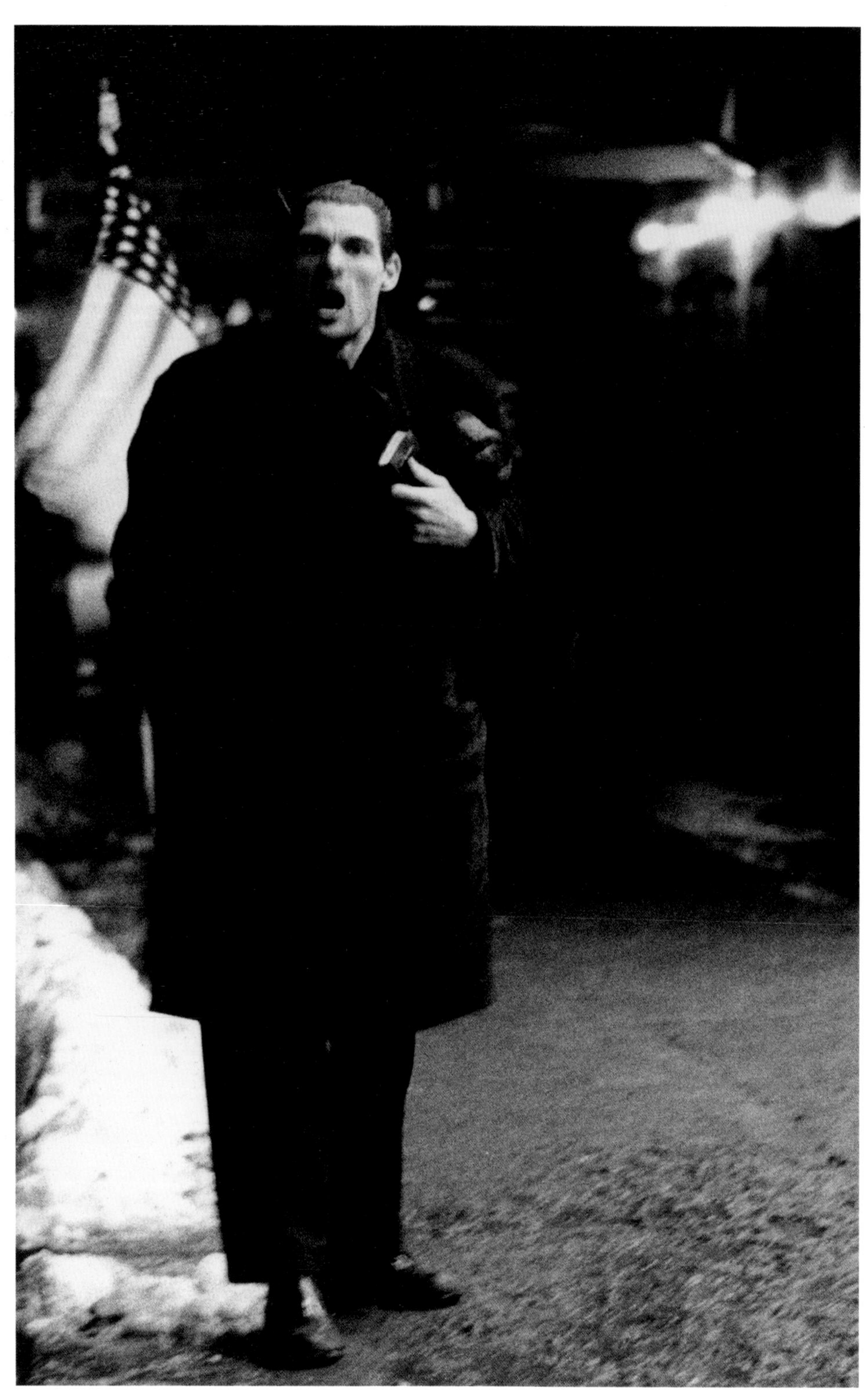

 Man yelling in Times Square, N.Y.C. 1958

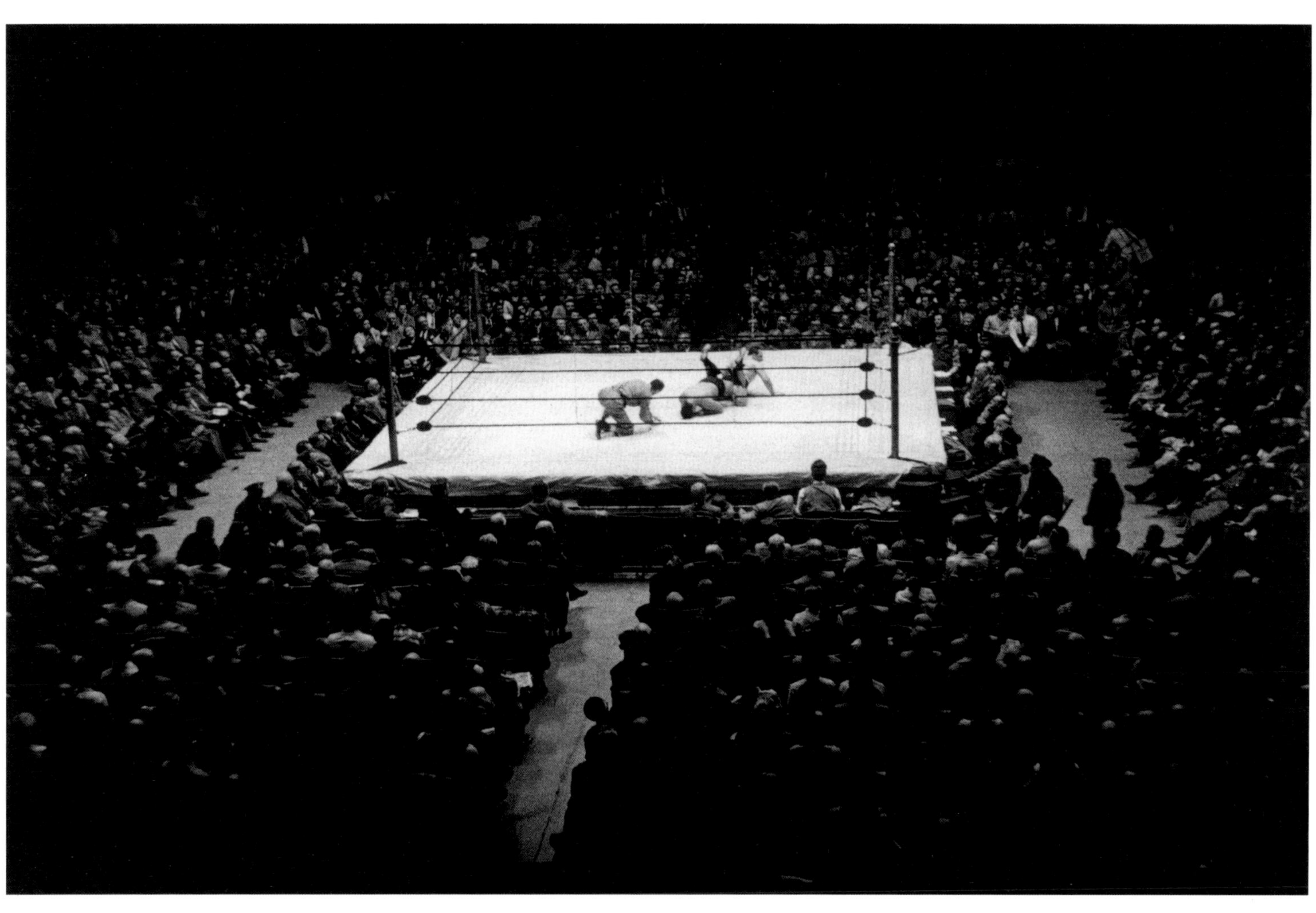

Wrestlers in the ring, N.Y.C. 1958

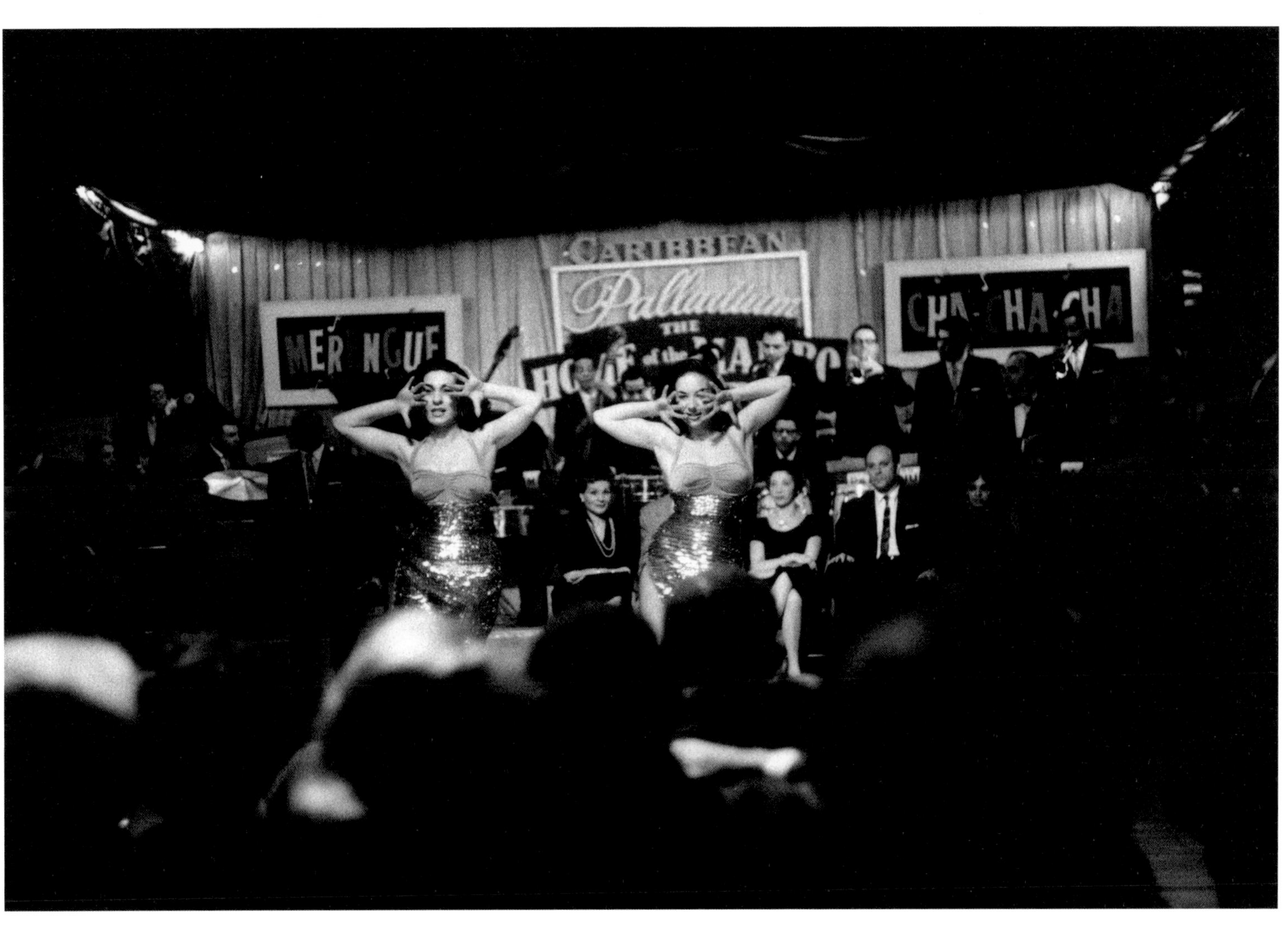

Two Cha-Cha dancers performing for an audience, N.Y.C. 1958

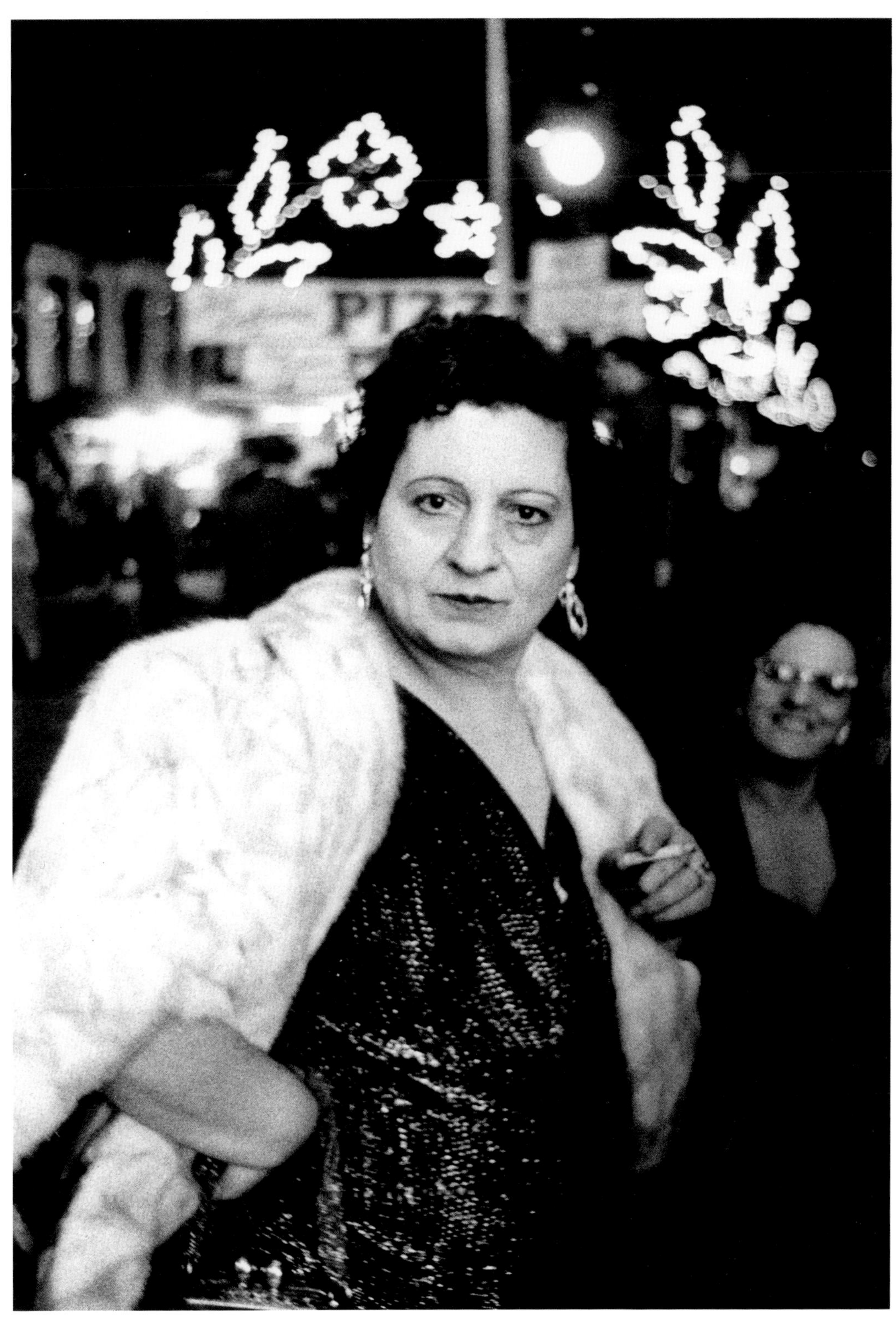

Woman in white fur with a cigarette, Mulberry Street, N.Y.C. 1958

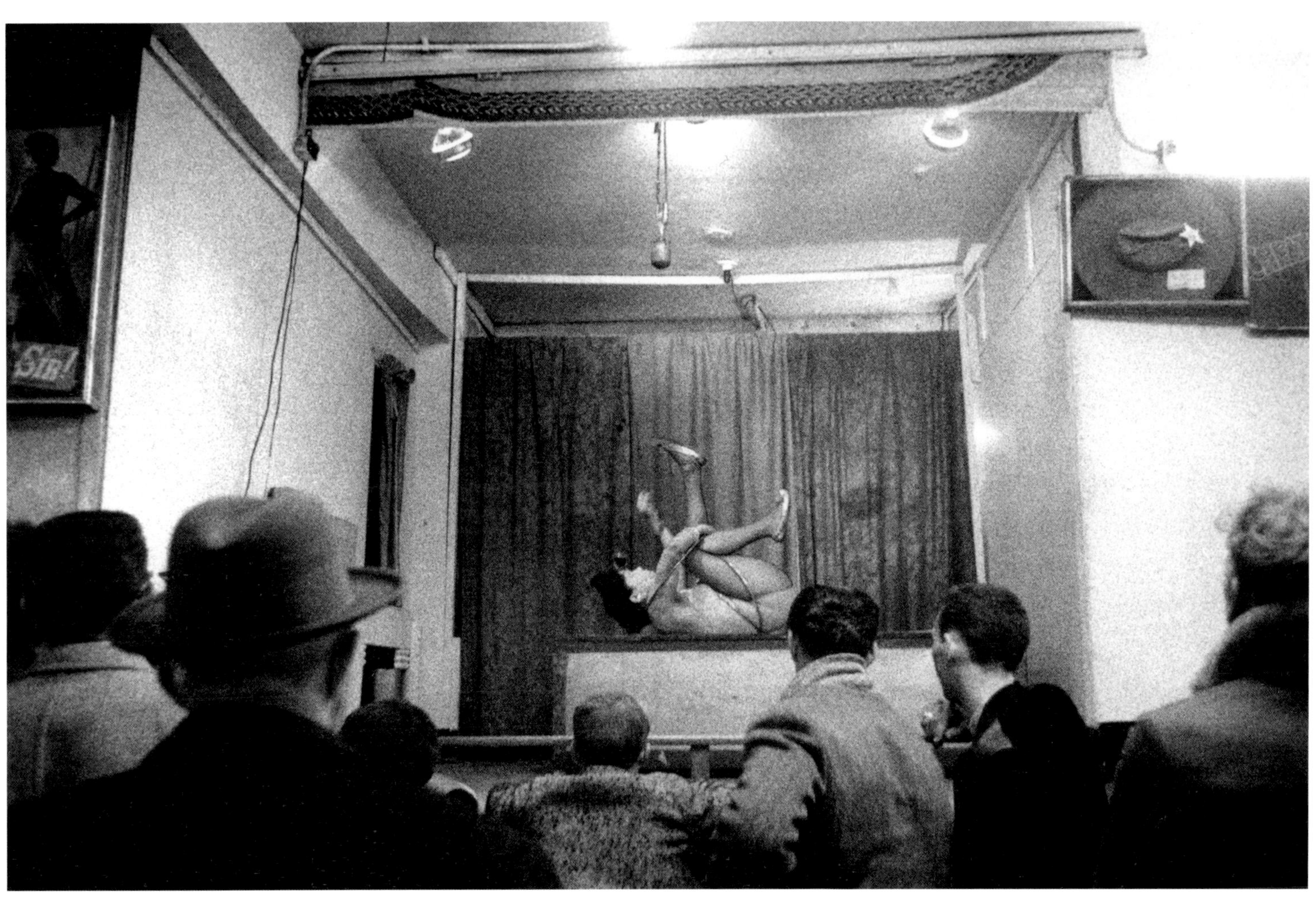

Contortionist Lydia Suarez performing for an audience, Hubert's Museum, N.Y.C. 1958

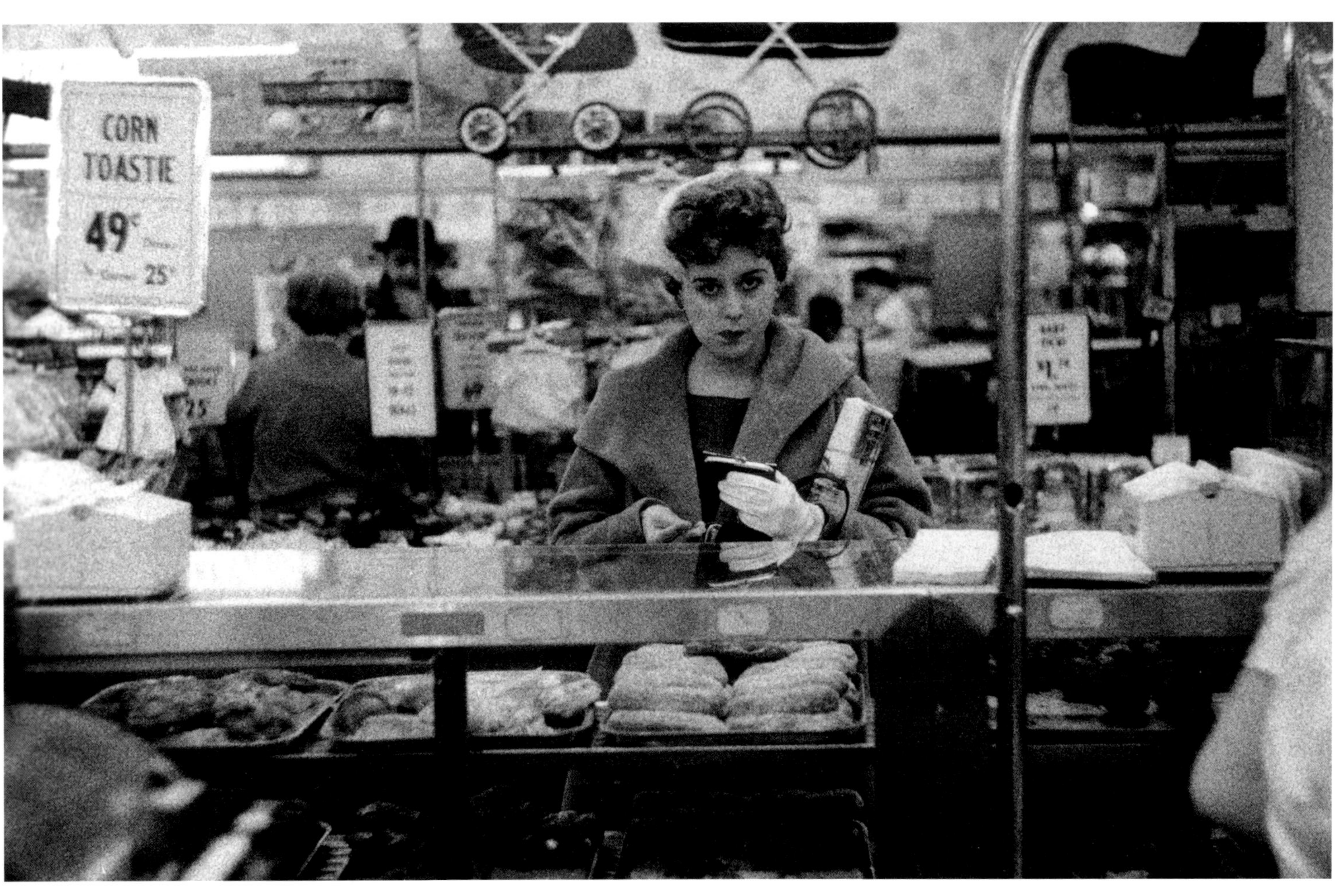

Woman with a change purse at a pastry counter, N.Y.C. 1958

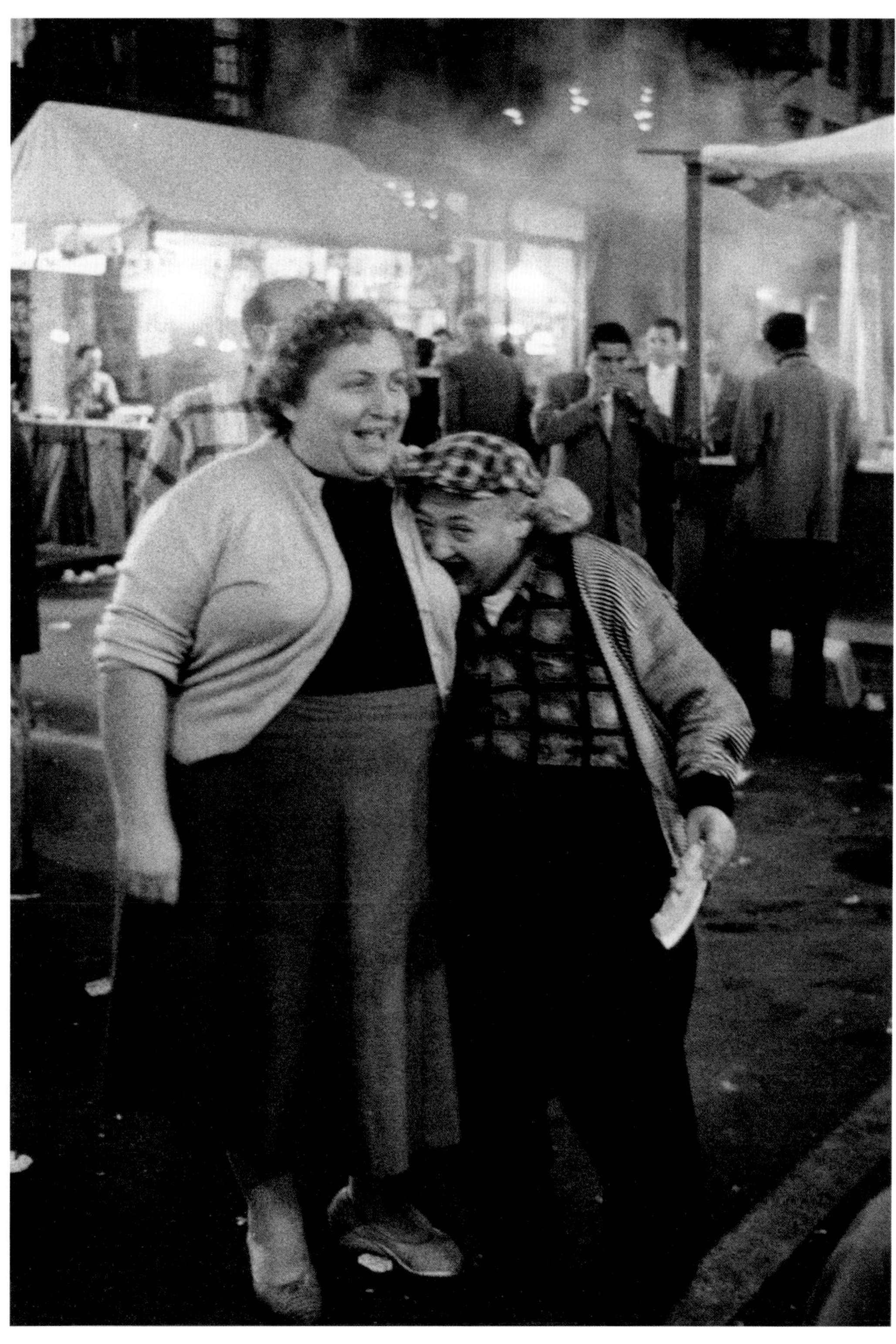

Little man biting woman's breast, N.Y.C. 1958

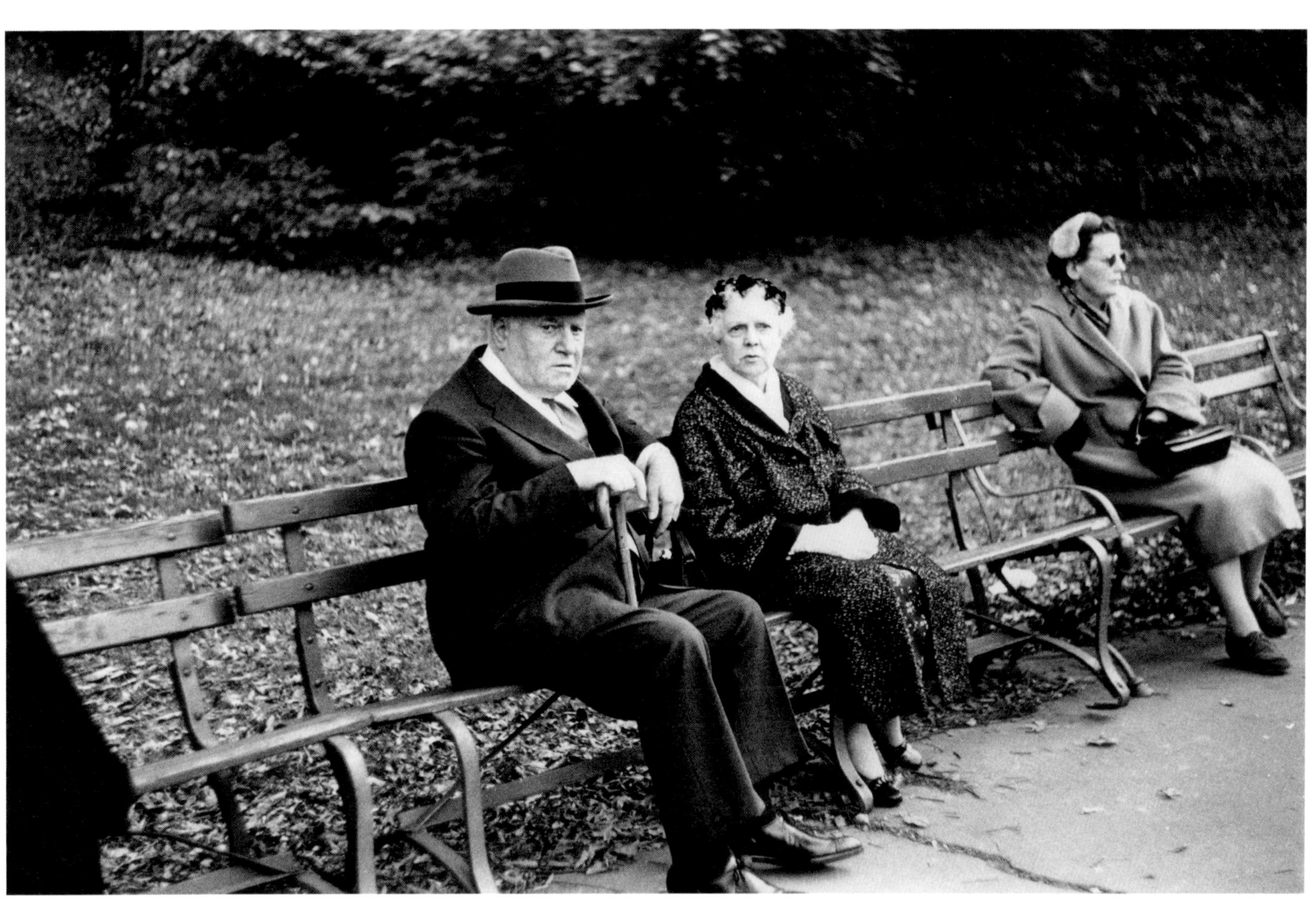

Old couple on a park bench, N.Y.C. 1958

Audience with projection booth, N.Y.C. 1958

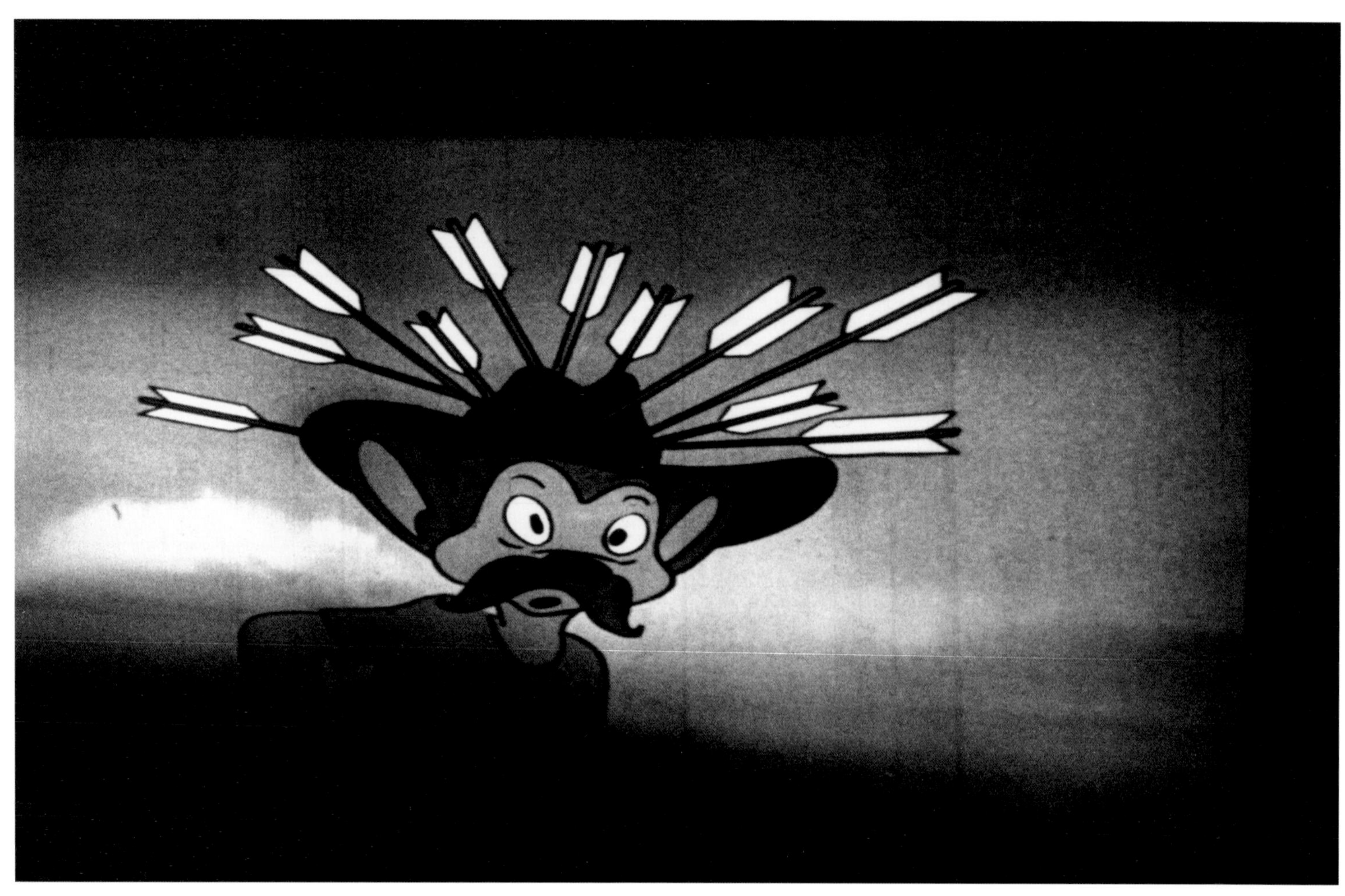

 Mighty Mouse western cartoon 1958

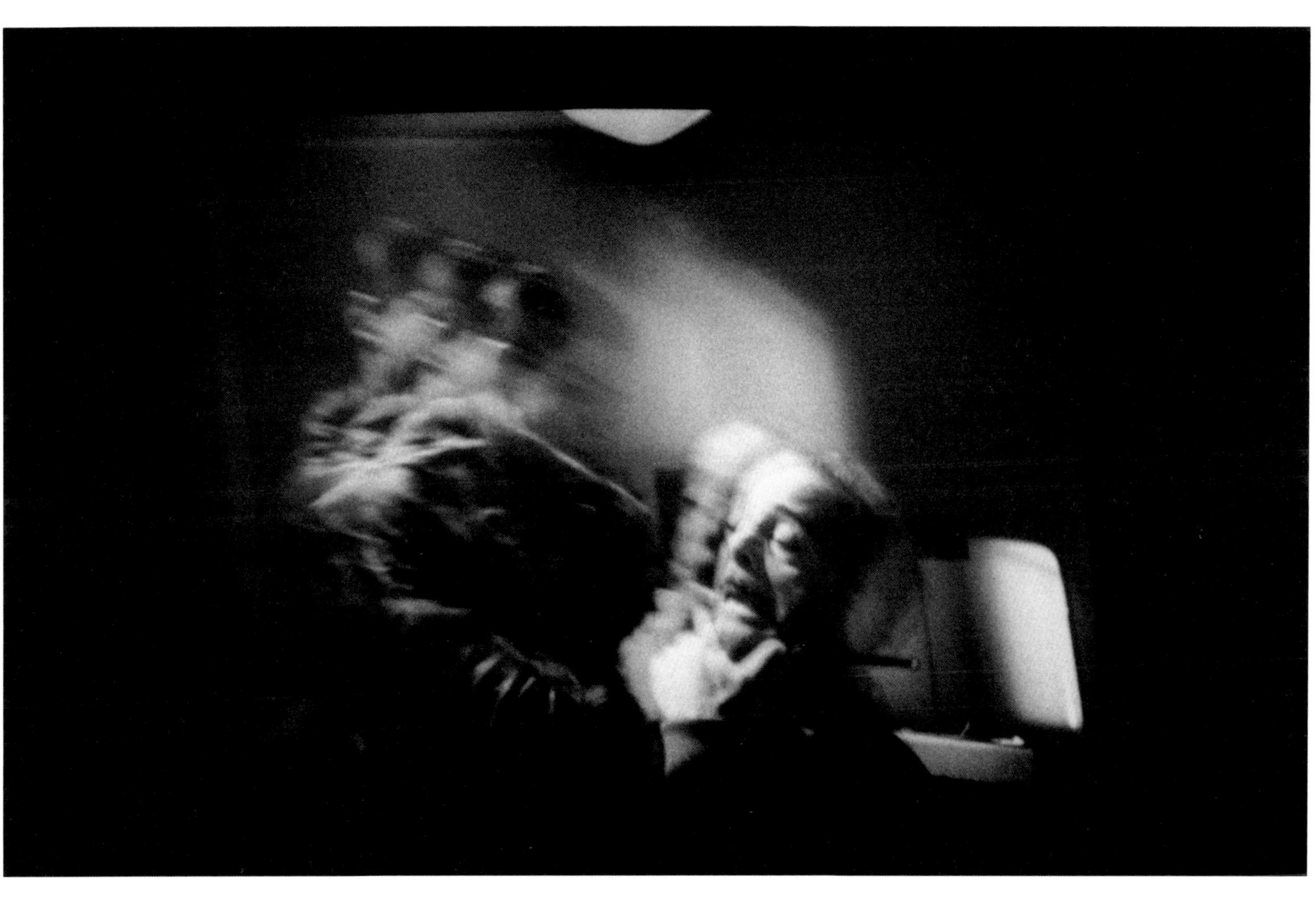

Man on screen being choked 1958

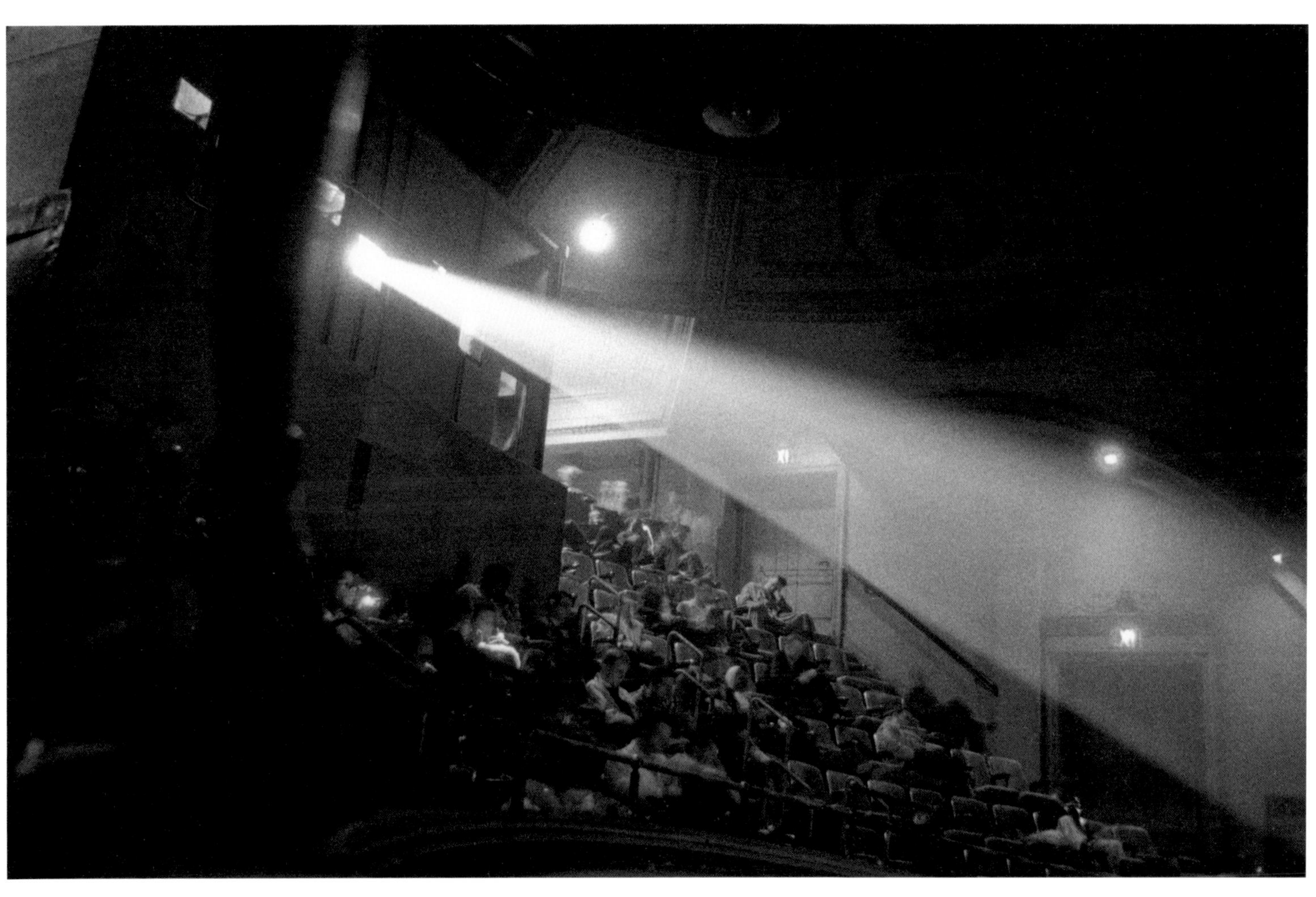

42nd Street movie theater audience, N.Y.C. 1958

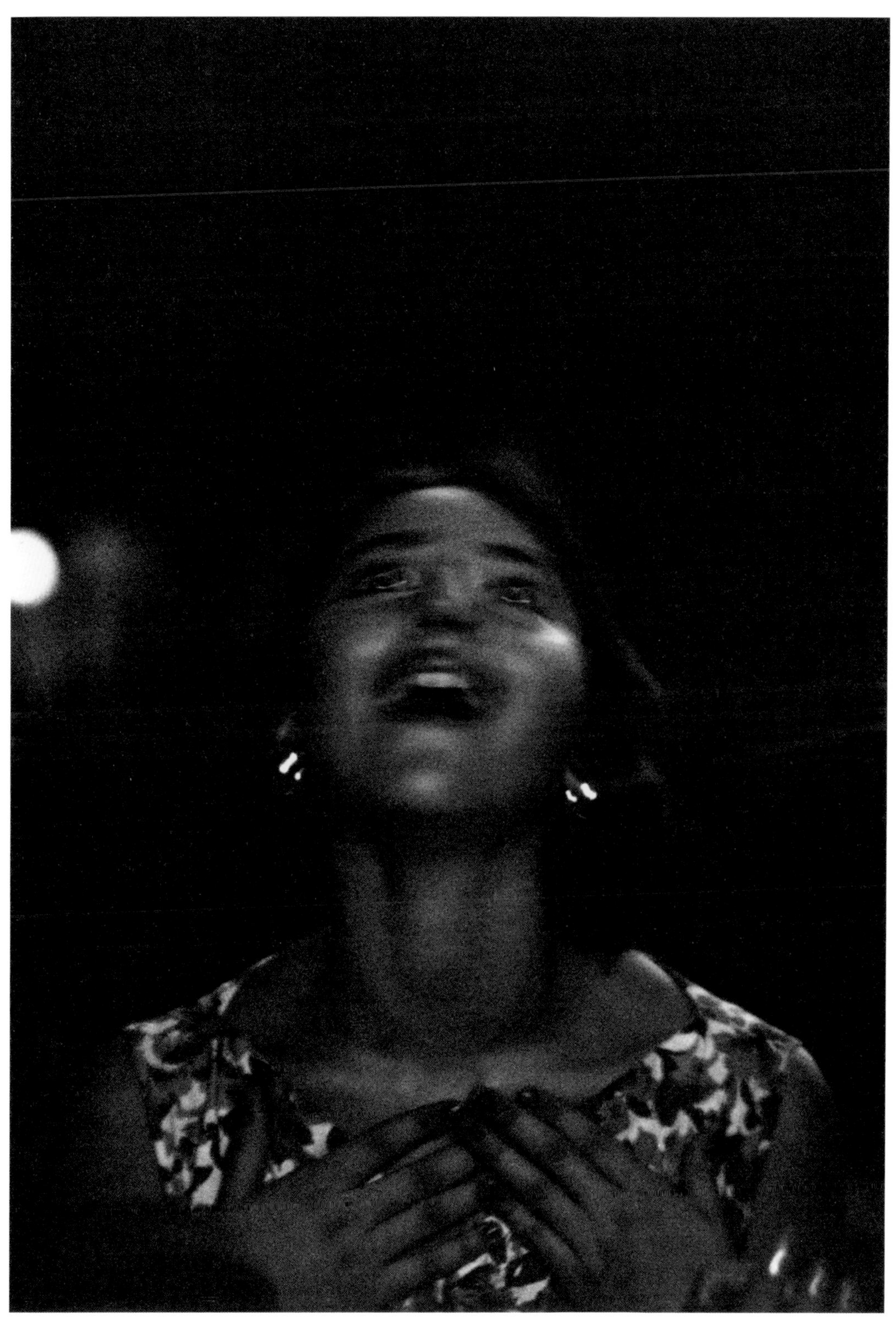

Blurry woman gazing up smiling, N.Y.C. 1957–58

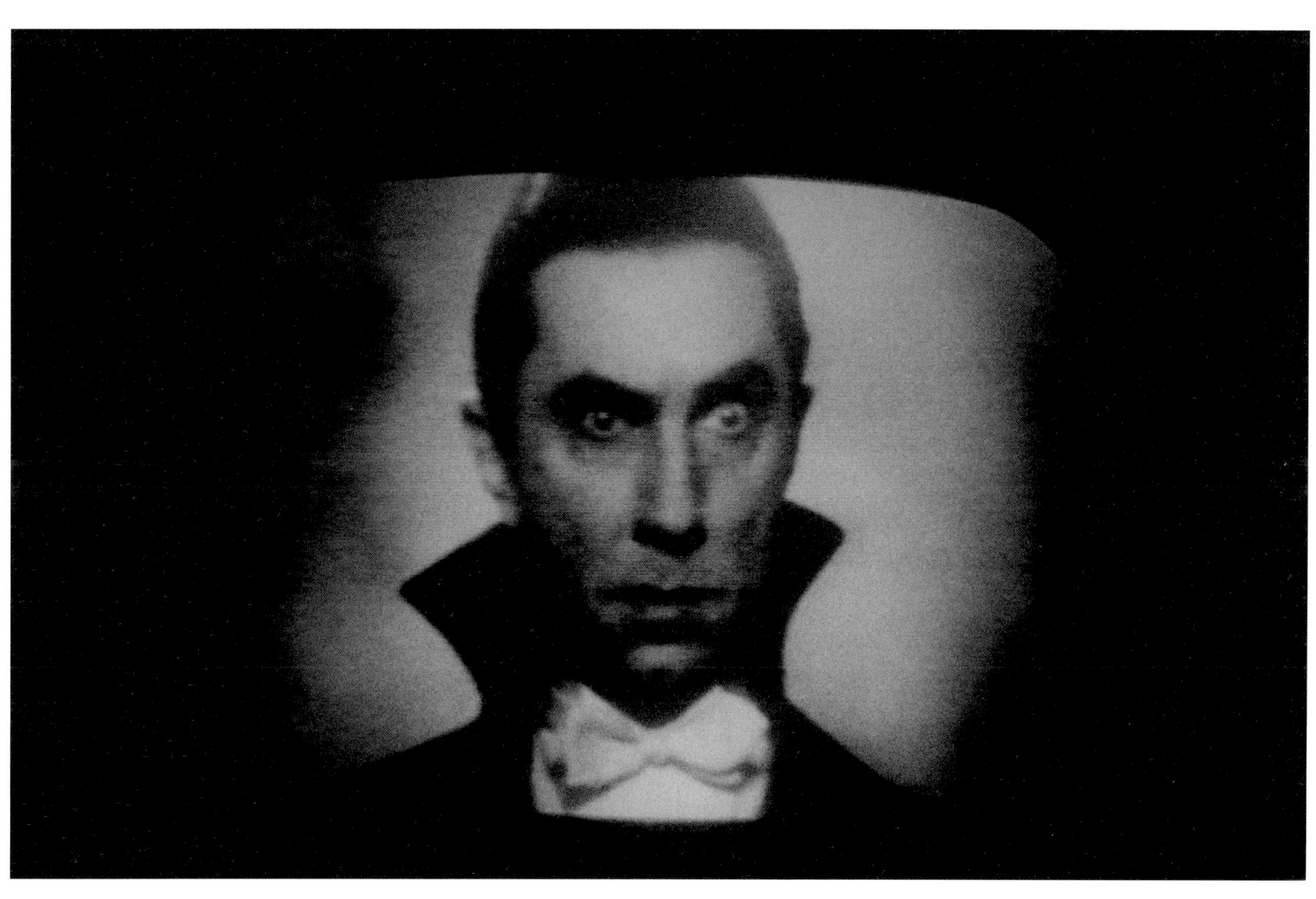

Bela Lugosi as Dracula on television 1958

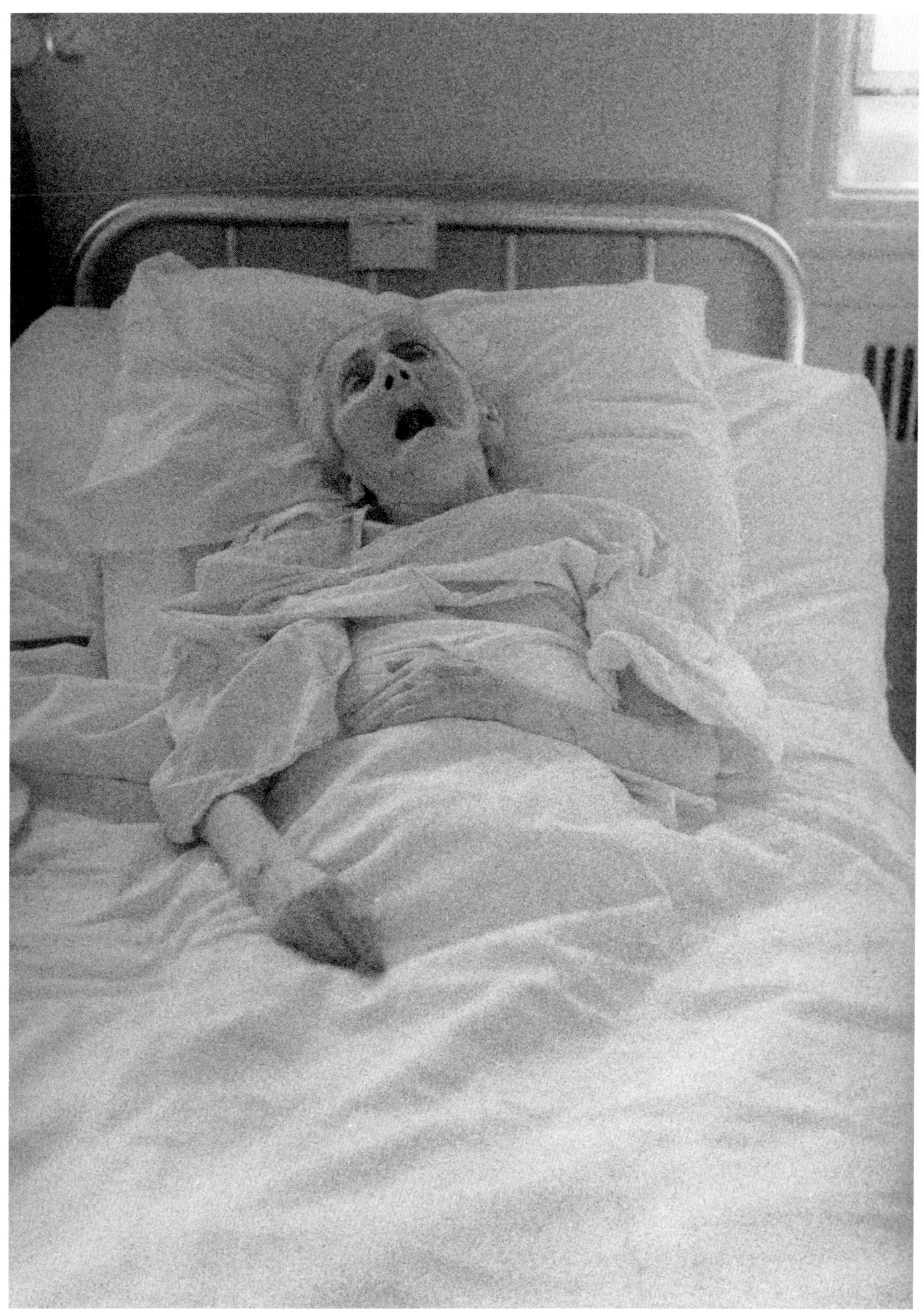

Old woman in a hospital bed, N.Y.C. 1958

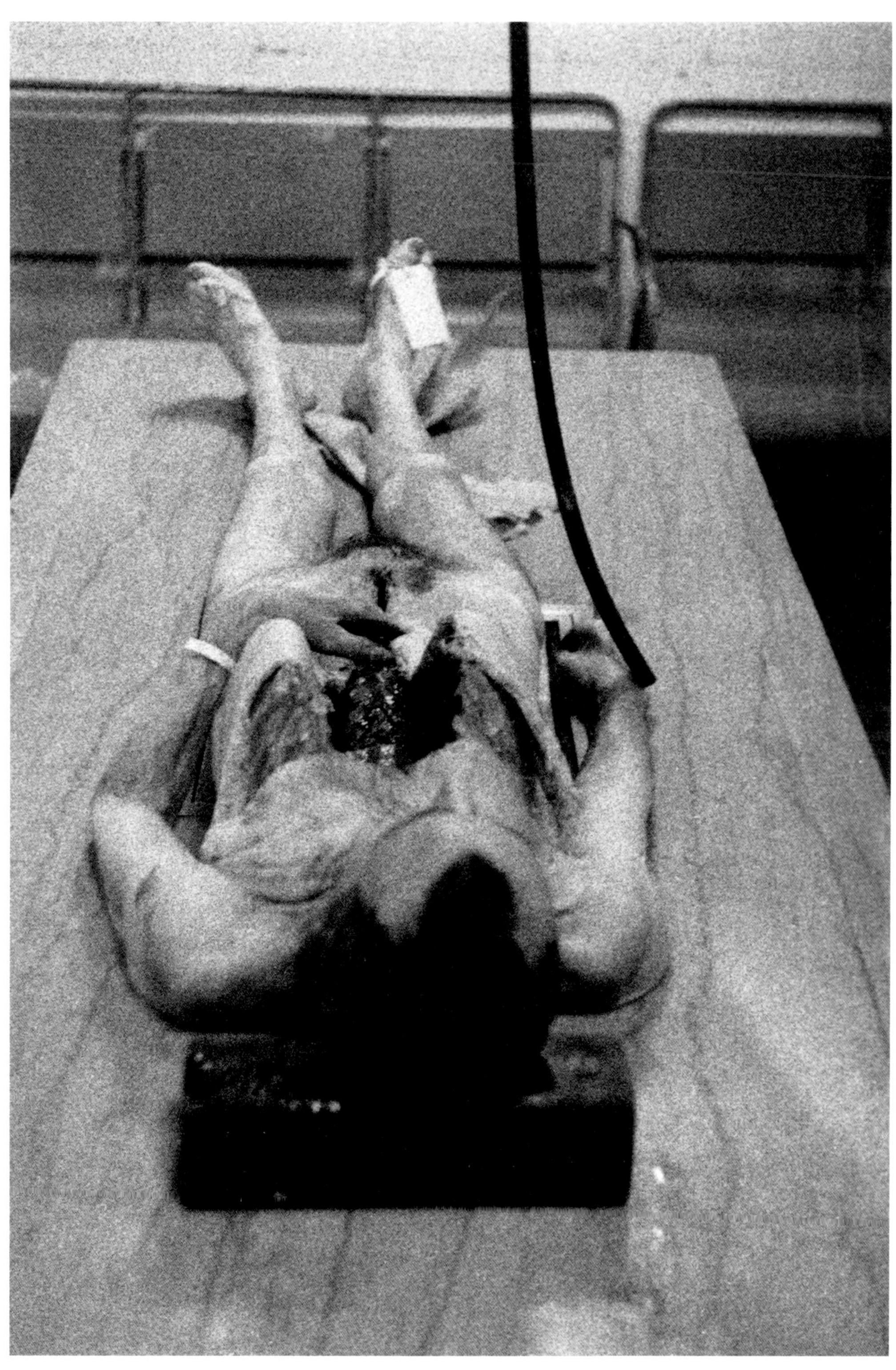

Corpse with receding hairline and a toe tag, N.Y.C. 1959

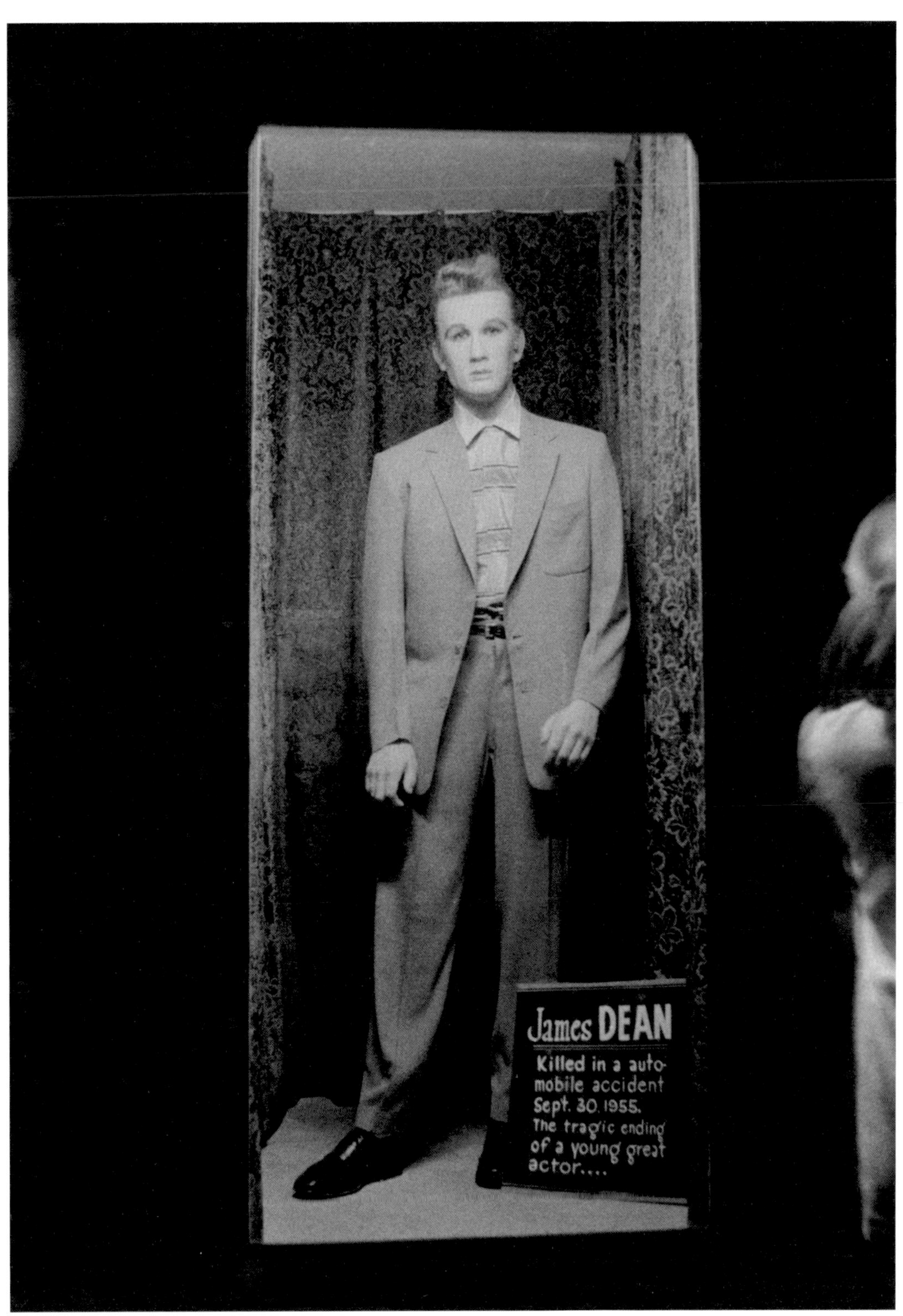

James Dean in the wax museum, Coney Island, N.Y. 1959

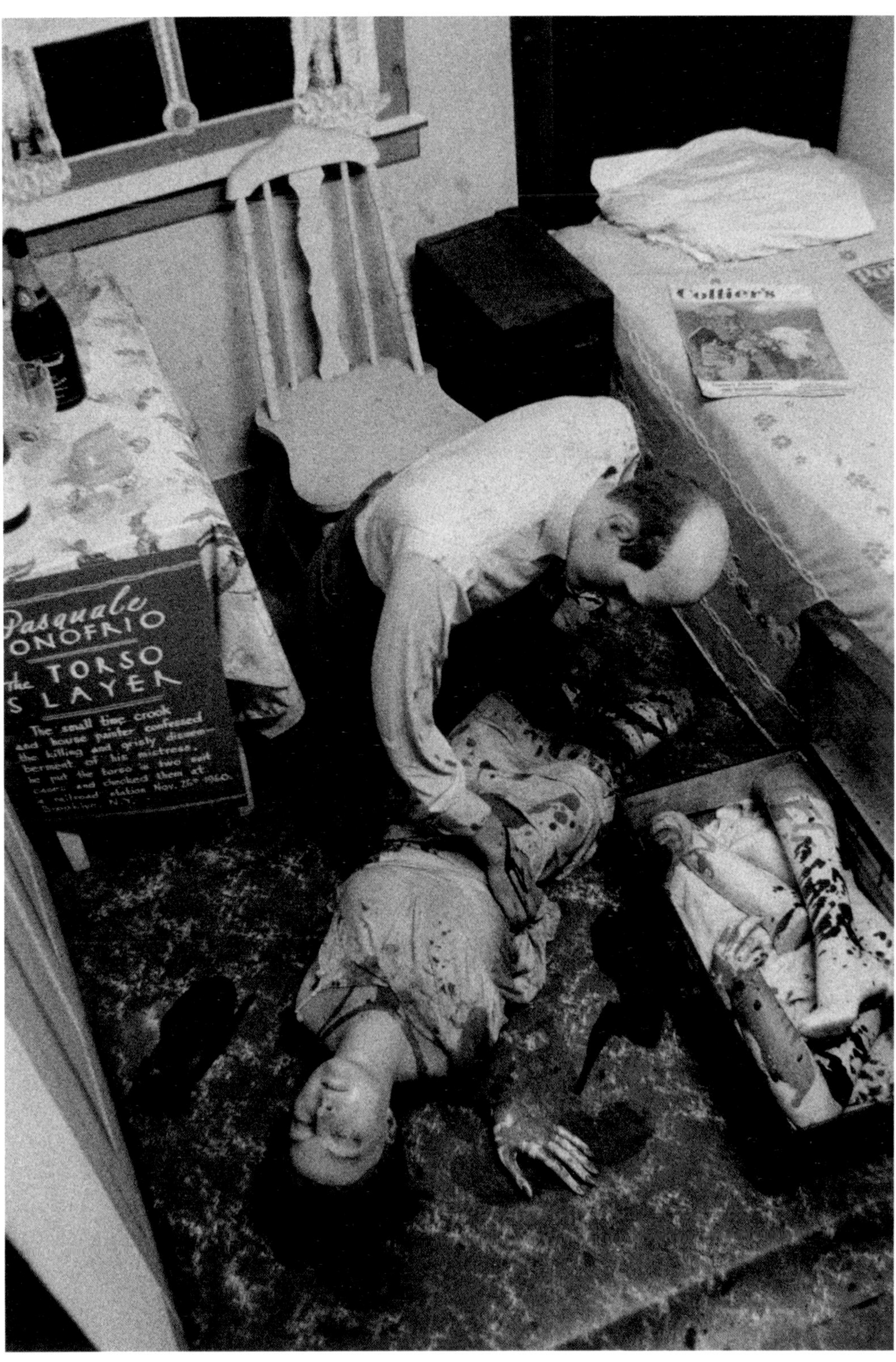

Wax museum axe murderer, Coney Island, N.Y. 1959

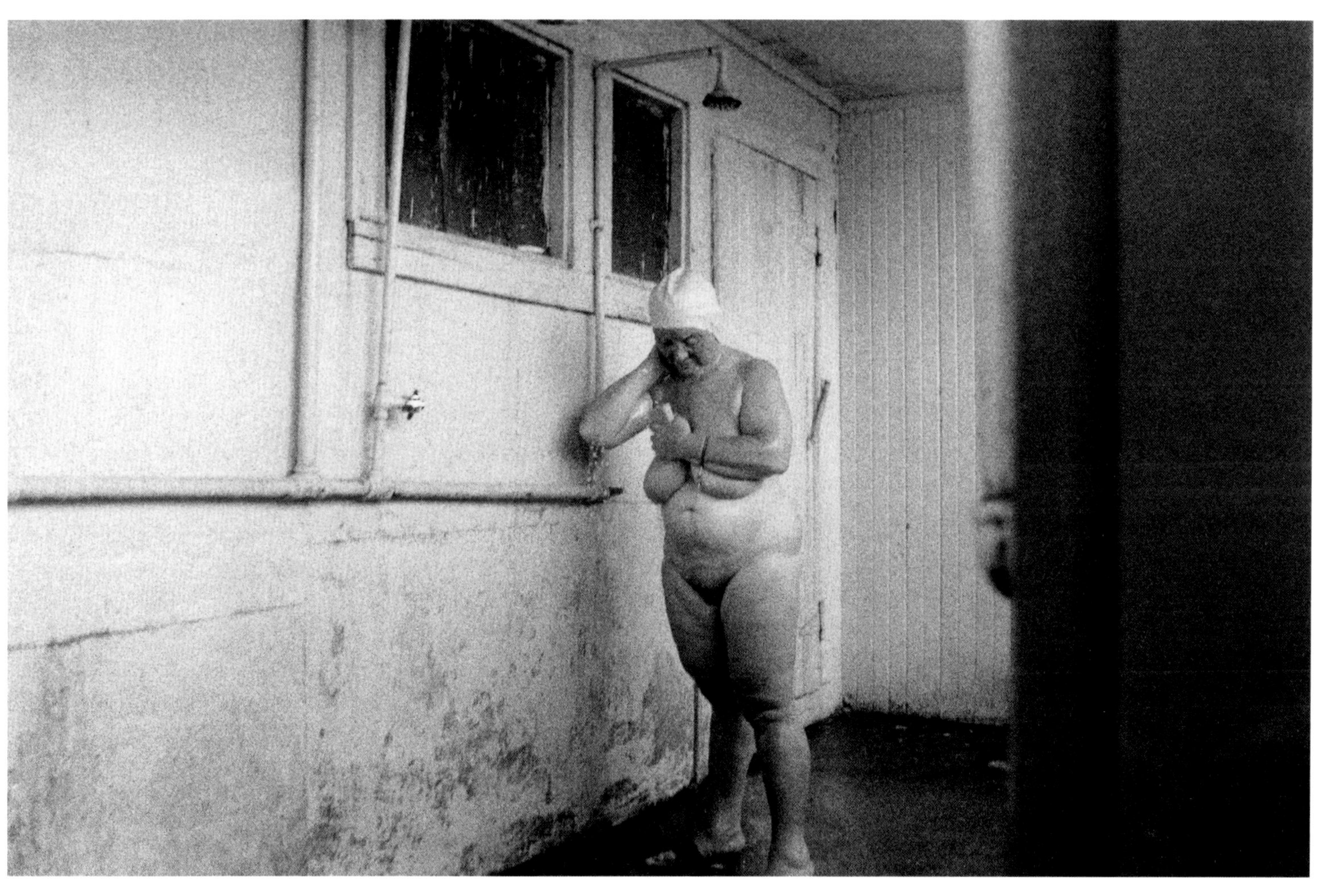

Lady in the shower, Coney Island, N.Y. 1959

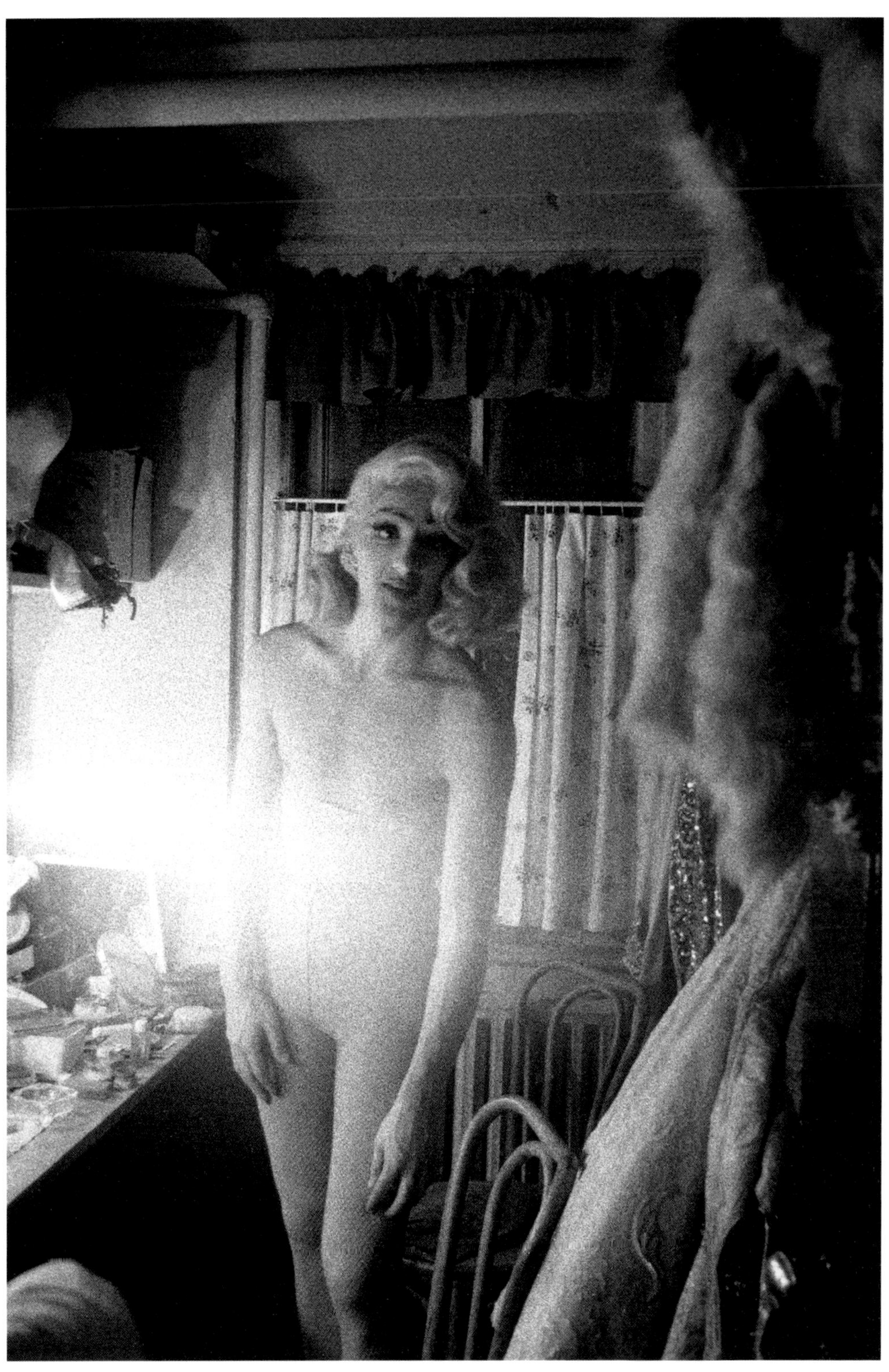

Blonde female impersonator standing by a dressing table, Hempstead, L.I. 1959

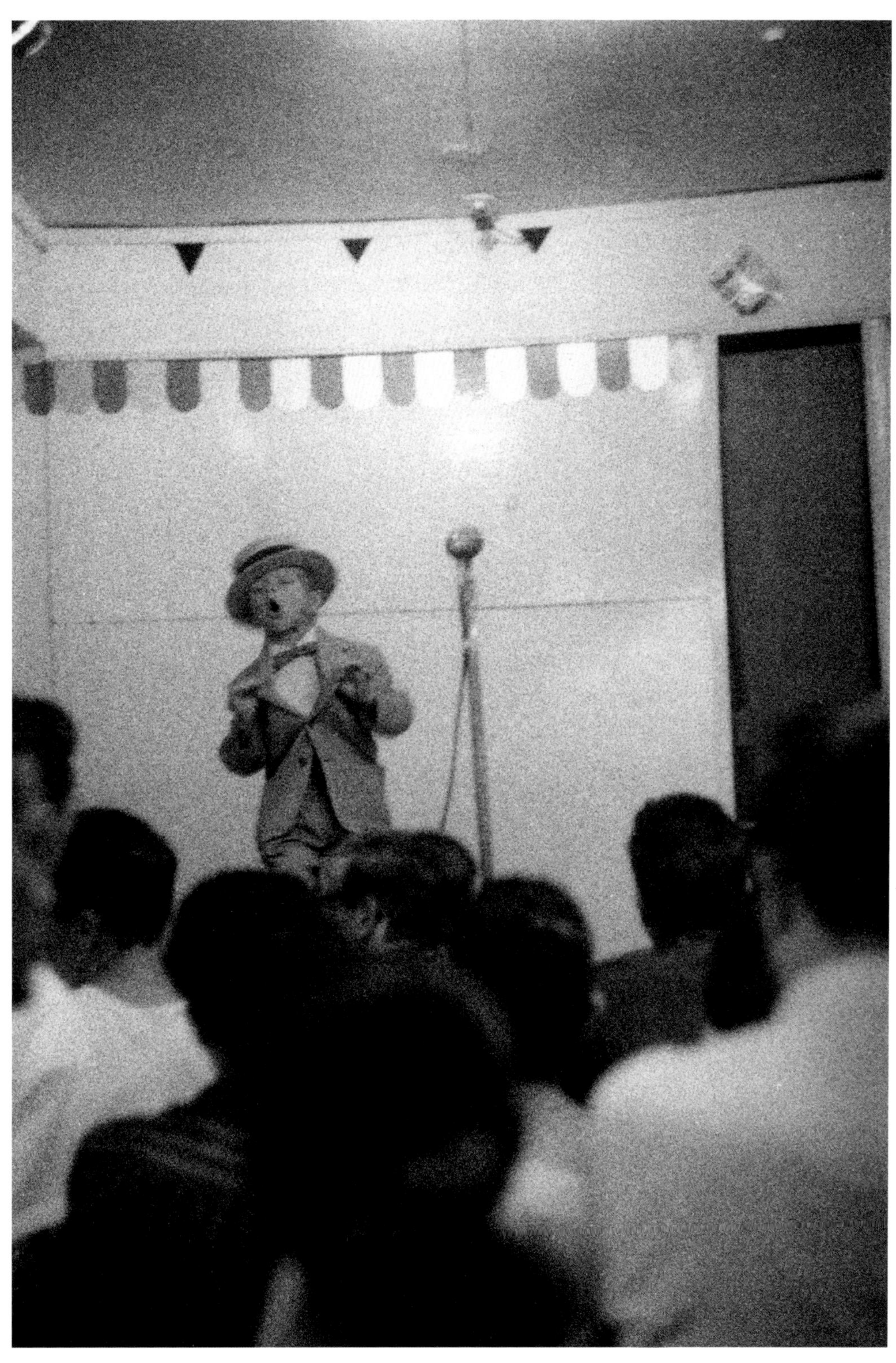

Andy "Potato Chips" Ratoucheff doing his Maurice Chevalier impersonation,
Hubert's Museum, N.Y.C. 1959

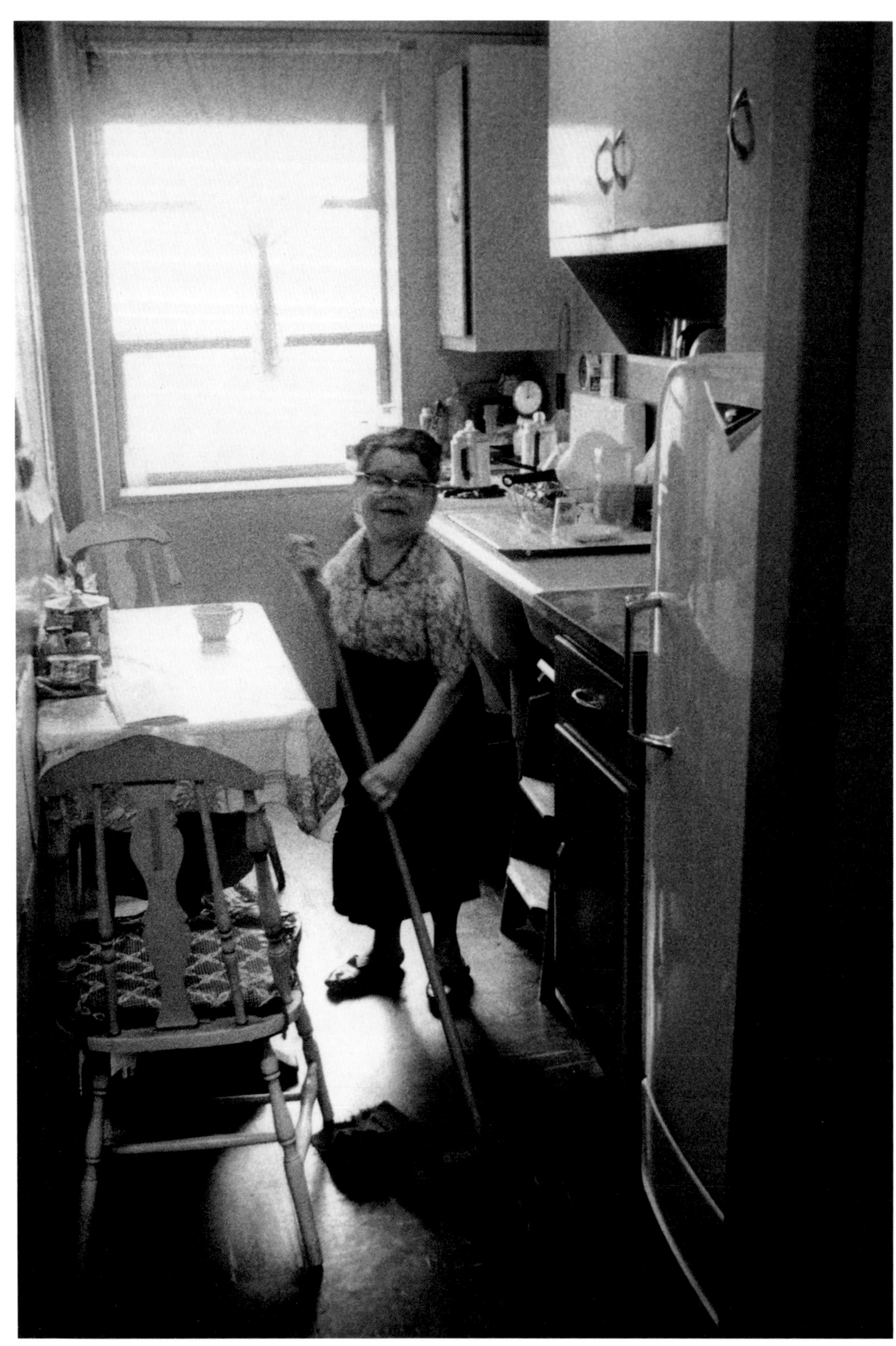

Miss Makrina, a Russian midget, in her kitchen, N.Y.C. 1959

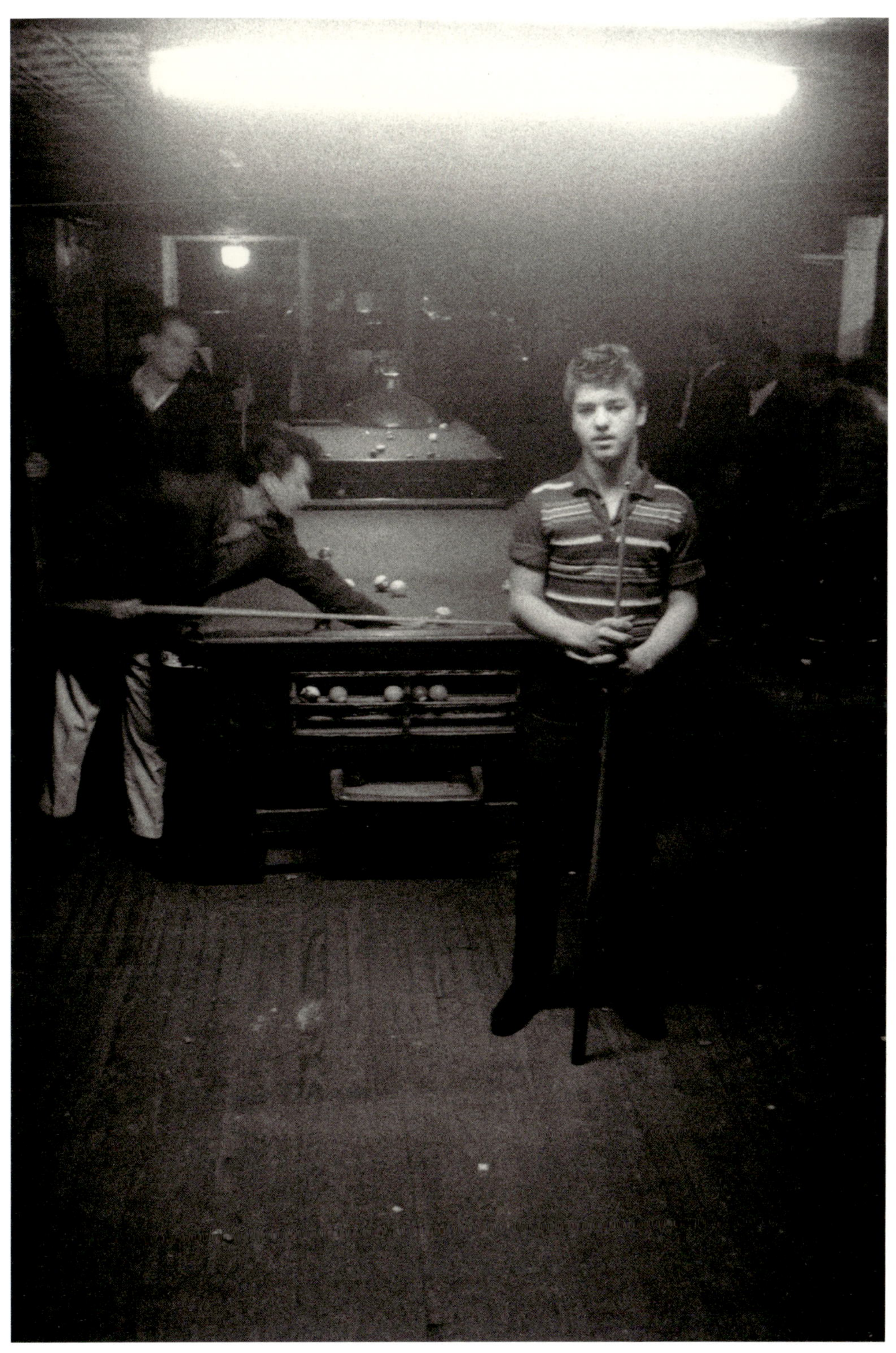

Boy at a pool hall, N.Y.C. 1960

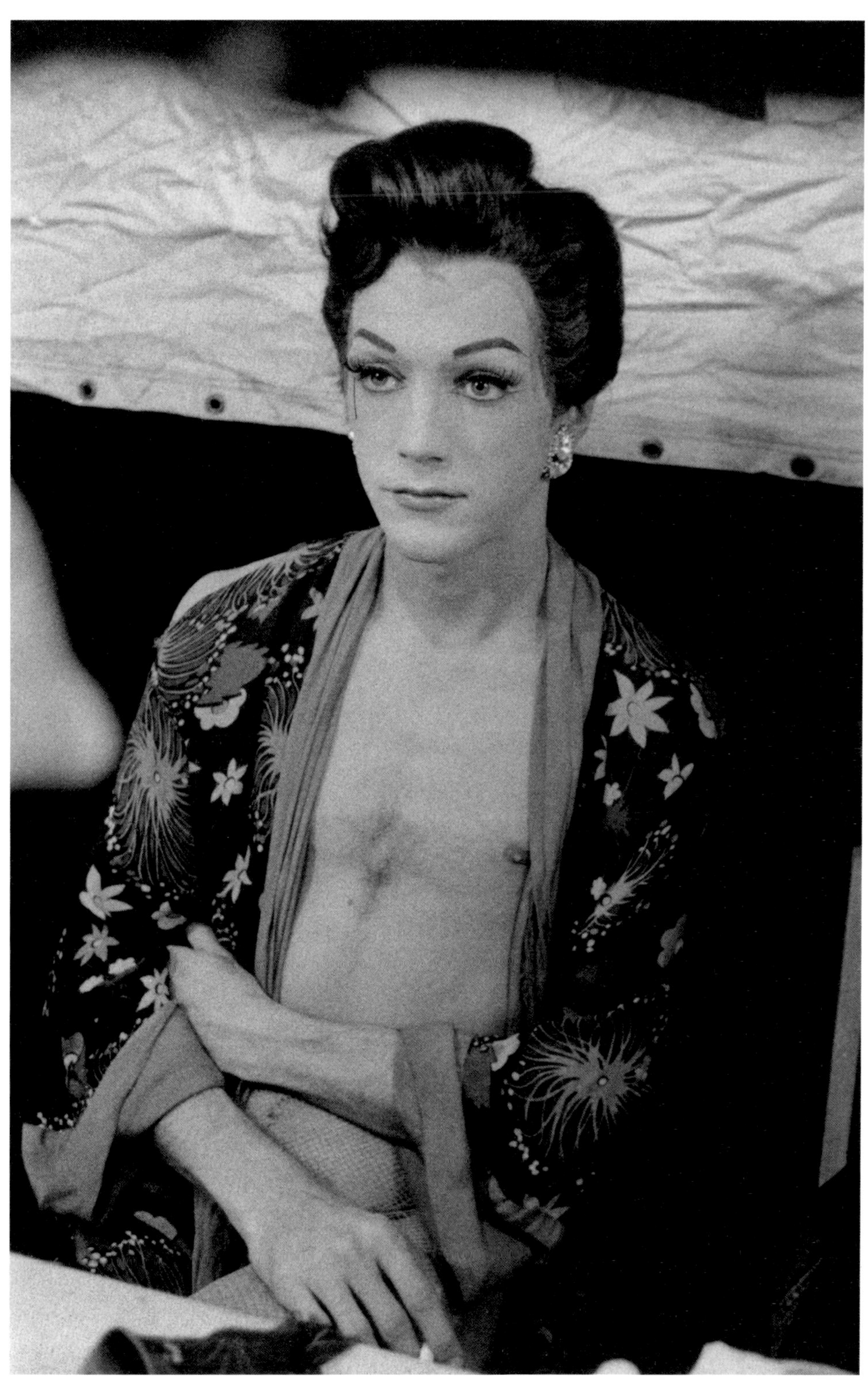

Seated female impersonator in an open kimono, Hempstead, L.I. 1959

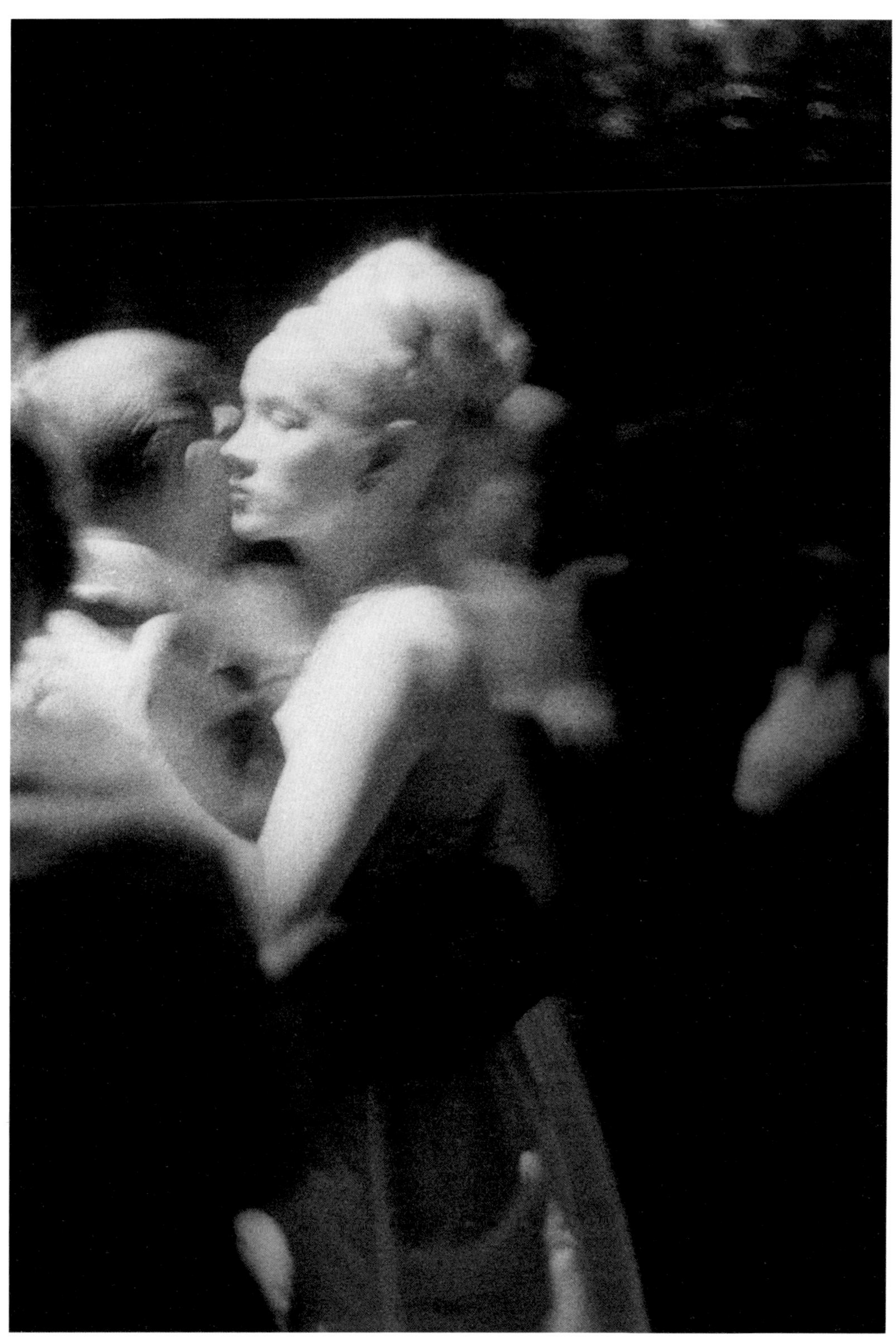

Miss Marian Seymour dancing with Baron Theo Von Roth at the Grand Opera Ball, N.Y.C. 1959

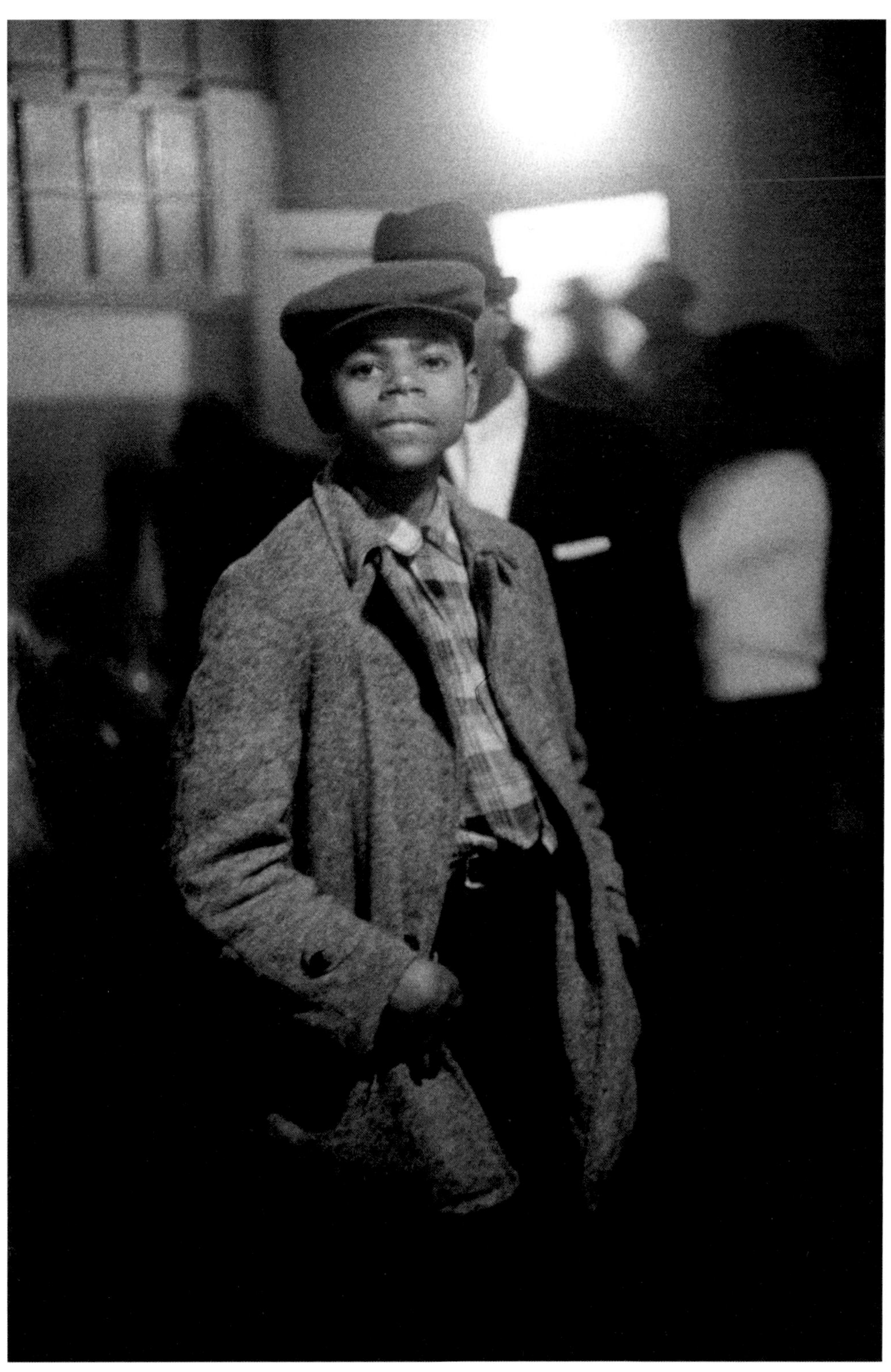

Boy in a cap at a dance, N.Y.C. 1960

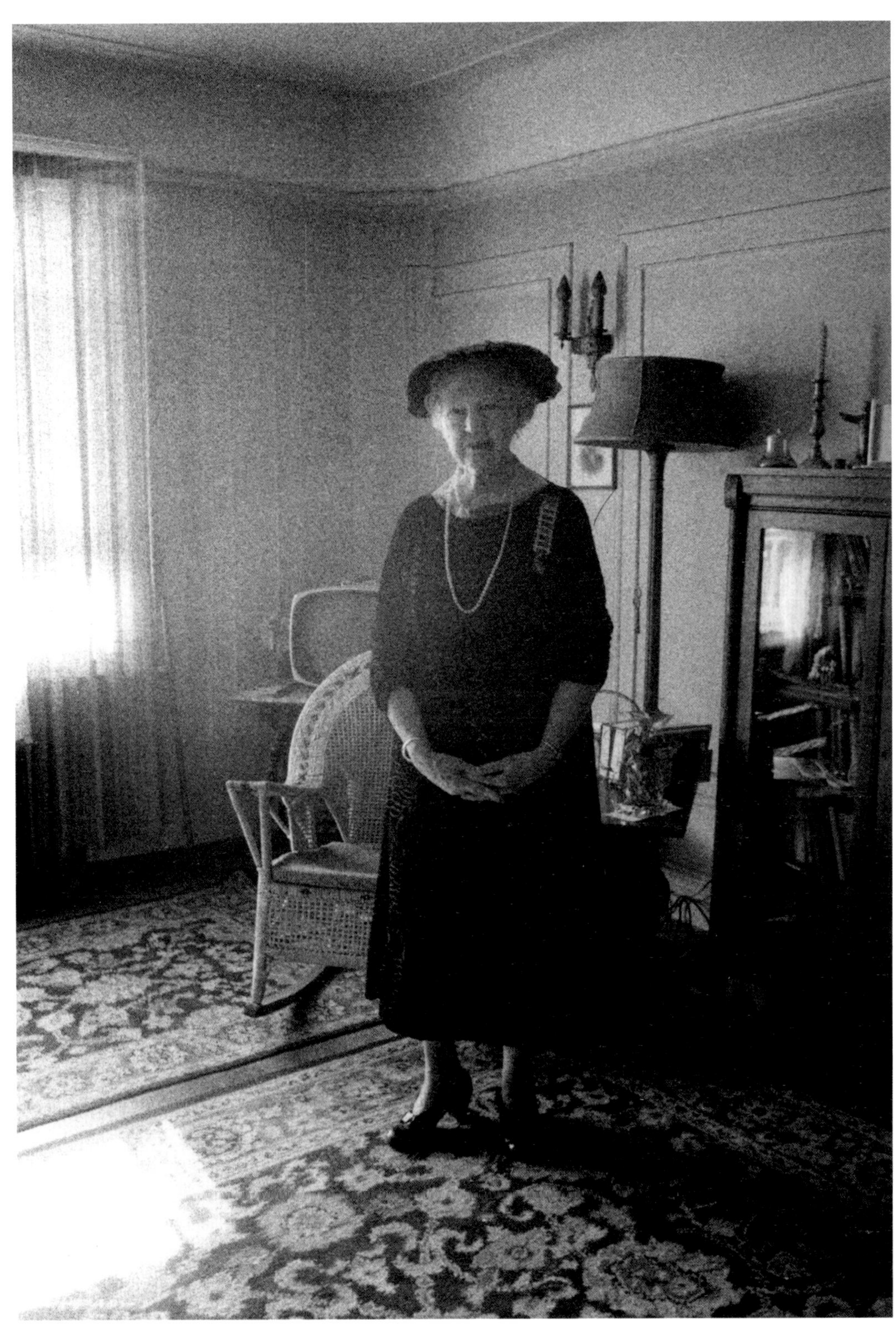

Flora Knapp Dickinson, Honorary Regent of the Washington Heights Chapter
of the Daughters of the American Revolution, N.Y.C. 1960

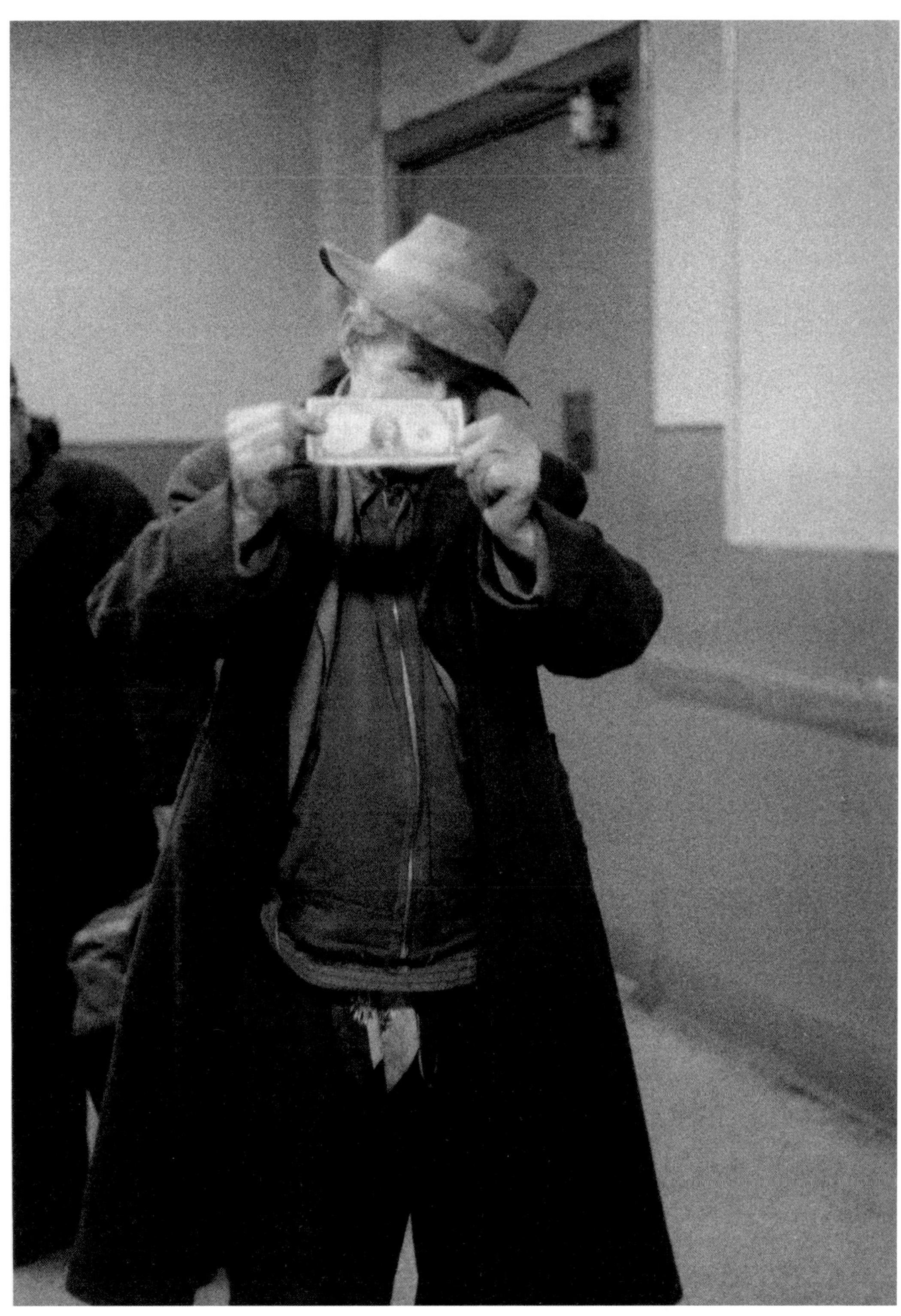

Man at the Municipal Shelter, holding up a dollar bill, N.Y.C. 1960

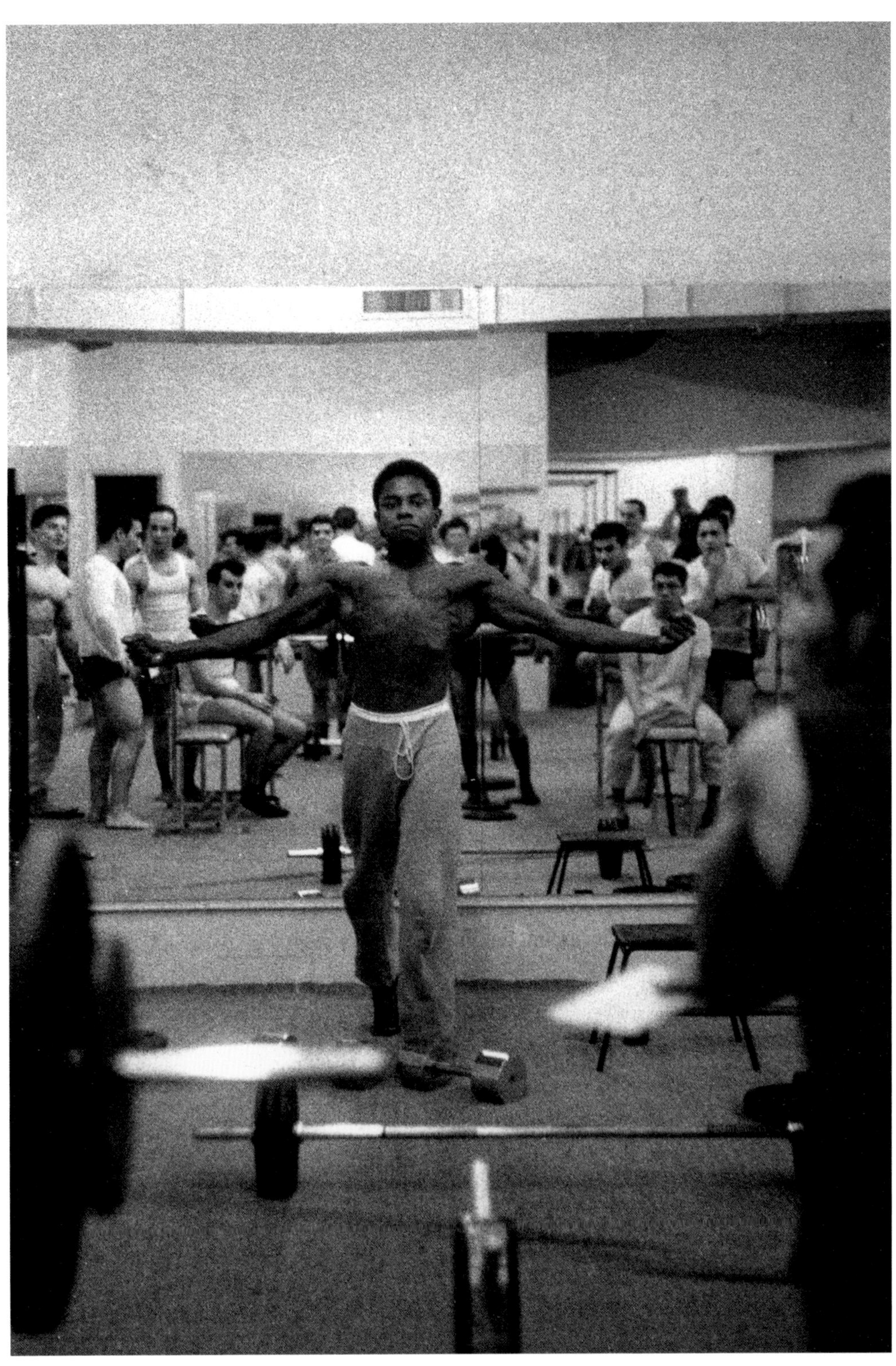

A boy practicing physique posing at the Empire Gym, N.Y.C. 1960

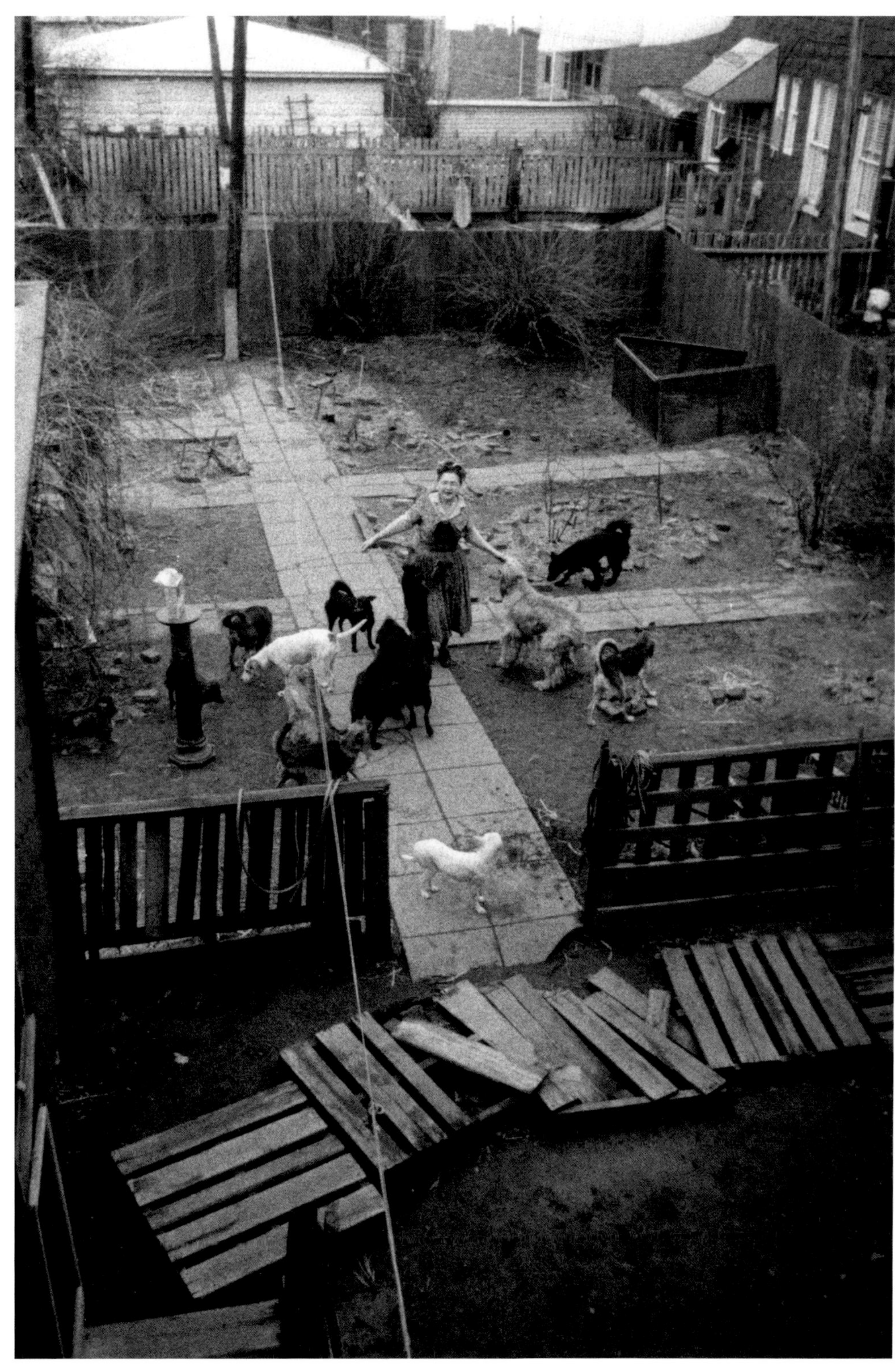

Miss Katheryn Lambert with her dogs in the backyard, Brooklyn, N.Y. 1960

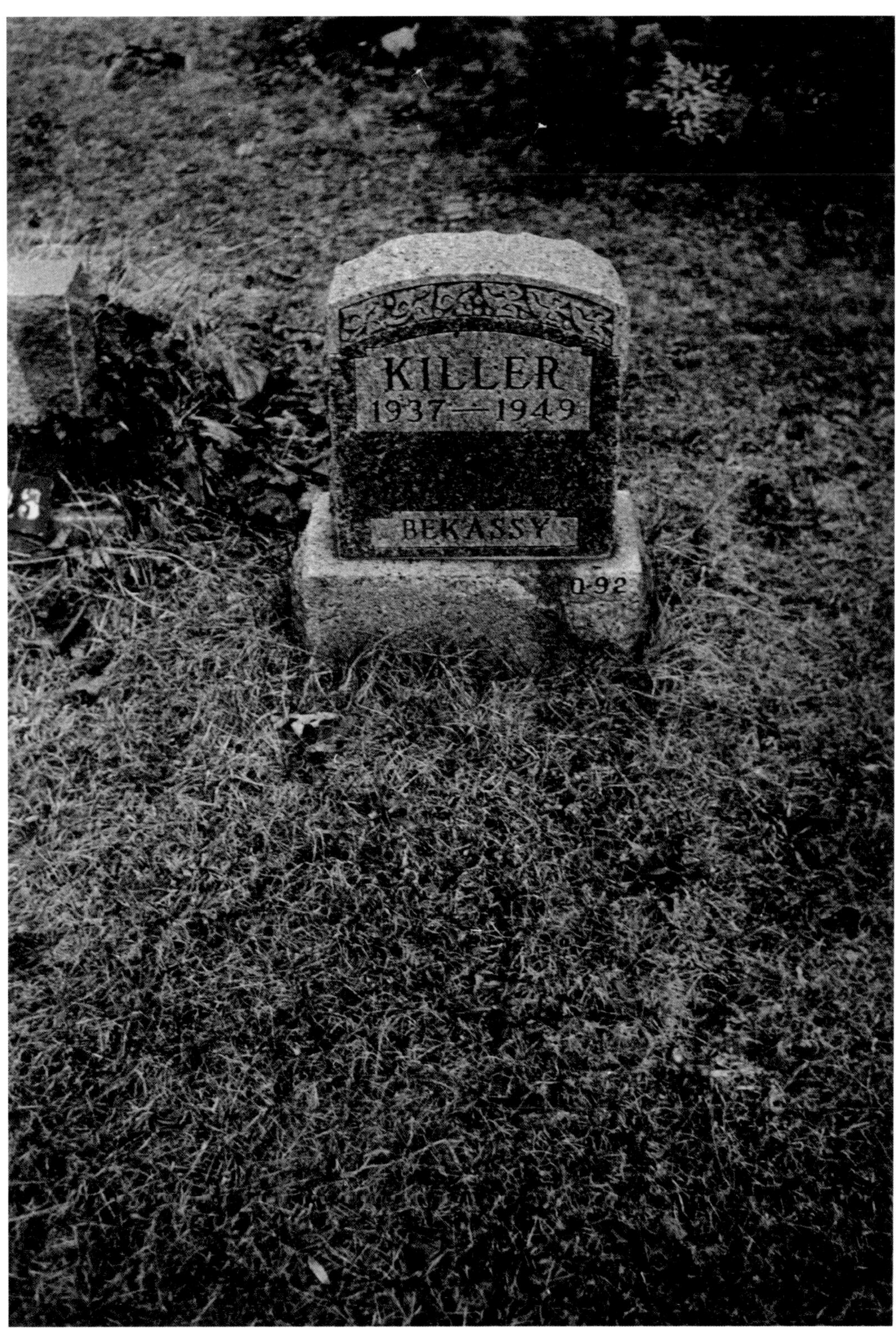

Headstone for "Killer" at Bide a Wee Cemetery, Wantagh, N.Y. 1960

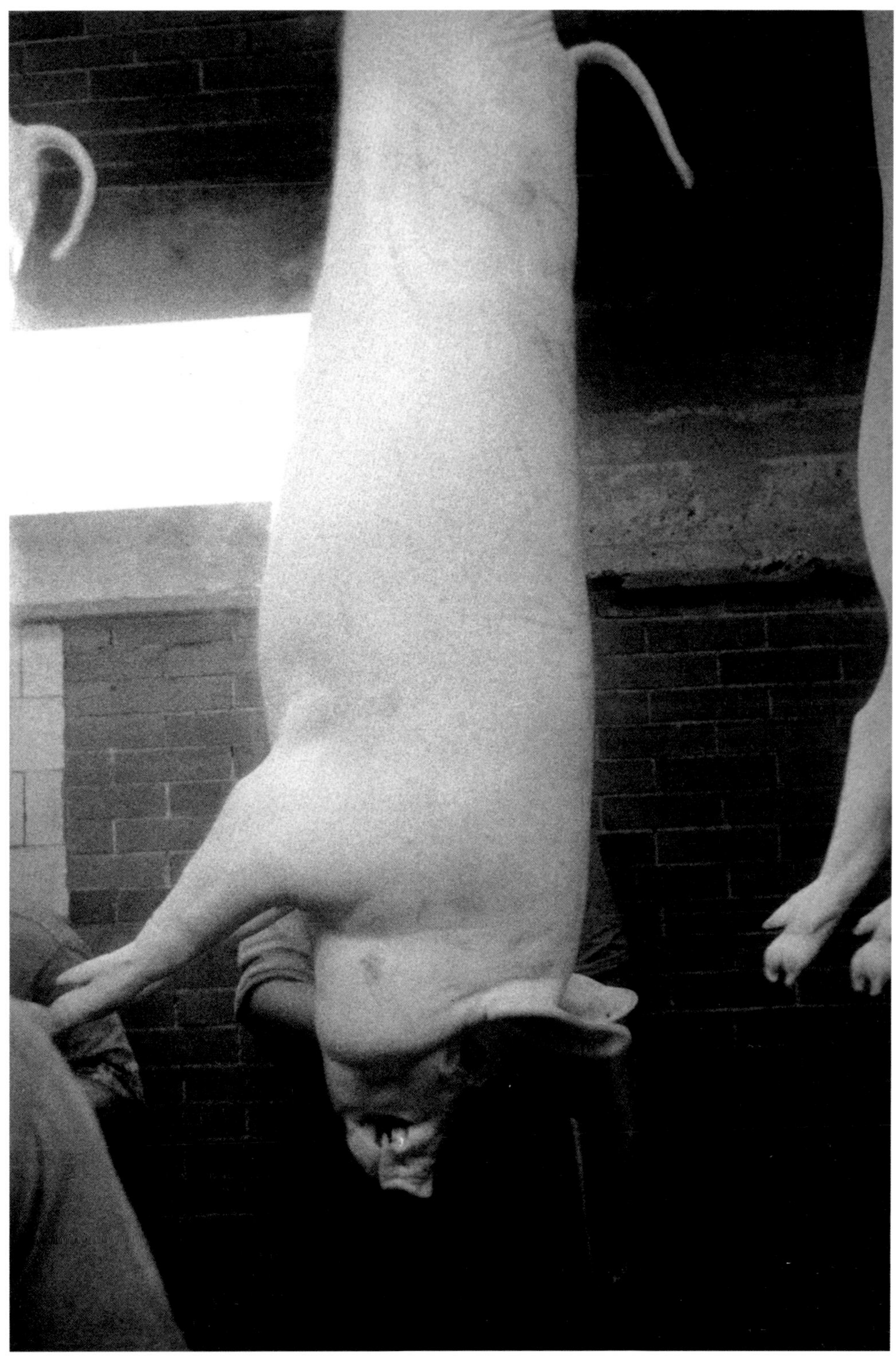

Dead pigs hanging, N.Y.C. 1960

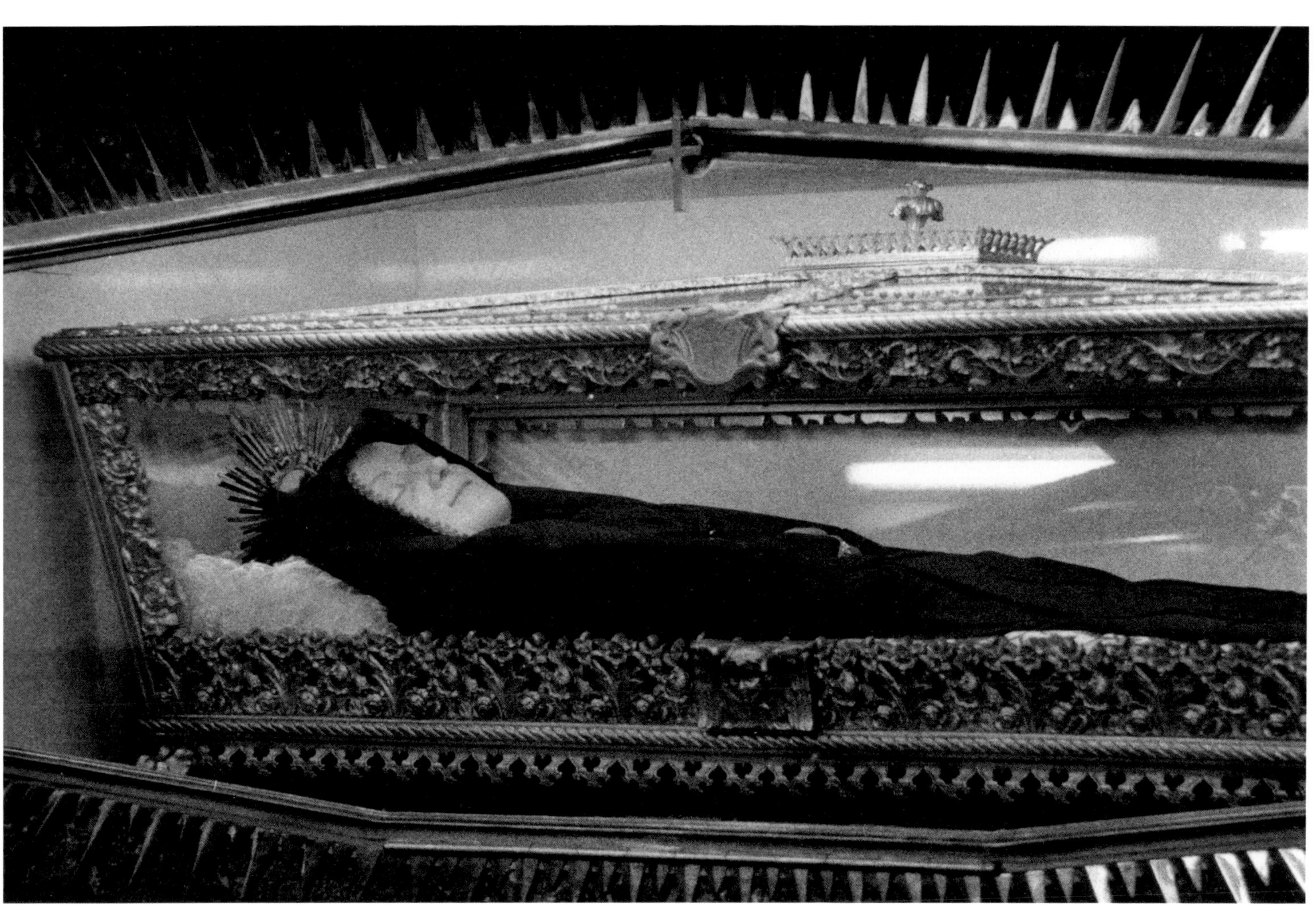

Mother Cabrini, a disinterred saint in her glass and gold casket, N.Y.C. 1960

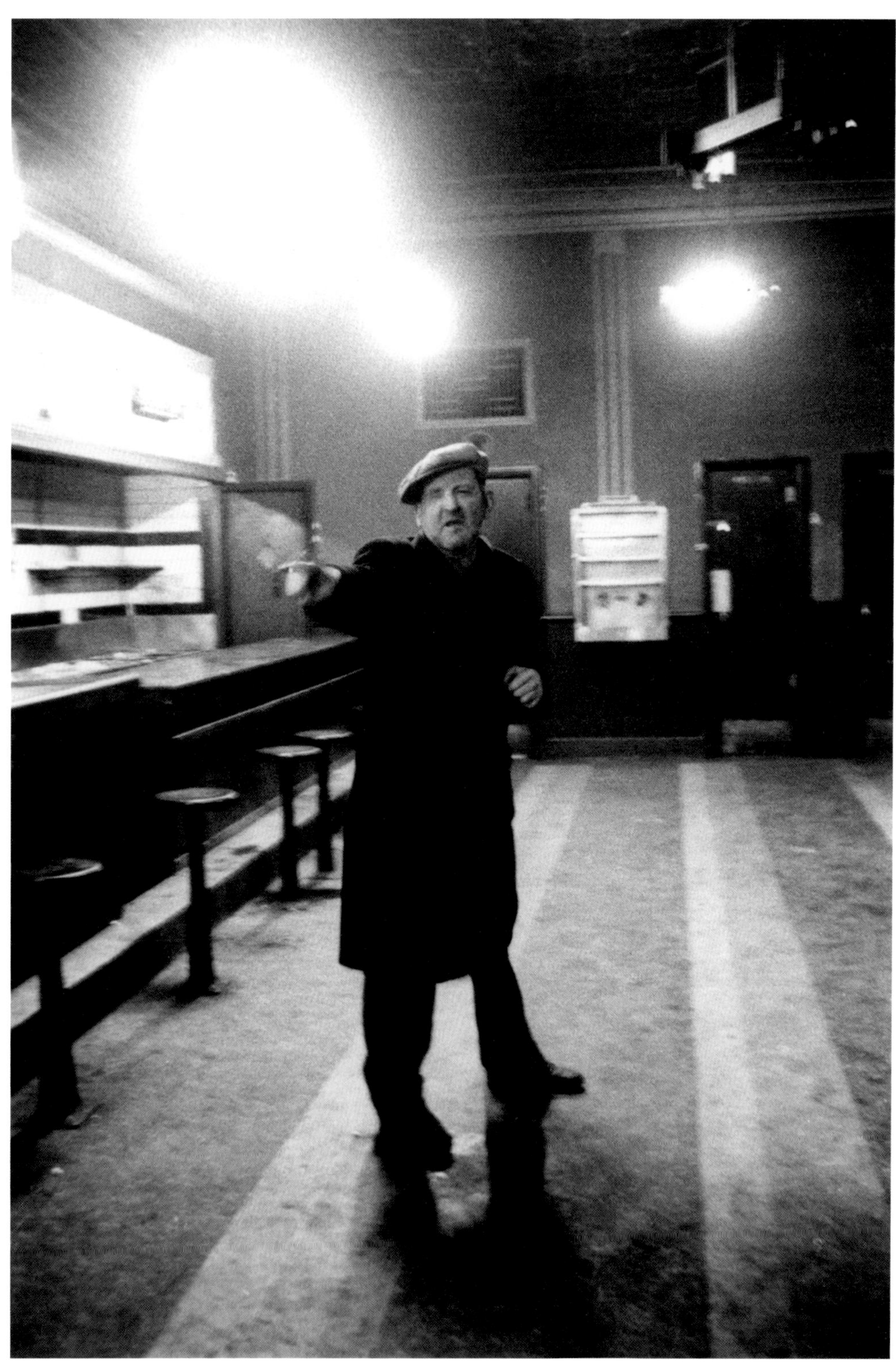

The Madman from Massachusetts in an empty bar, N.Y.C. 1960

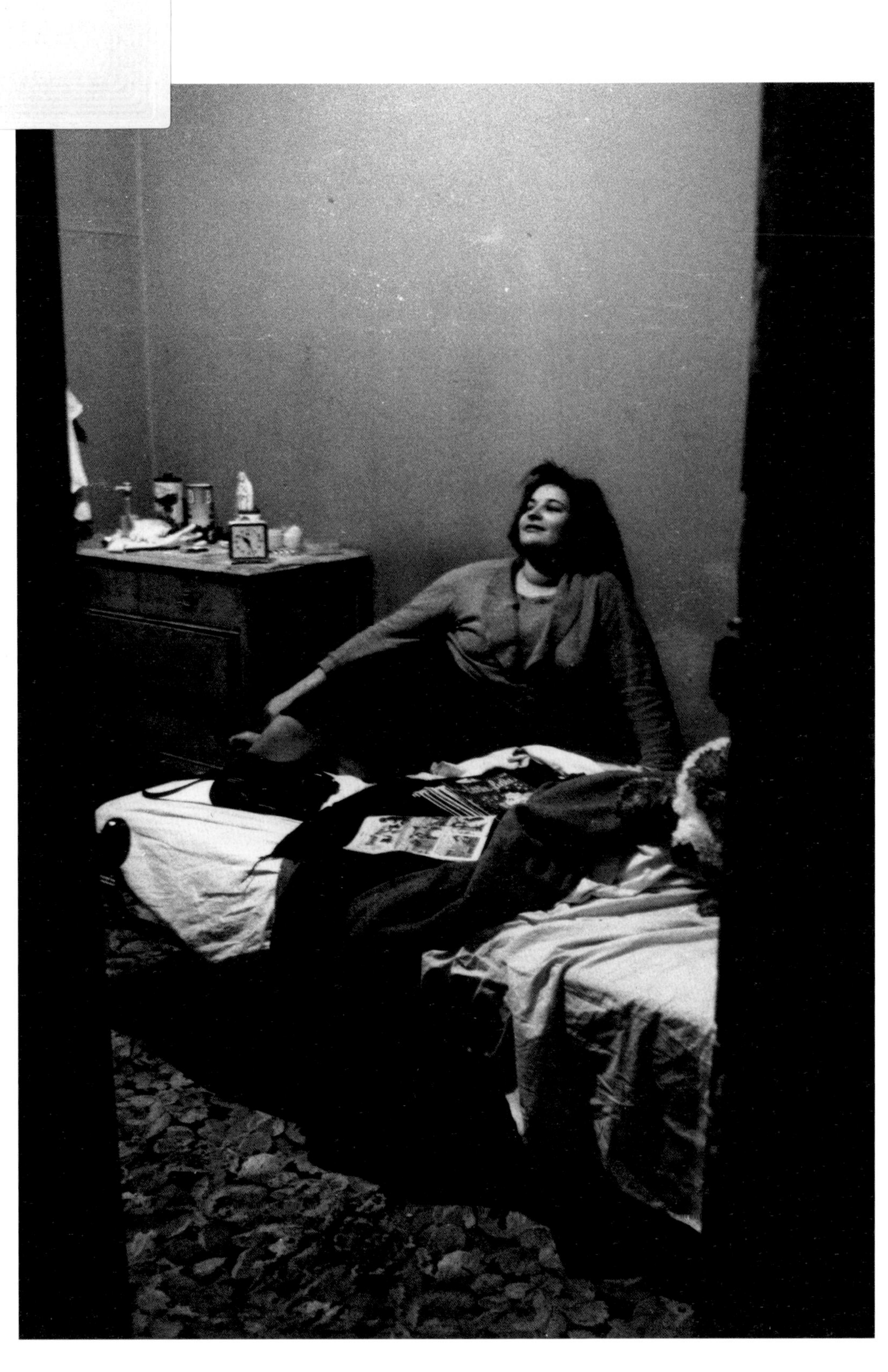

Patti, a resident of the New Holland Hotel seated on her bed, N.Y.C. 1960

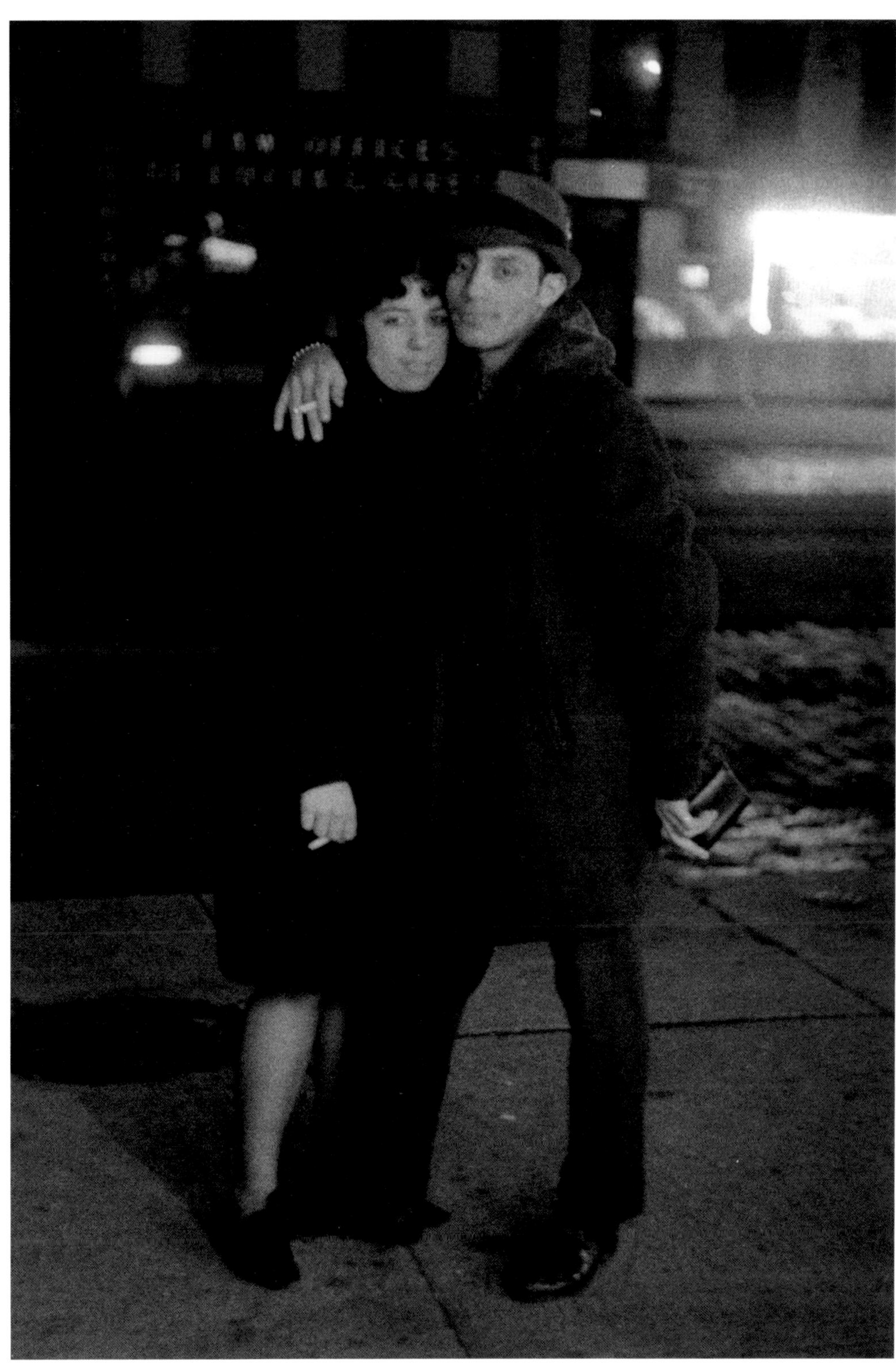

Norma and Gallo, members of a Brooklyn teen gang, N.Y.C. 1960

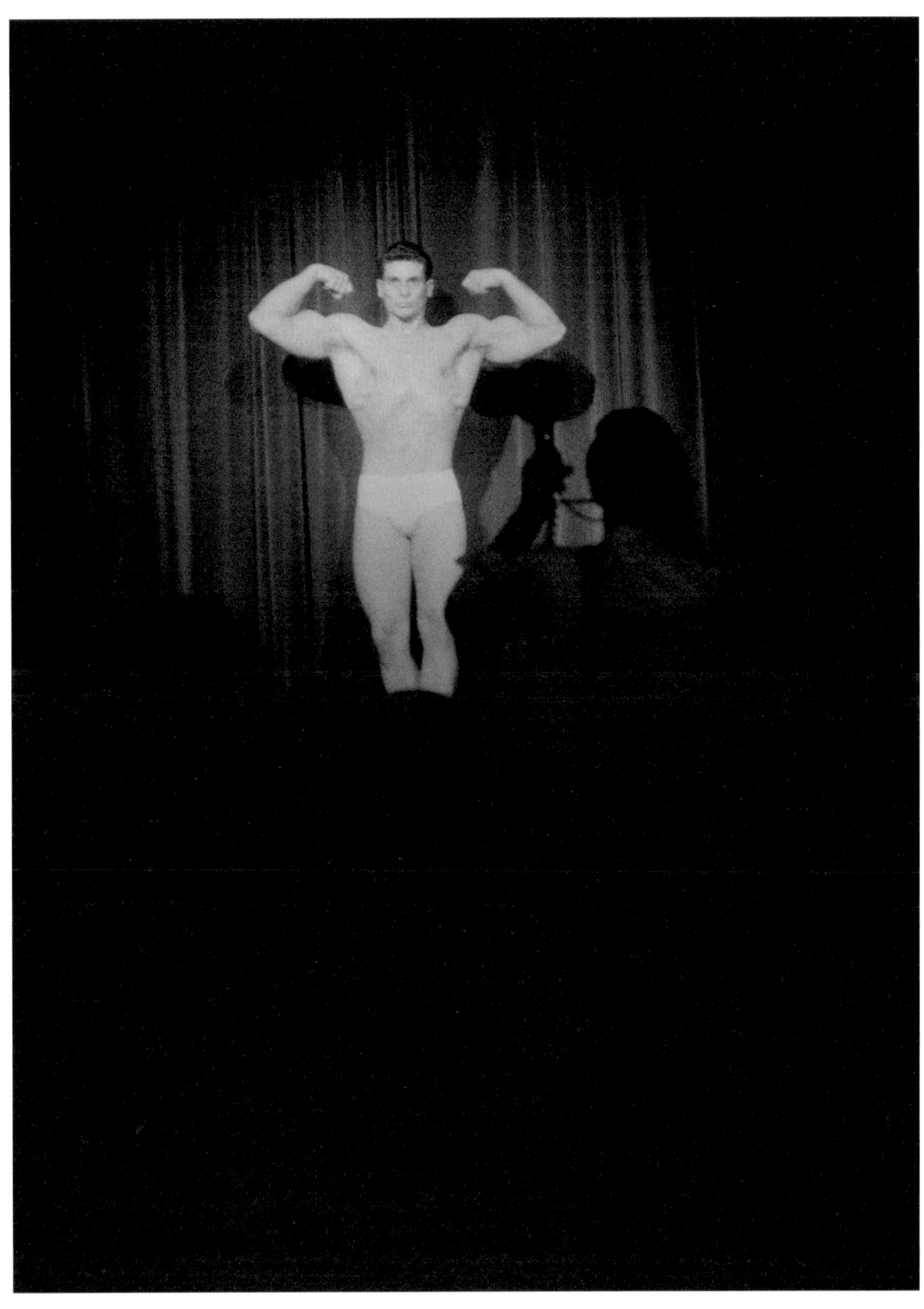

Contestant in a physique contest, N.Y.C. 1960

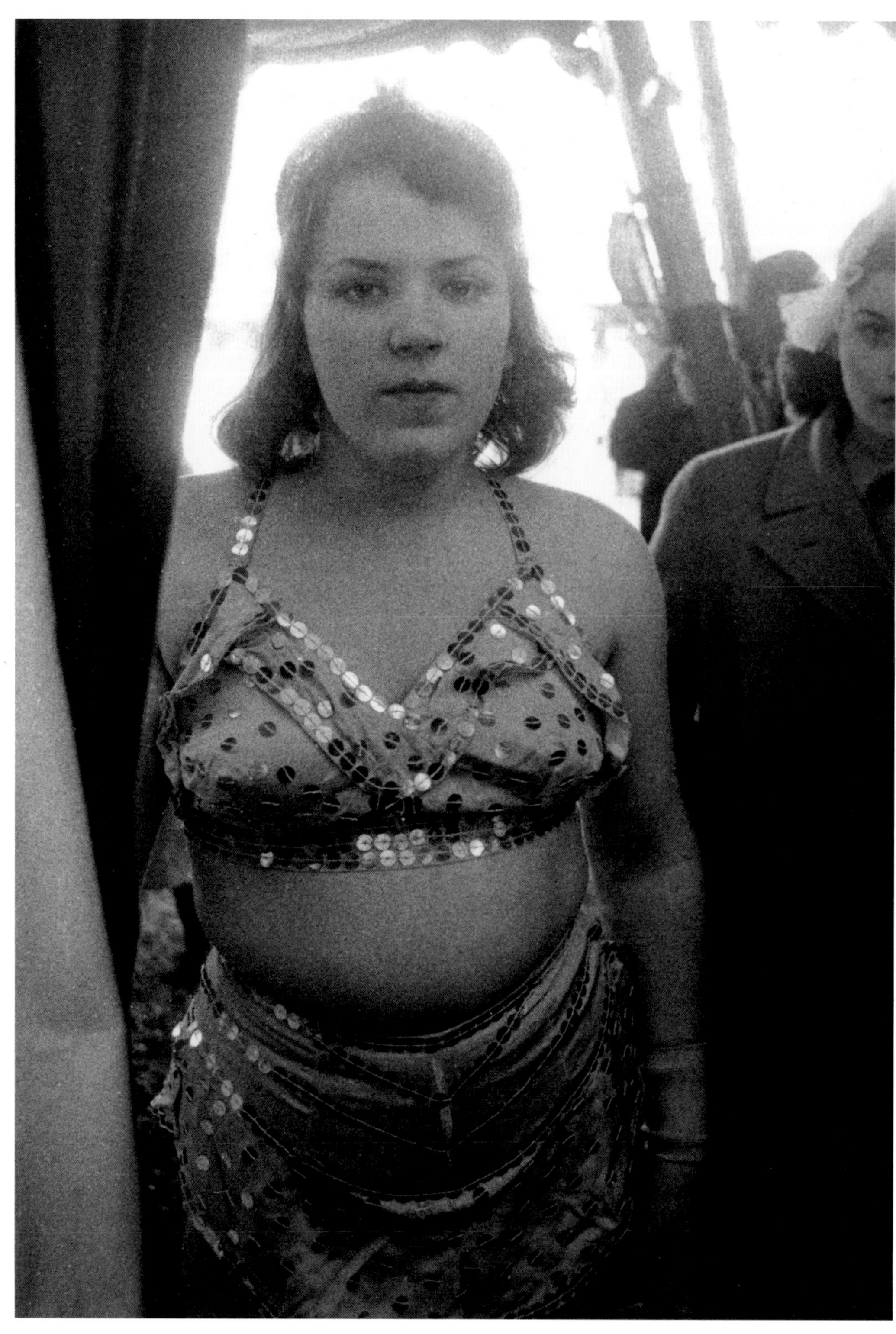

  Girl in her circus costume backstage, Palisades Park, N.J. 1960

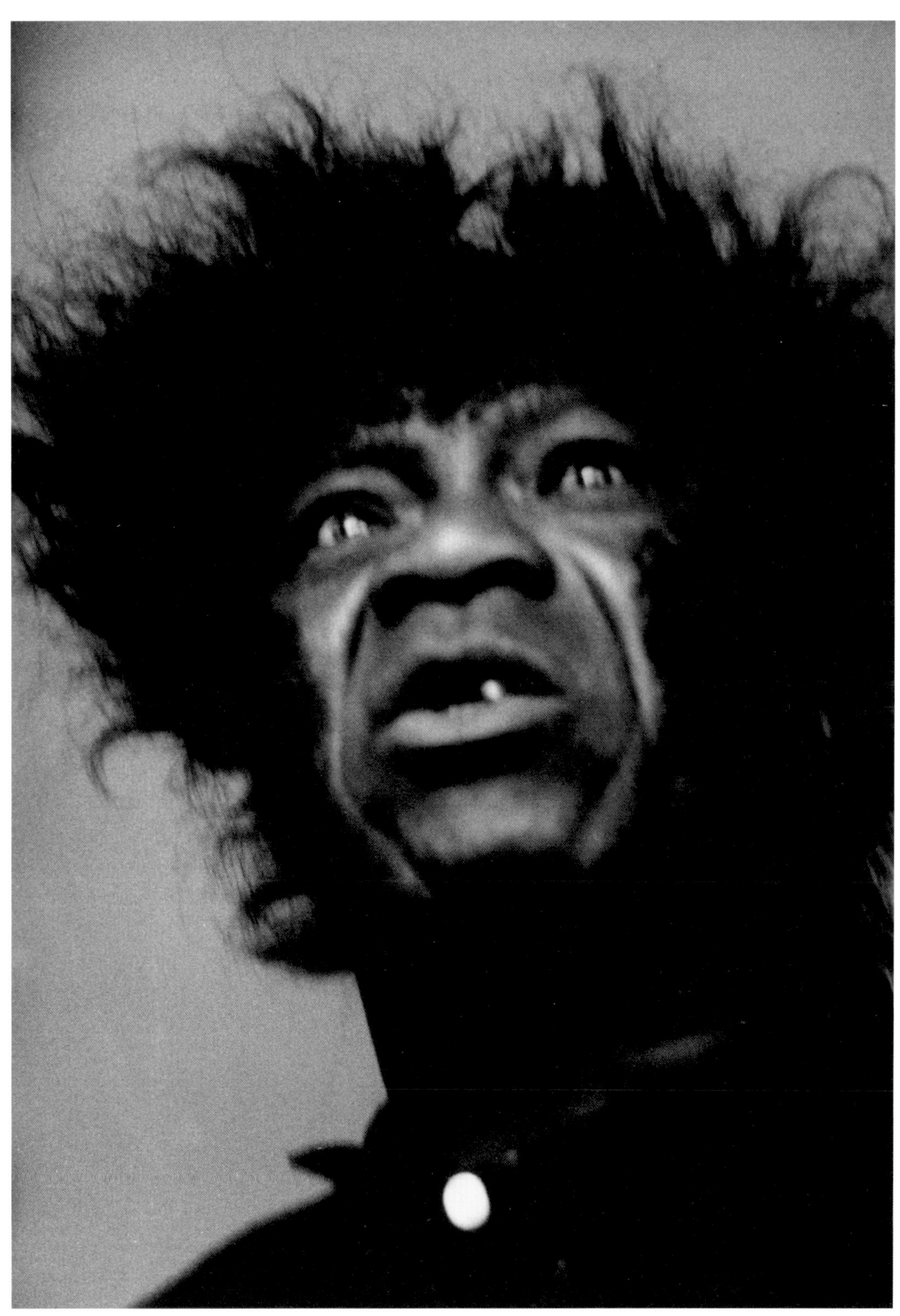

Hezekiah Trambles, "The Jungle Creep," on stage at Hubert's Museum, N.Y.C. 1960

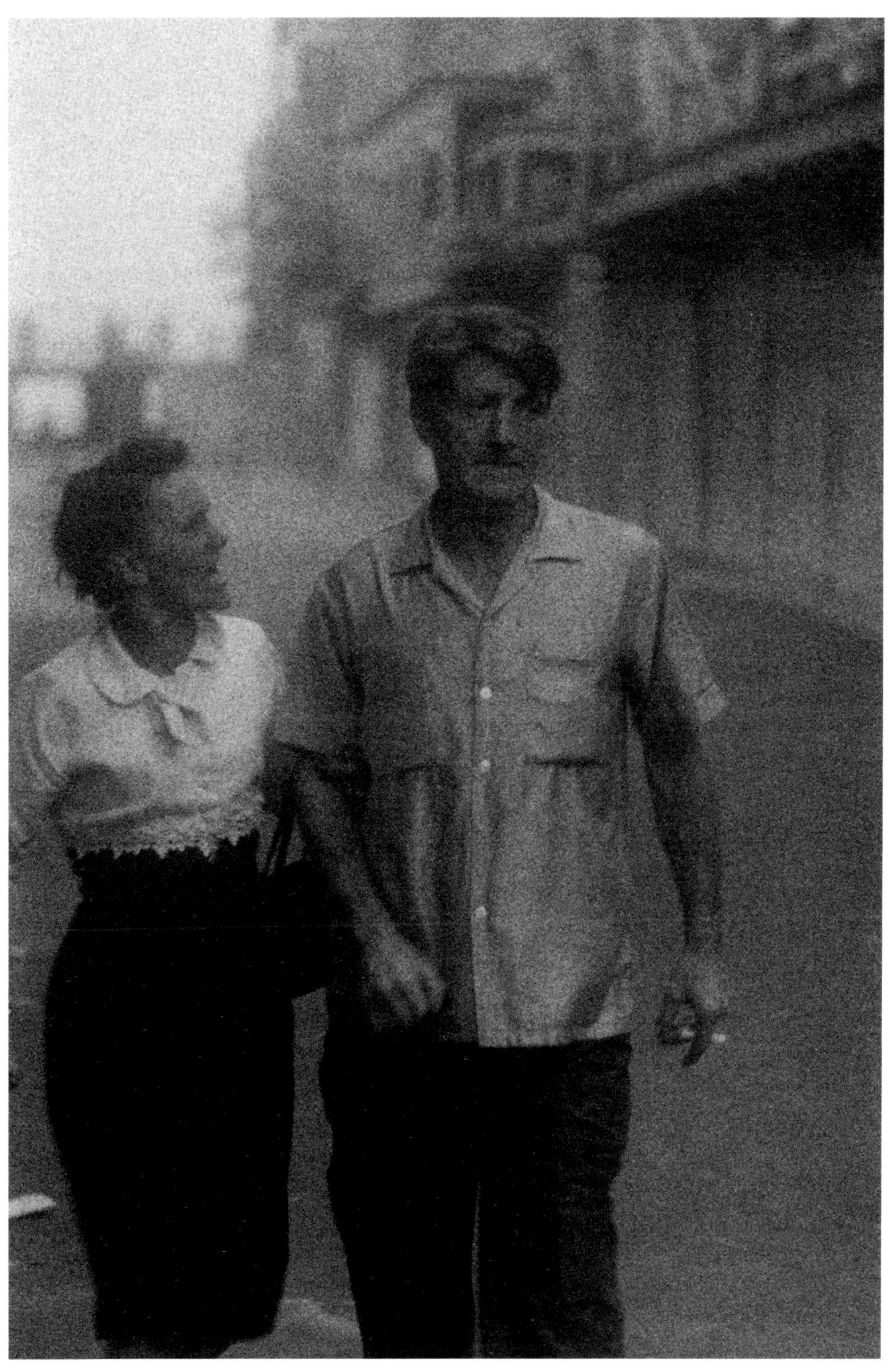

Couple arguing, Coney Island, N.Y. 1960

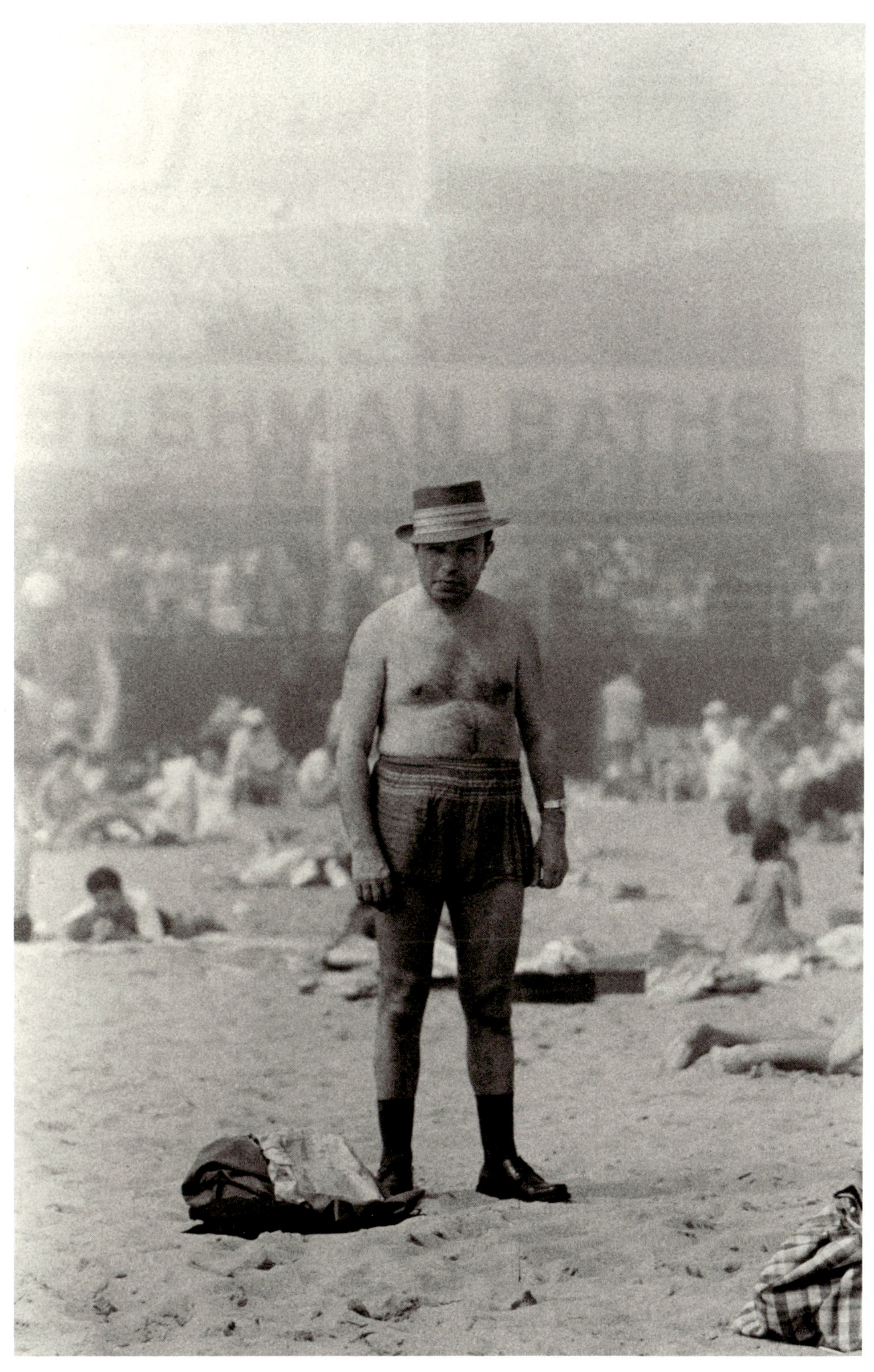

Man in hat, trunks, socks and shoes, Coney Island, N.Y. 1960

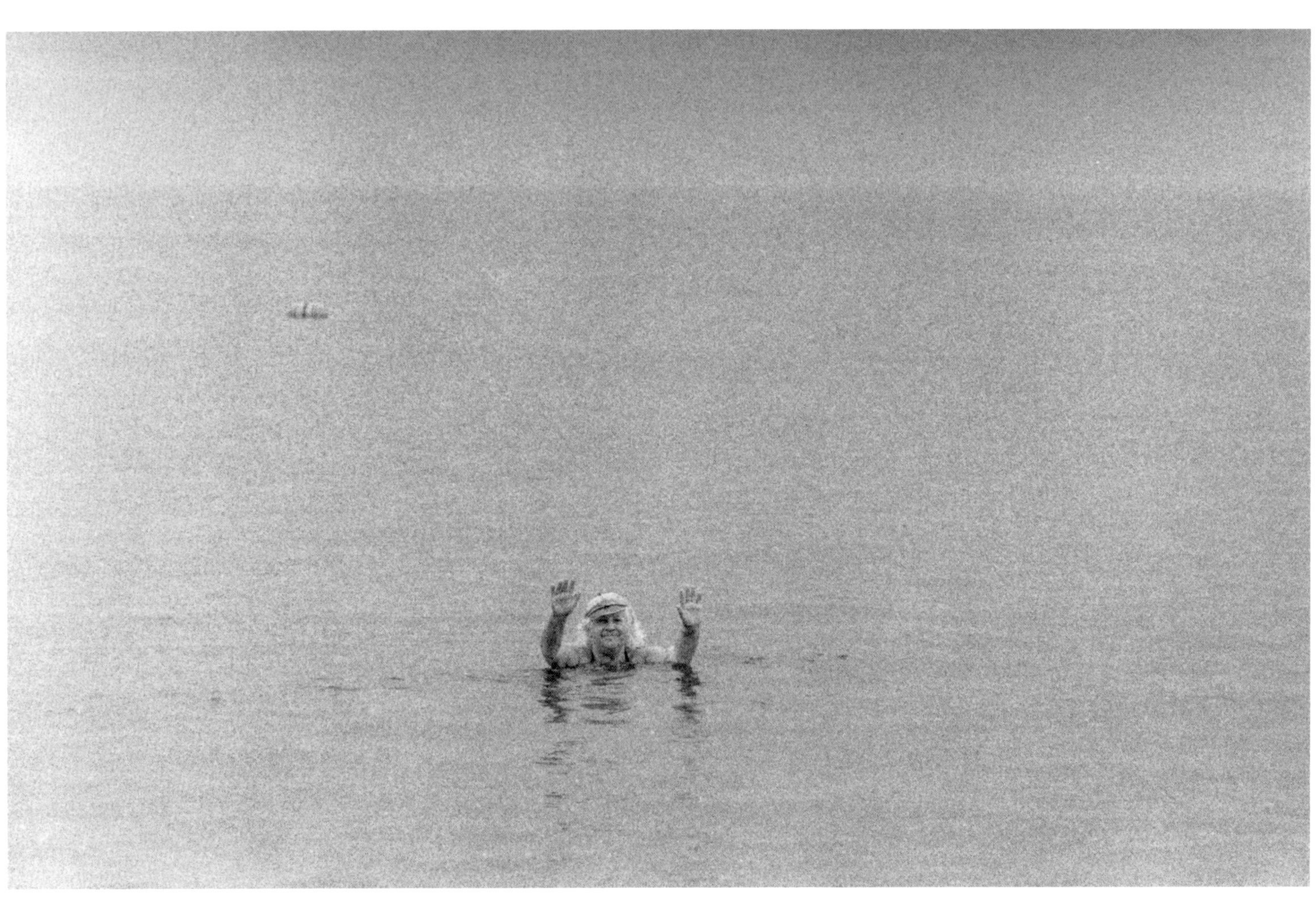

Old woman with hands raised in the ocean, Coney Island, N.Y. 1960

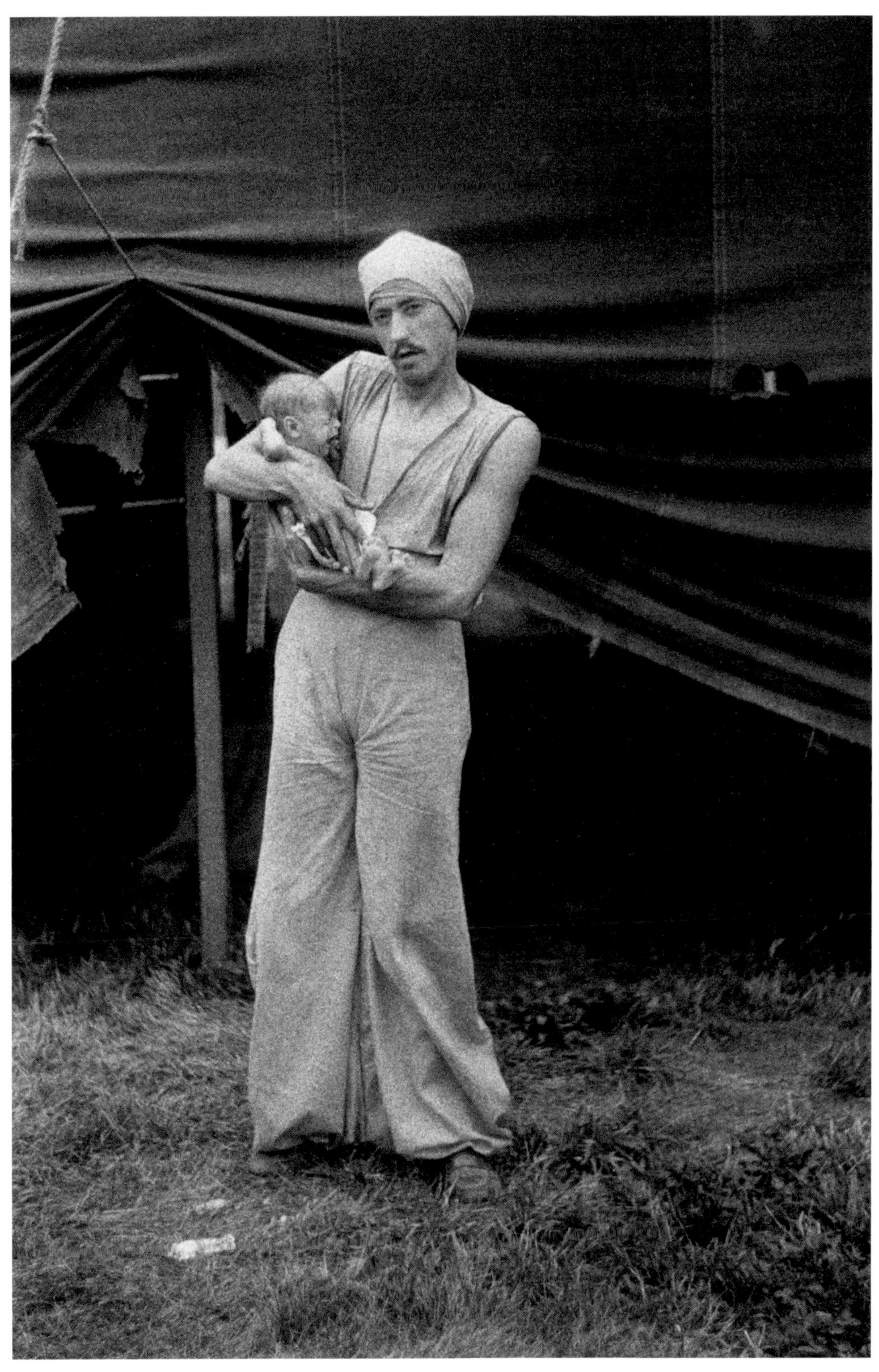

The Man Who Swallows Razor Blades, Hagerstown, Md. 1960

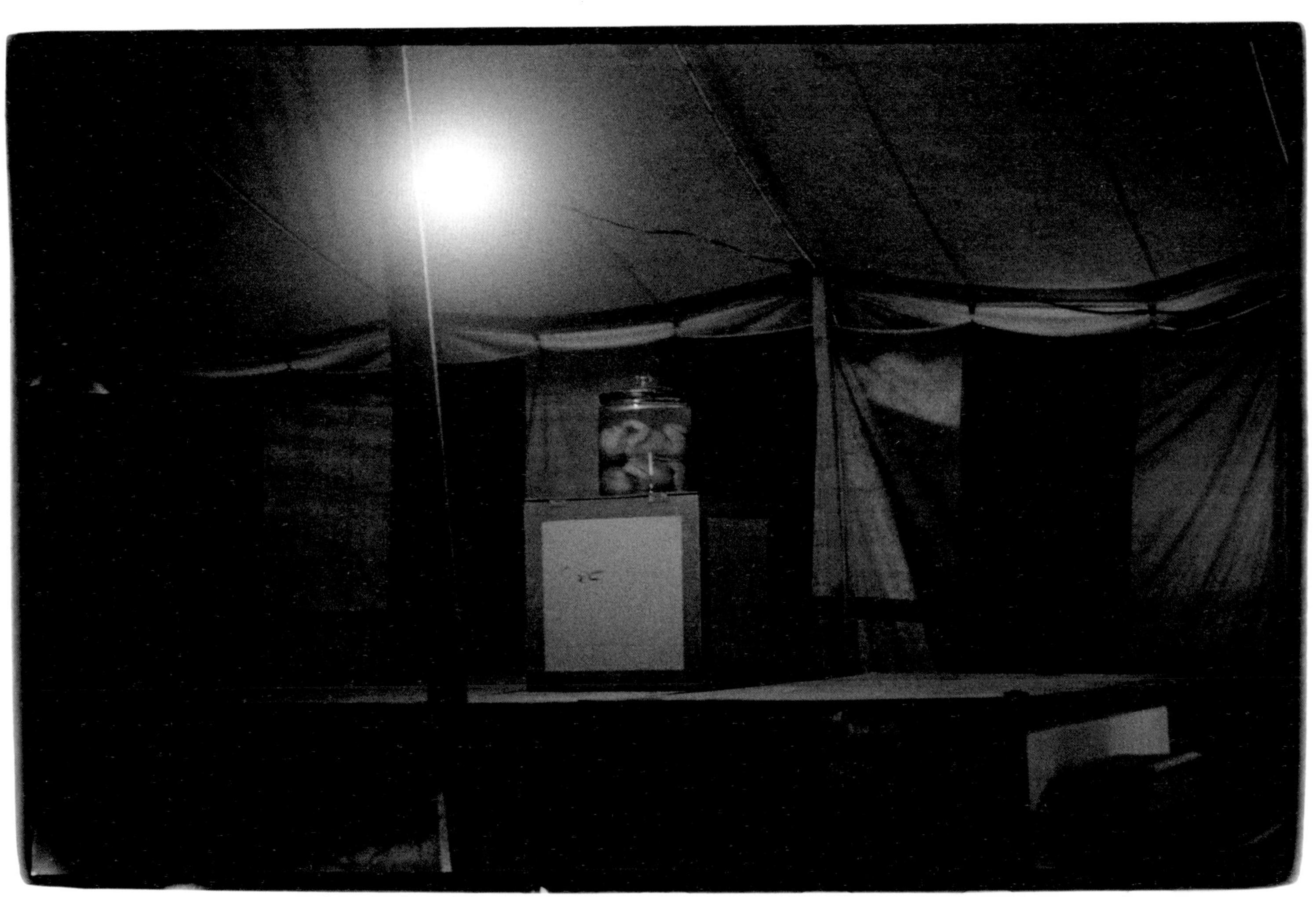

Siamese twins in a carnival tent, N.J. 1960

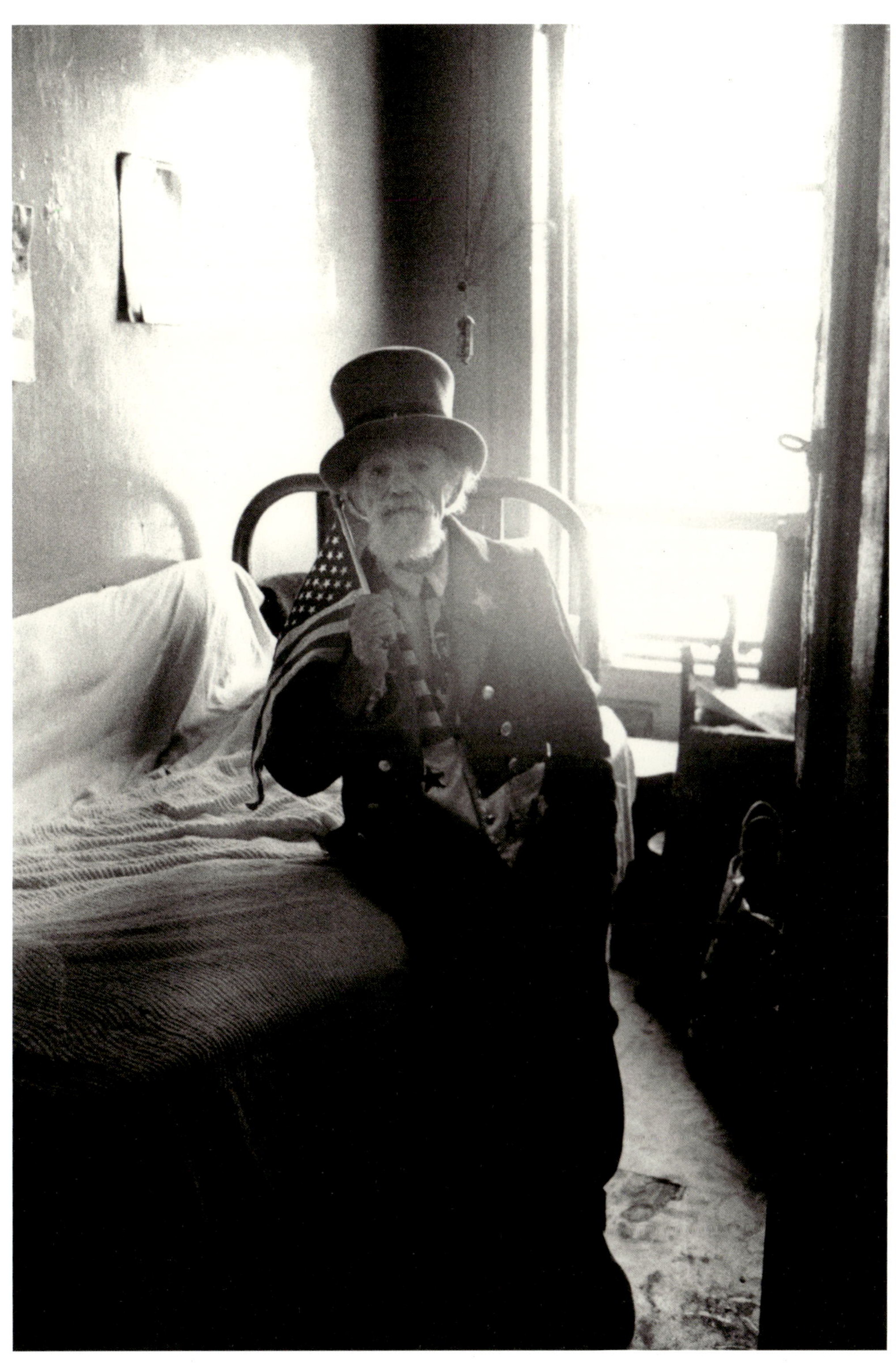

Uncle Sam leaning on a cot at home, N.Y.C. 1960

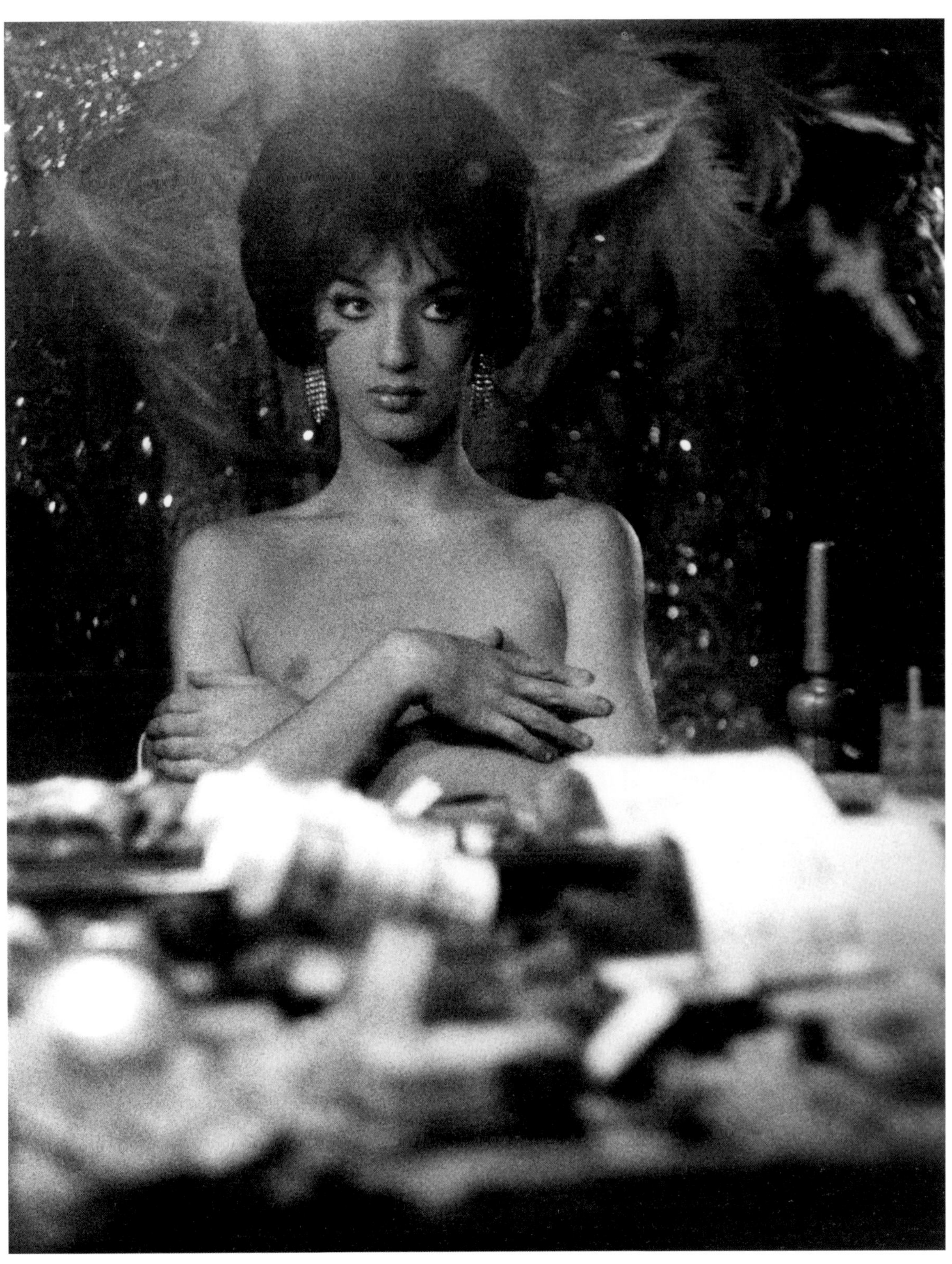

Seated female impersonator with arms crossed on her bare chest, N.Y.C. 1960

Bring for sg.   call H.W. { panoraleas of people
                                 { archetypes
DON'T FORGET POLLY   { villains
AND THE PRINCES   { Baby Joyce
ARTIFACT   { Female Impersonator

                    Camera *
                    { second doesn't work
                    { dark bottom bunc
                    {   contact
                    { Self timer ↑

call Linda to call Elefante
say Allan may not
              make it

like are —
uncongious
parodies of our human comedy

take John need for shot

print for Leo
Nimick
JACK 2
A. SINATRA.

call off J and Storme

10:00 ESQUIRE

call Bishop

3:00 SHOW.

Joe Allen is a metaphor for
human destiny — walking blind into
the future ~~while we will view~~
~~while we view our past~~
with an eye on the past.

call Storme.

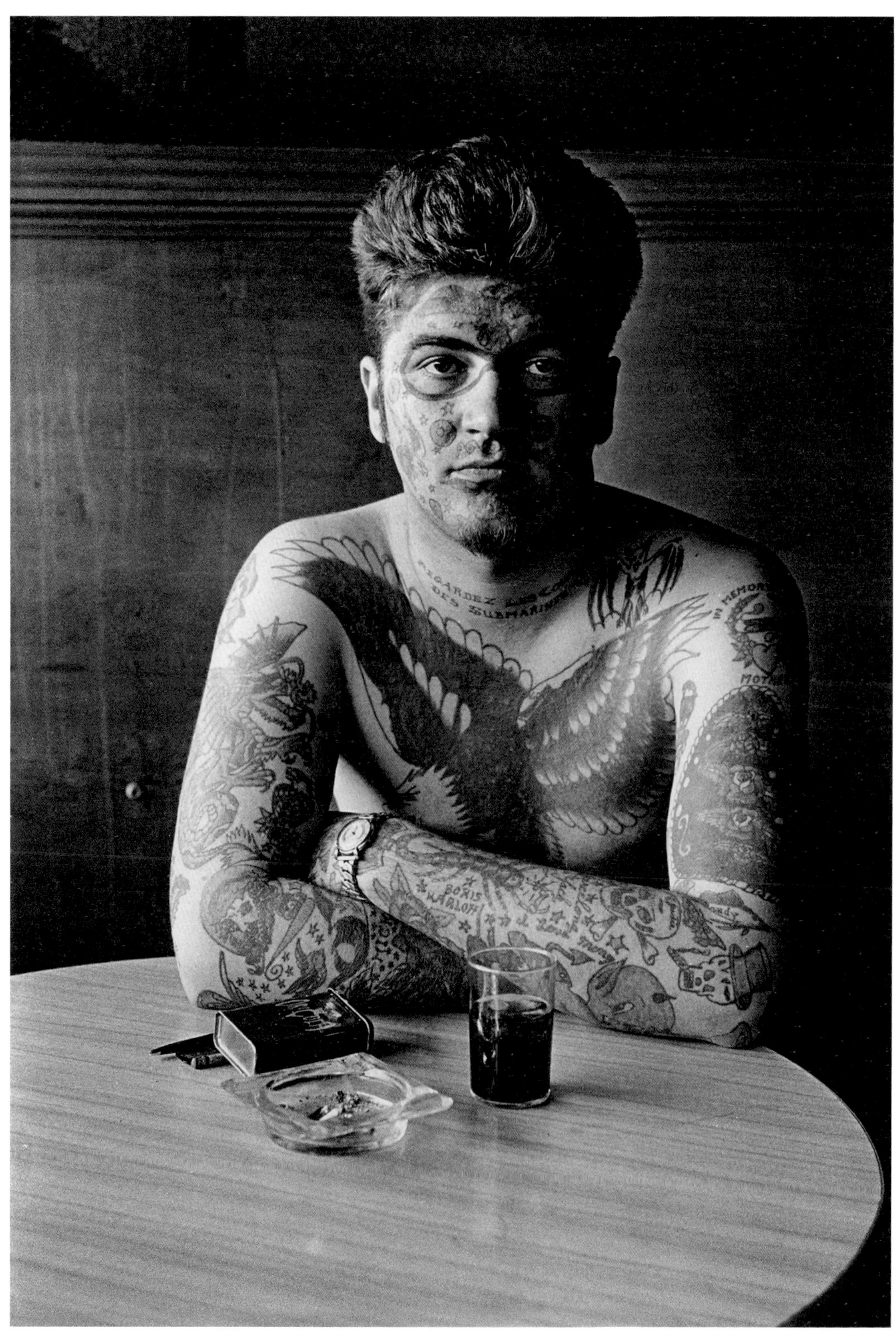

Jack Dracula at a bar, New London, Conn. 1961

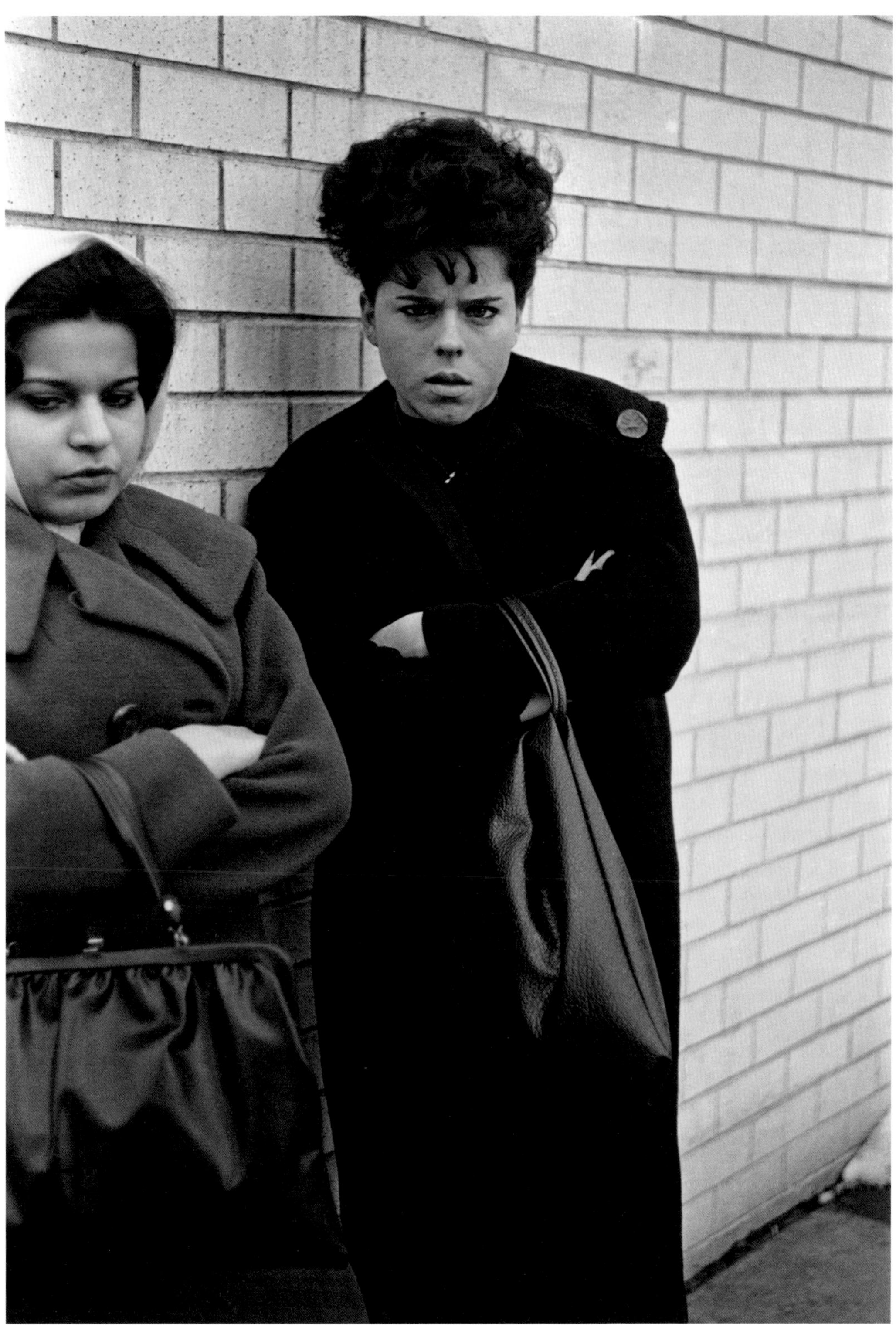

Two girls by a brick wall, N.Y.C. 1961

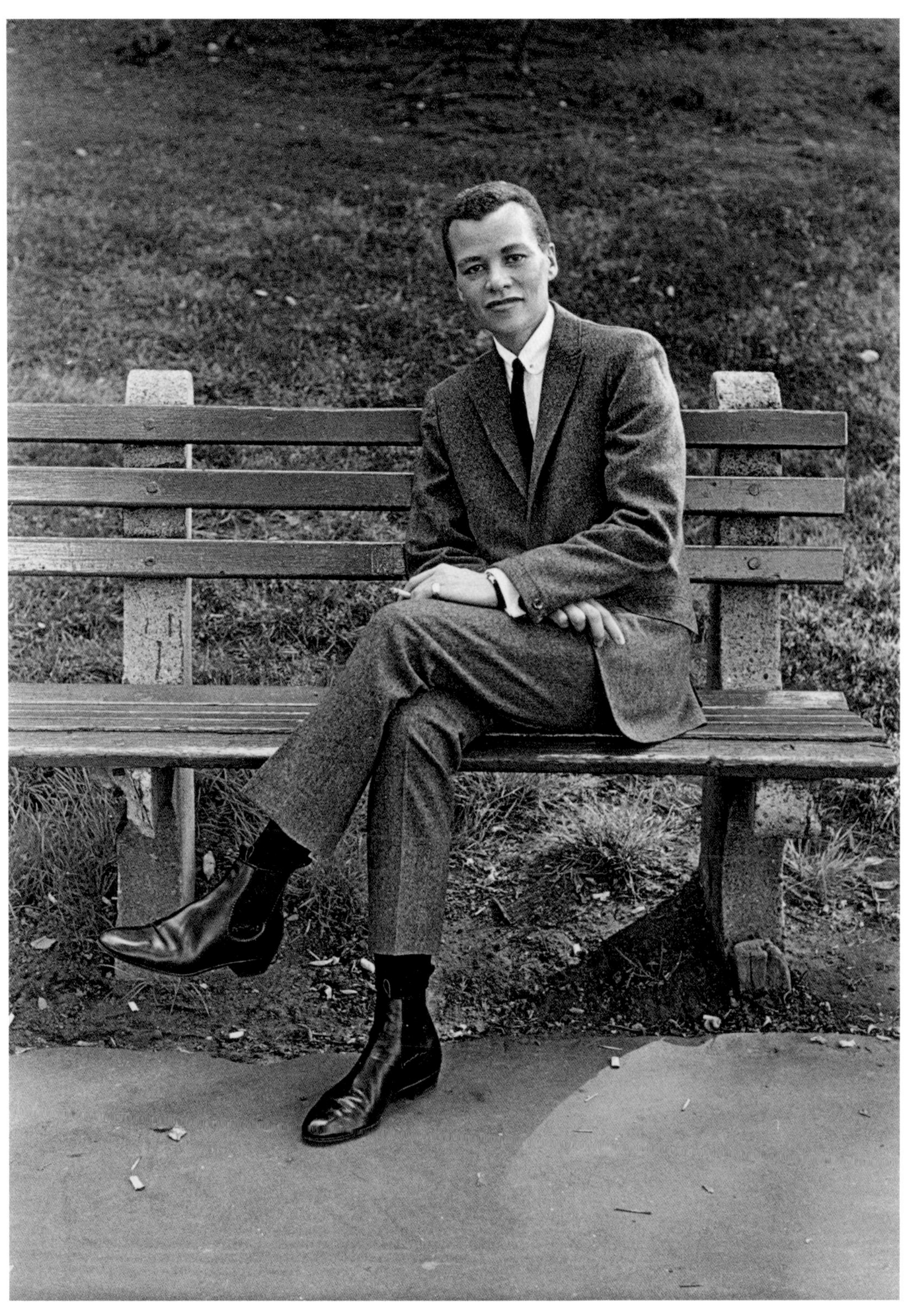

Miss Stormé de Larverie, the Lady Who Appears to be a Gentleman, N.Y.C. 1961

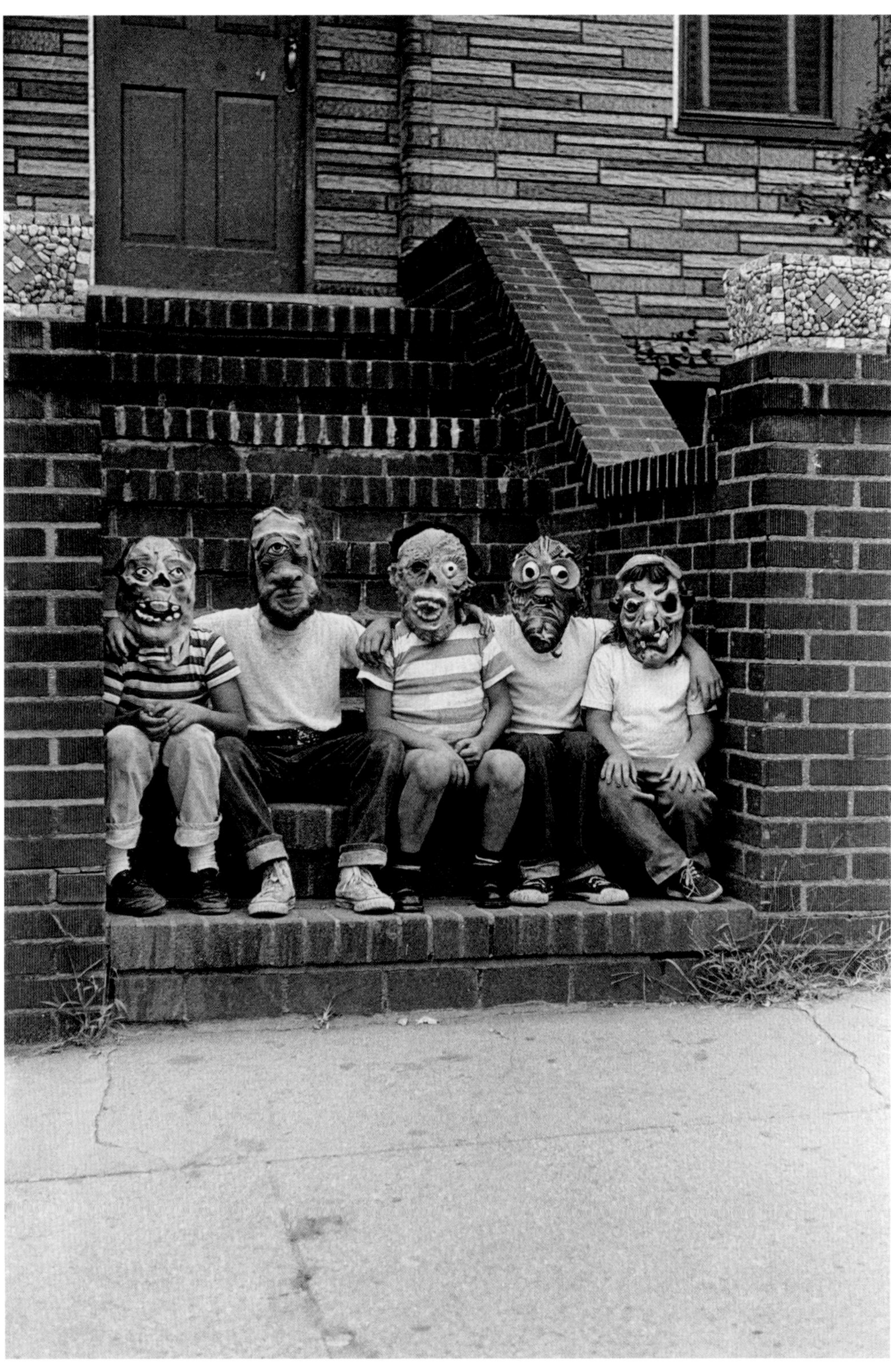

Five members of The Monster Fan Club, N.Y.C. 1961

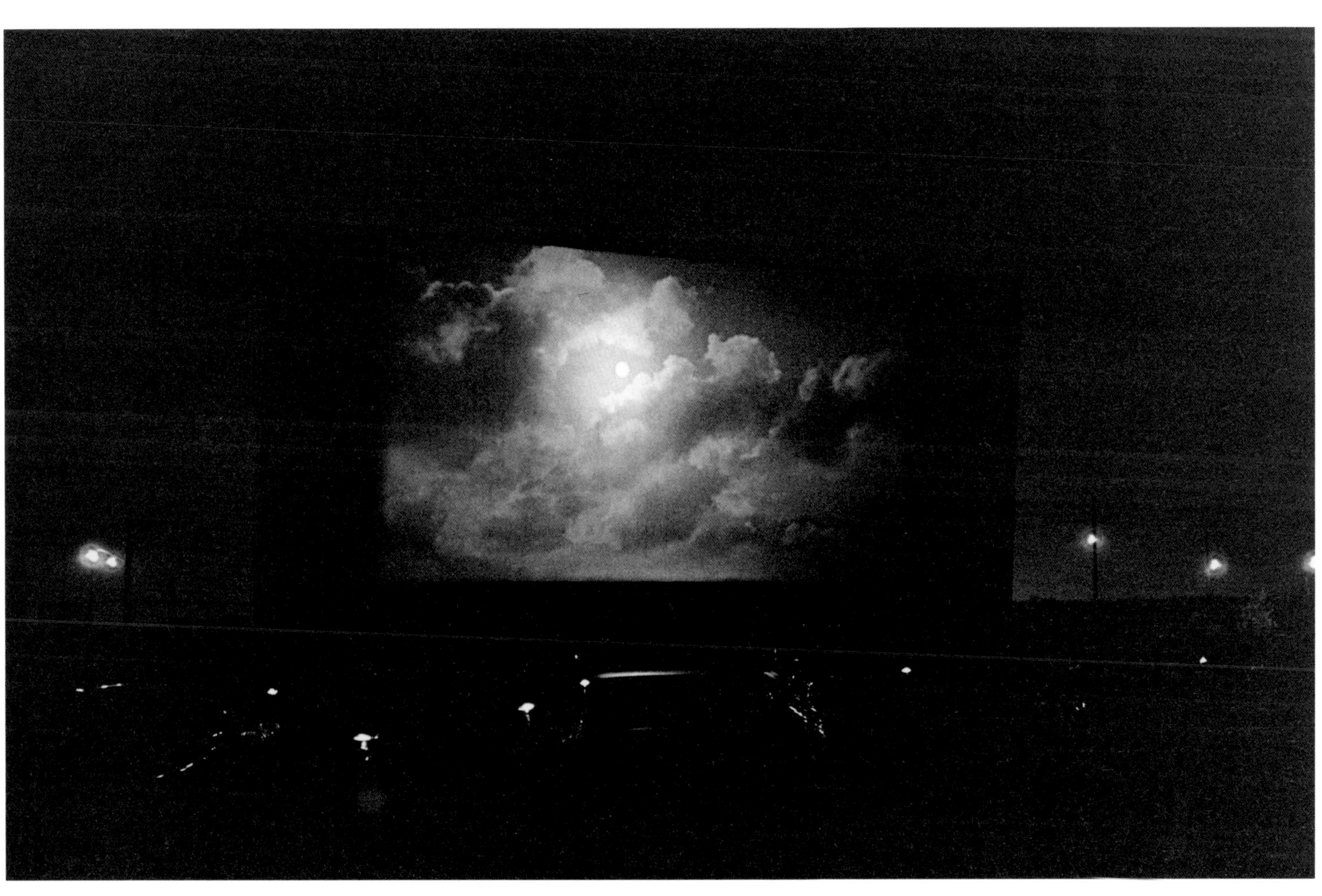

Clouds on screen at a drive-in movie, N.J. 1961

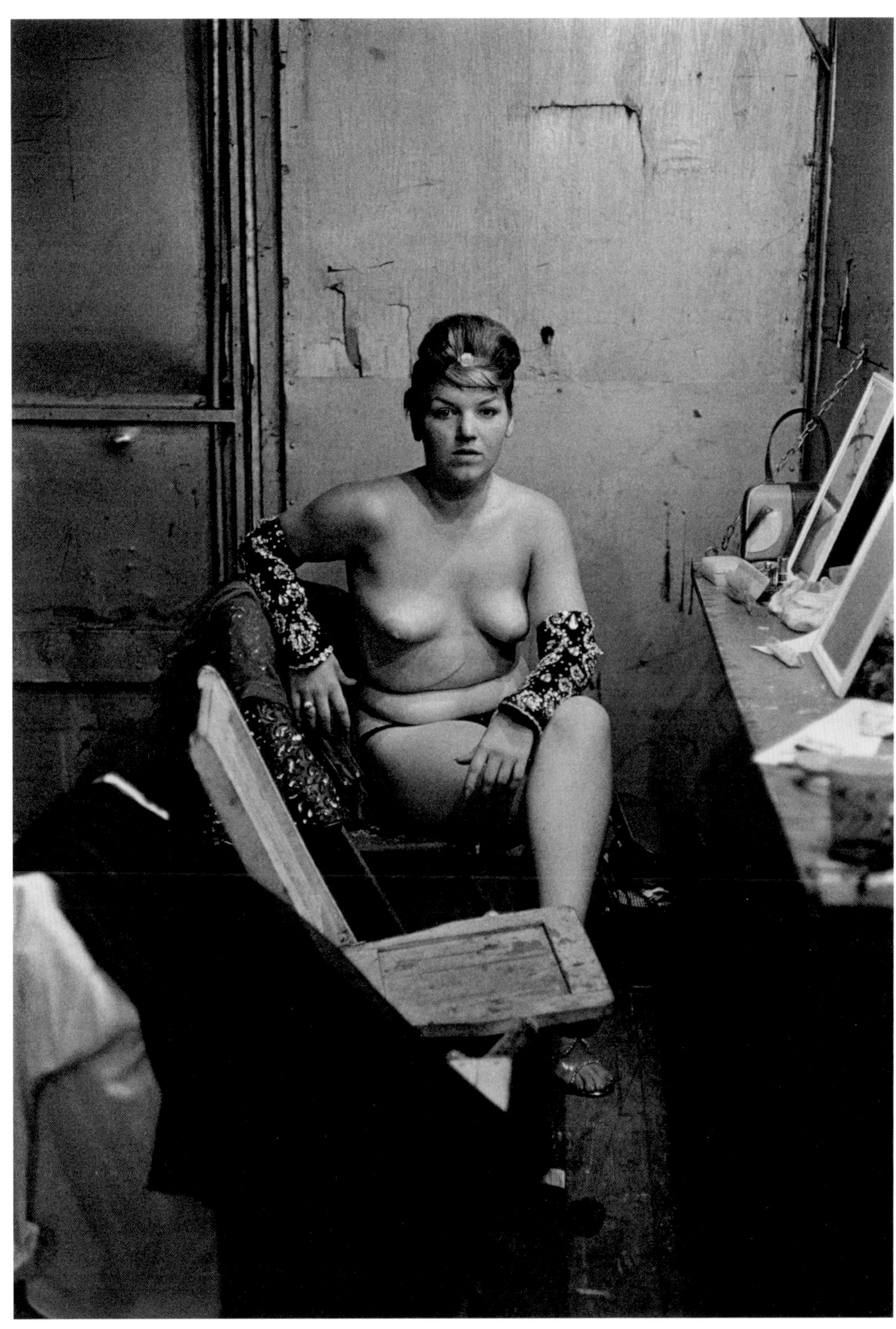

Stripper with bare breasts sitting in her dressing room, Atlantic City, N.J. 1961

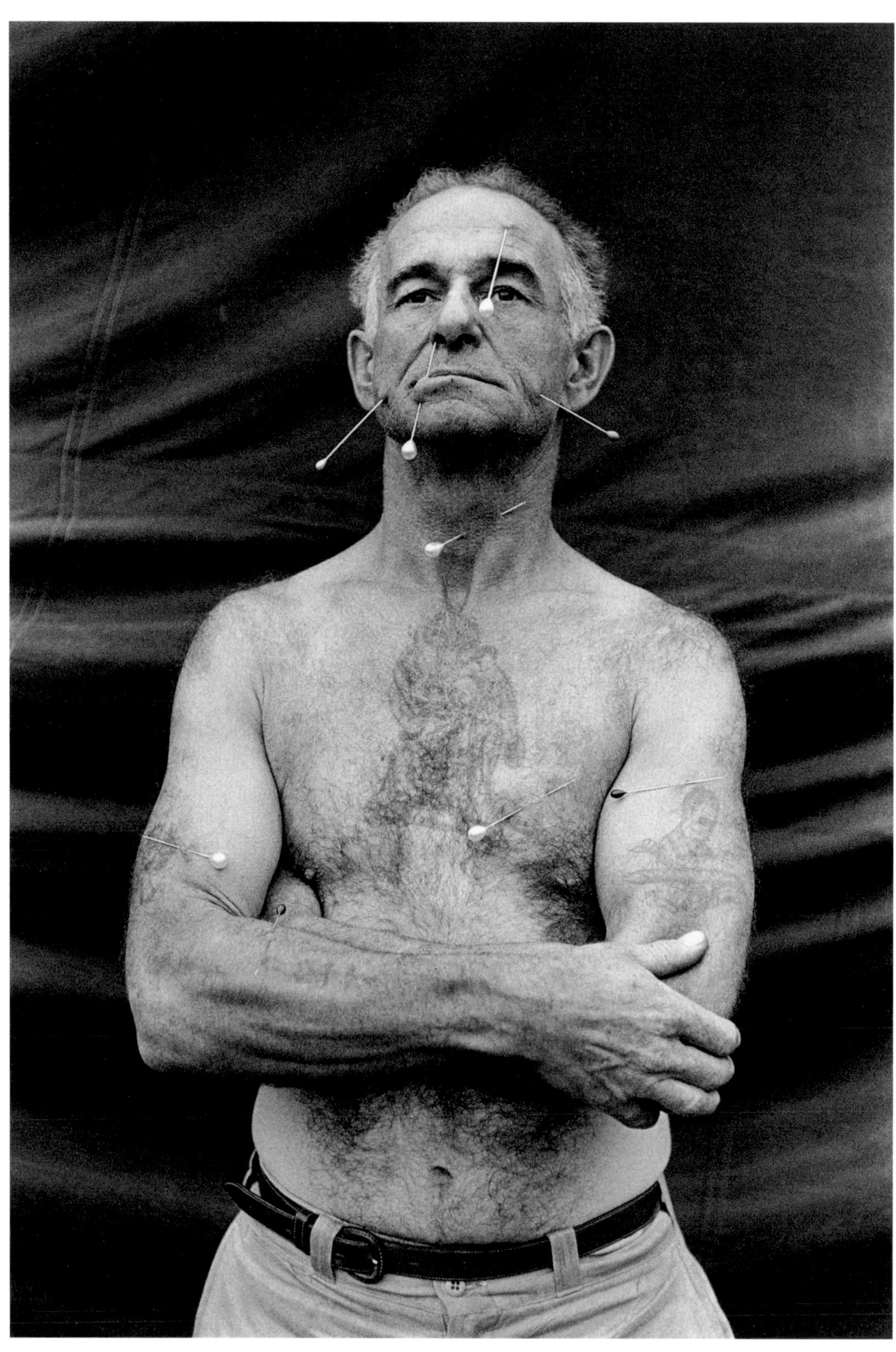

The Human Pincushion, Ronald C. Harrison, N.J. 1961

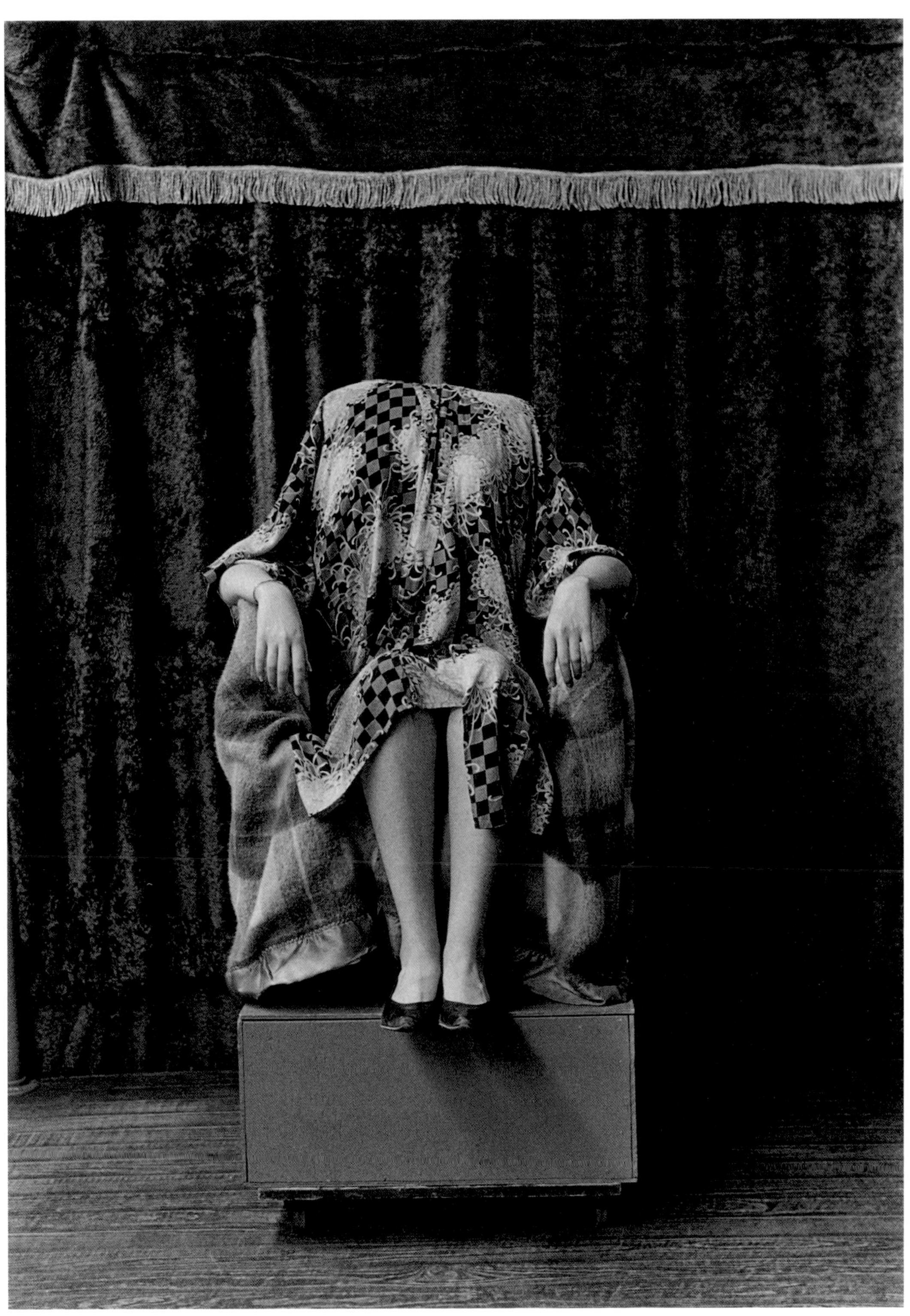

Headless woman, Palisades Park, N.J. 1961

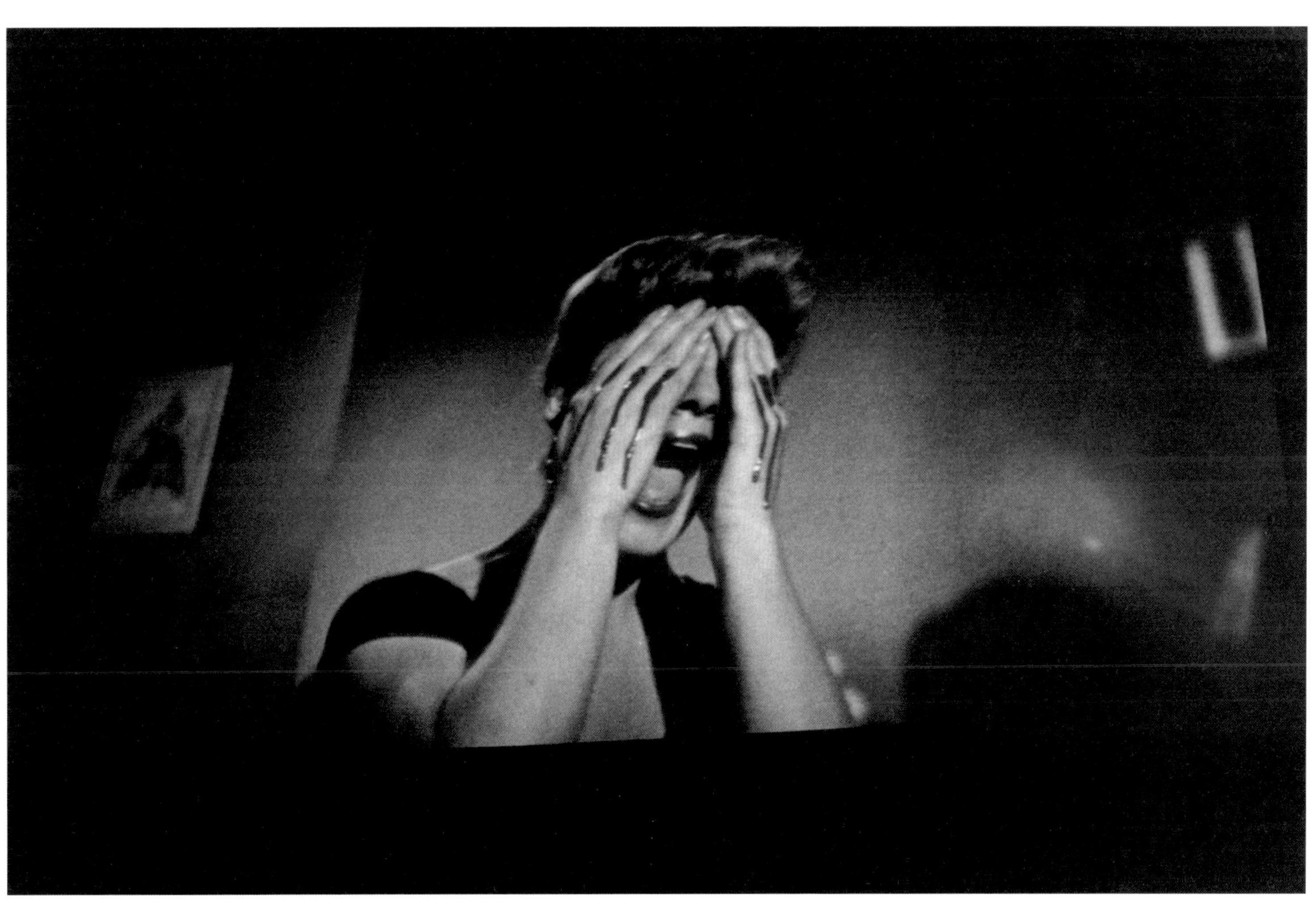

Screaming woman with blood on her hands 1961

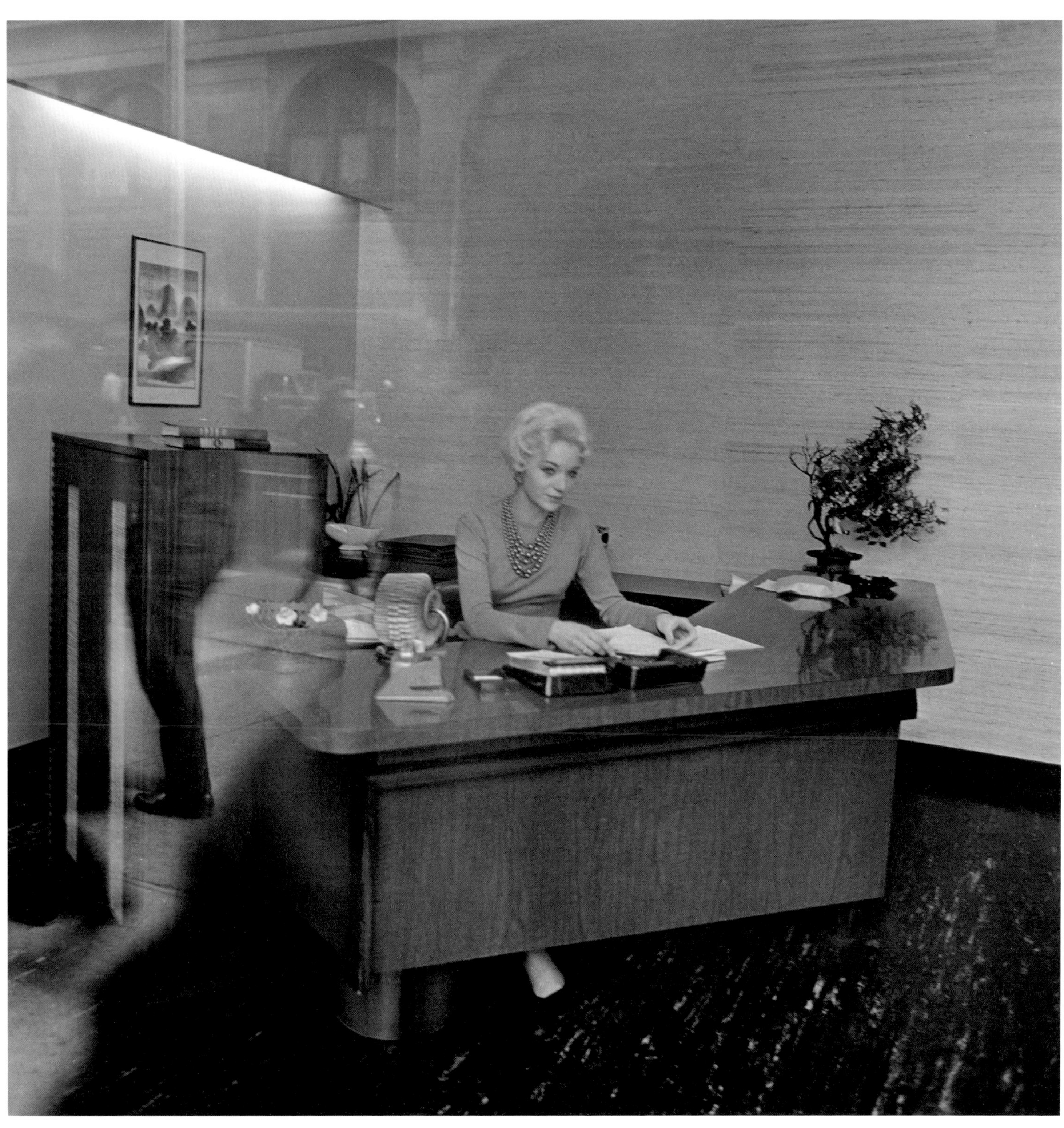

Blonde receptionist behind a picture window, N.Y.C. 1962

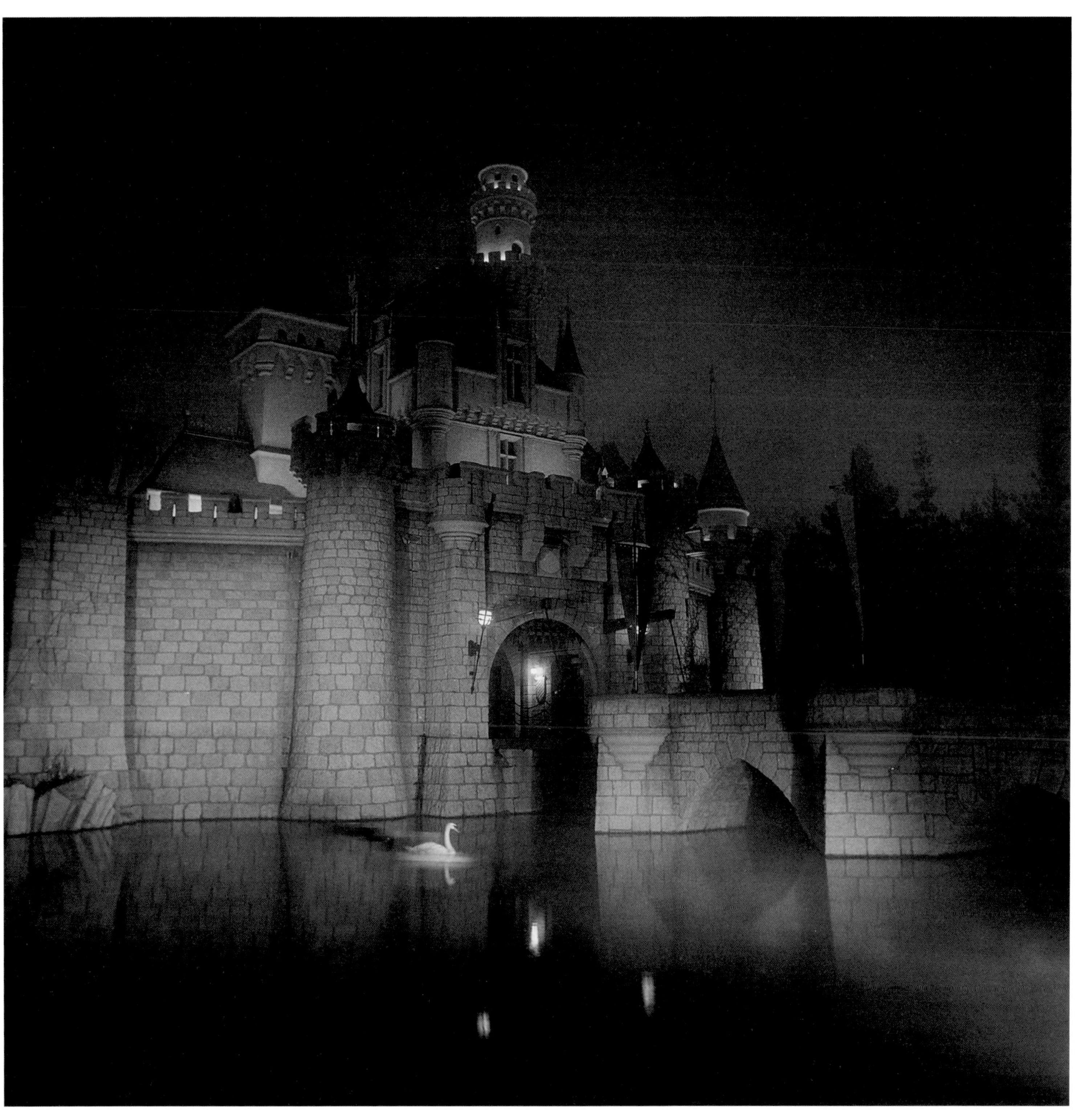

A castle in Disneyland, Cal. 1962

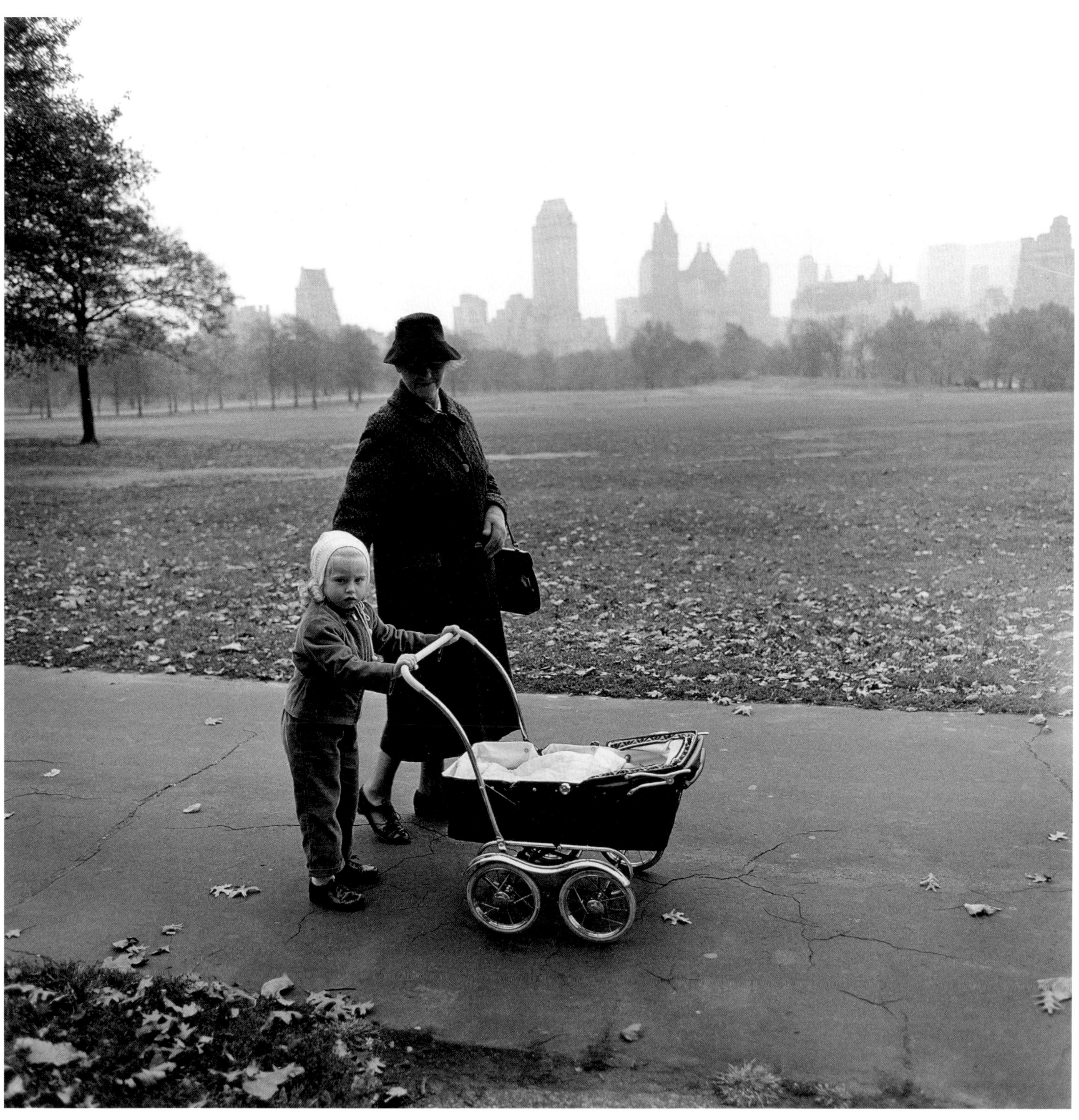

Girl and governess with baby carriage, N.Y.C. 1962

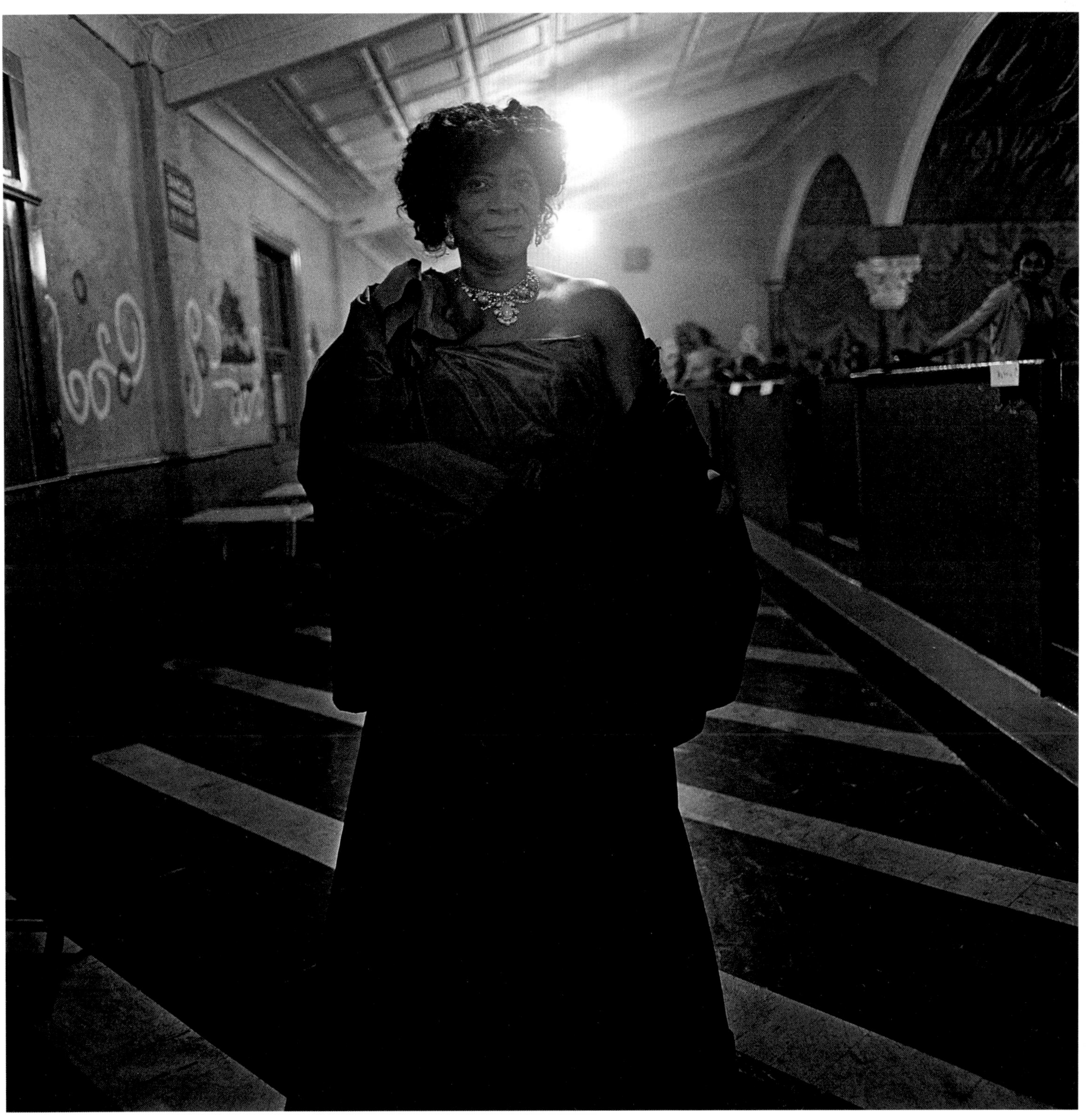

Tall partygoer in a taffeta dress, N.Y.C. 1962

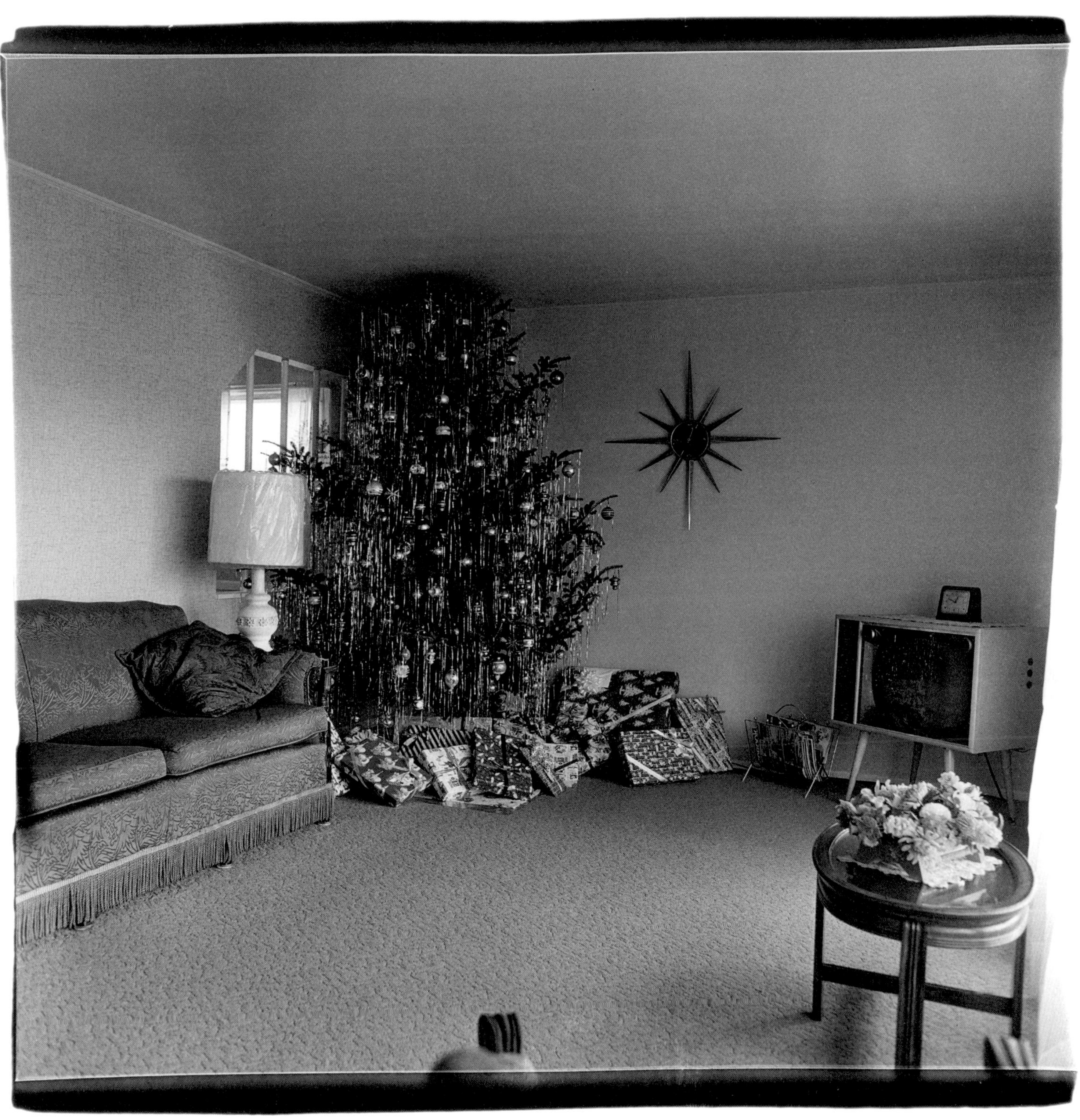

Xmas tree in a living room in Levittown, L.I. 1962

rehearsal hall W.57 ~~in town~~ Alexandros

design something 415 E 53

suburbs

bus trip

train trip

stations - trains

opera -   (intmsg) Amati.

séance (sunday religuousads)

gypsies

tattoo

opera opening (presspass?)

backstage (yannopoulos?)

theater backstage Sybil? Lois?
Bob?

rehearsal

testimonial dinner

ballet class - 57. +

collection?

church meeting Pentecostal?)

antique show 34 th St Armory. 1 - 11 P.M.
th. Sun. Oct. 19

aquarium 10-5 exc mon tues.
columbus day open
state fair
special 5+10 28th + 45th Ave
Rose Cummins
wrestlers backstage.
Palladium
Apollo
wedding
bowling Sterlings bway P.A. CY 3-1600
Home of the Daughters of Jacob
Dr Seltzer.
School
auction
oddshops - antique, exterminator
Holiday shop decor
driving in the rain.
cartoon movie
fashion show   library
                hotel rooms.

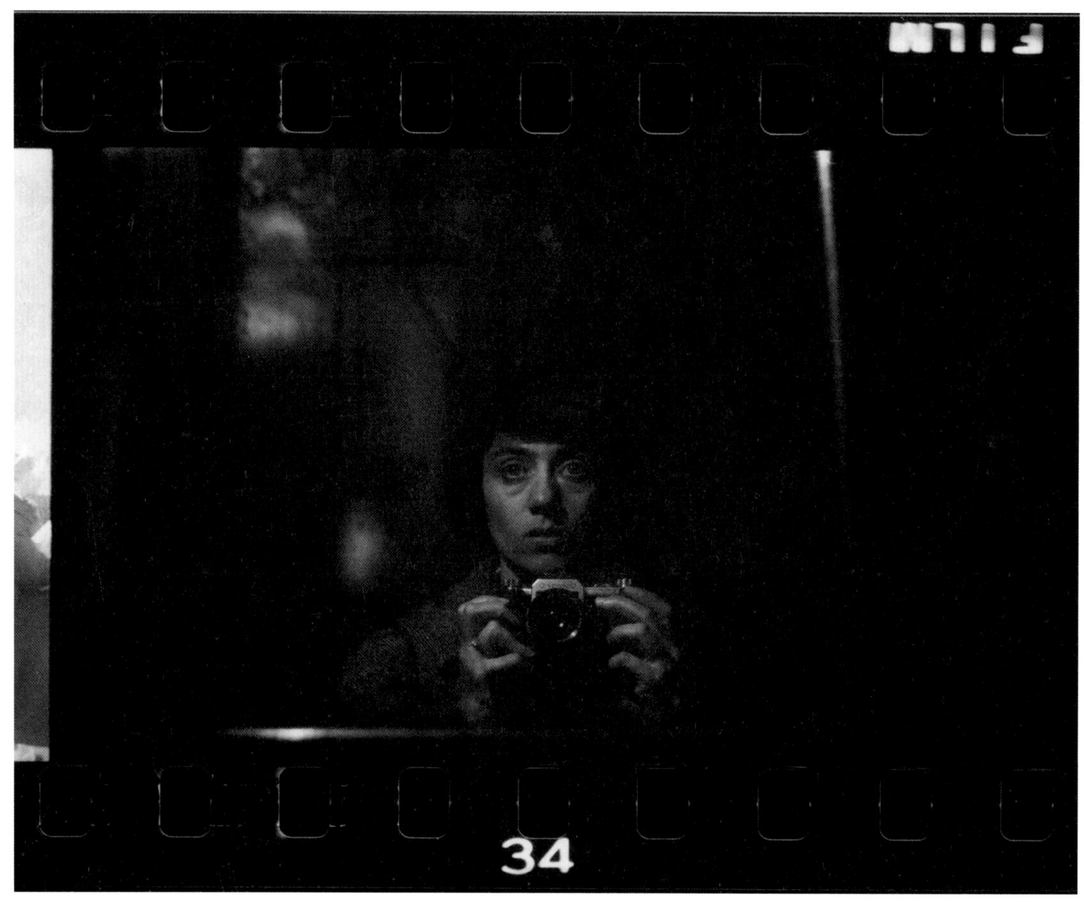

DIANE ARBUS
Self-portrait with 35mm Contax D camera, 1959. Contact sheet, roll 614 #34

in the beginning

JEFF L. ROSENHEIM

There are and have been and will be an infinite number of things on earth:
individuals all different, all wanting different things, all knowing
different things, all loving different things, all looking different.
Everything that has been on earth has been different from any other thing.
That is what I love: the differentness, the uniqueness of all things
and the importance of life.... I see something that *seems* wonderful;
I see the divineness in ordinary things.

DIANE ARBUS   HIGH-SCHOOL ESSAY ON PLATO, 1939[1]

In a high-school essay on Plato that she wrote at the age of sixteen, Diane Arbus described her sense of what was waiting to be discovered out there in the world. Her fascination with the differences between all things and, more significantly, between all people may have been part of what initially compelled her to pick up the camera. It certainly permeates her work from the beginning of her picture making in 1956 and sustains it to the end of her life fifteen years later.

Arbus had started making photographs in the early 1940s and continued to do so sporadically for well over a decade. During the same period, she and her husband, Allan, were engaged in a moderately successful career in fashion photography — she as the art director/stylist, he as the photographer/technician — using the credit line "Diane & Allan Arbus." In 1956, she left the business partnership and committed herself full-time to her own work.

When Arbus first ventured into the New York City streets to photograph, she was exploring much of the same terrain — pedestrians in Times Square, bathers at Coney Island, street fairs in Little Italy — as her predecessors and contemporaries, from Paul Strand and Walker Evans to

---

1. *Diane Arbus Revelations* (New York: Random House, 2003), p. 70. Diane Arbus (née Nemerov) graduated in 1940 from the Fieldston School in the Bronx, New York. She married Allan Arbus in April 1941.

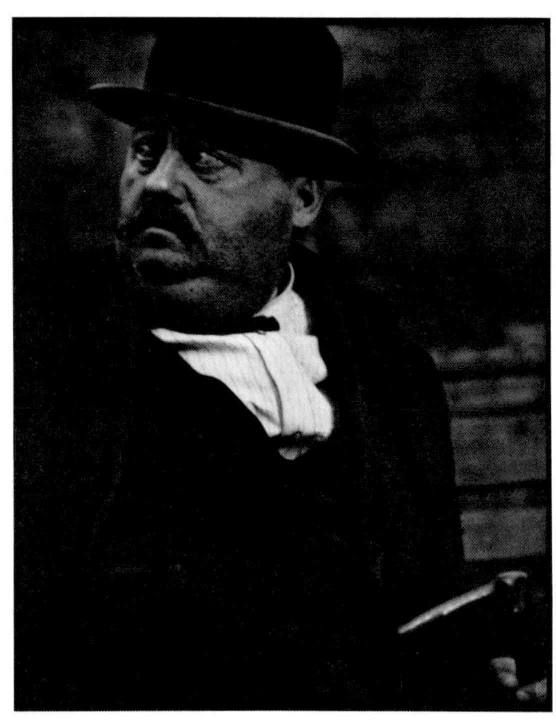

PAUL STRAND
Portrait—New York, 1916

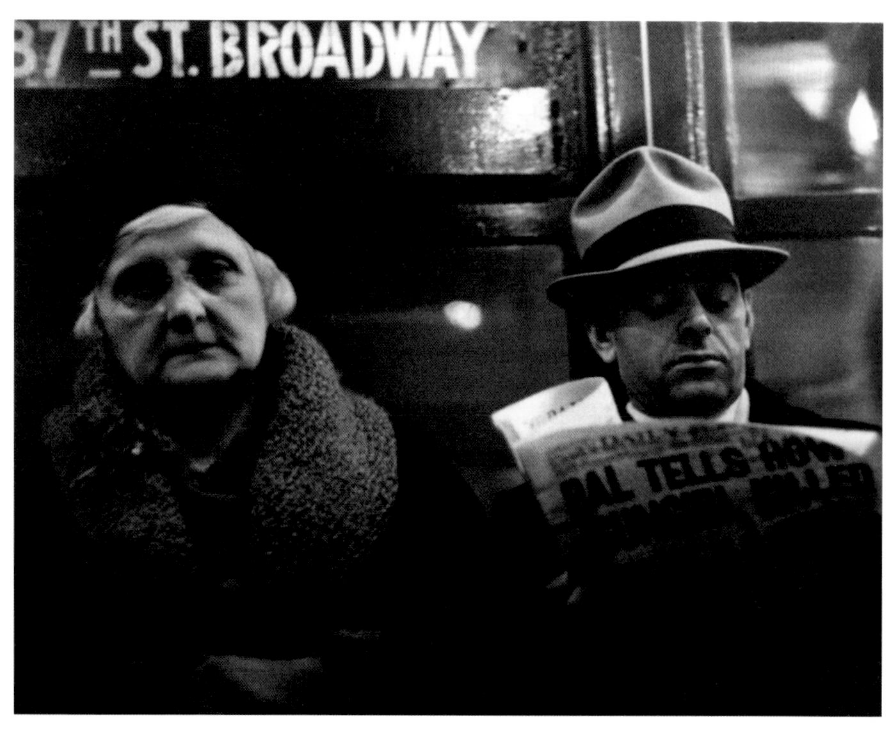

WALKER EVANS
Subway Passengers, 1938

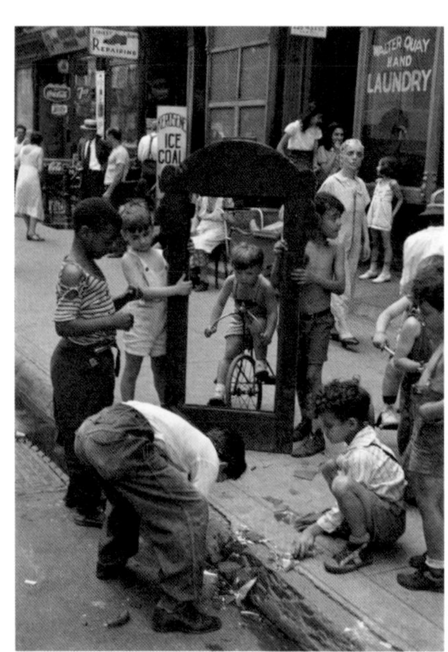

HELEN LEVITT
New York, ca. 1940

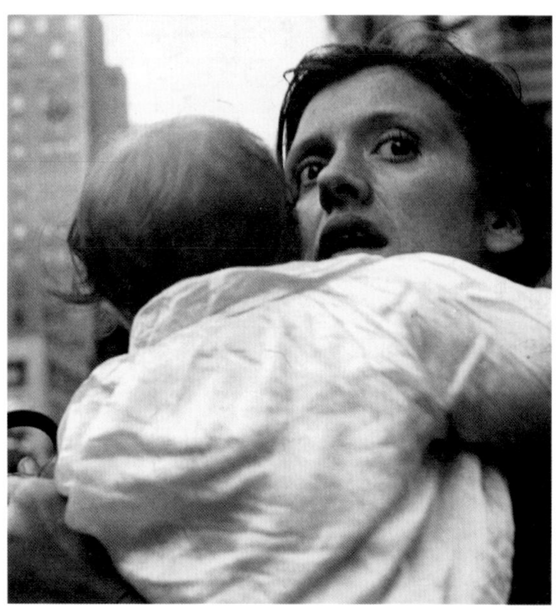

LEON LEVINSTEIN
New York, 1955

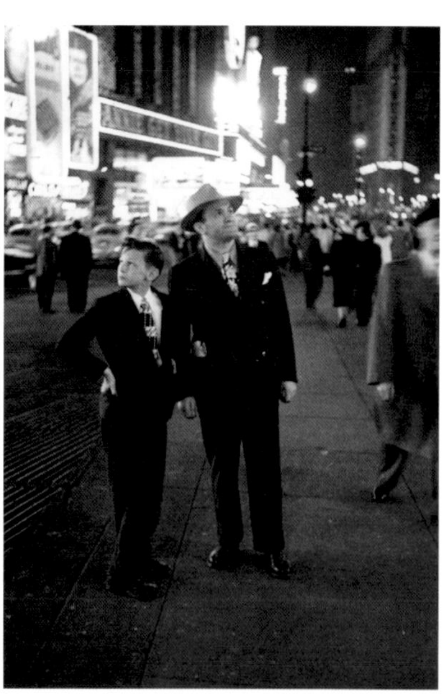

LOUIS FAURER
Times Square, NYC, 1947

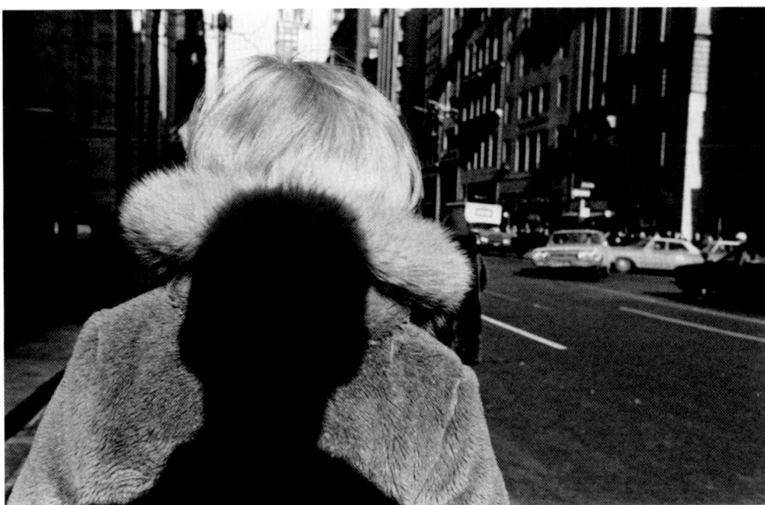

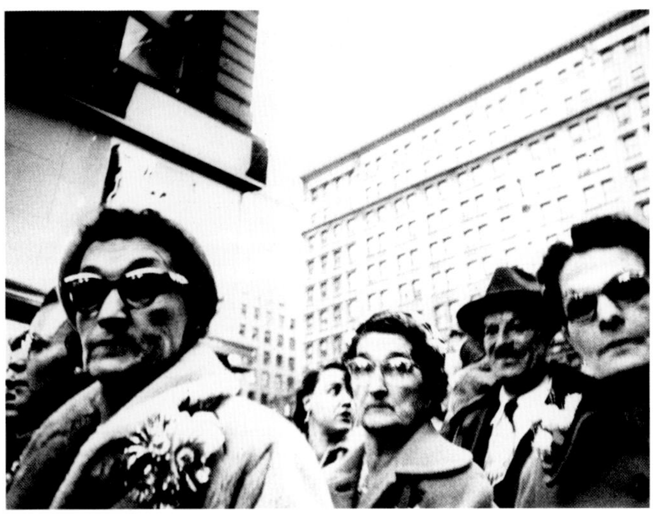

Garry Winogrand and Lee Friedlander, among others. Each had a distinct way of working and, with the striking exception of Arbus, a way of remaining anonymous. To hide his intentions and make candid portraits, Strand attached a fake lens to the side of his camera; Evans secreted his camera in the folds of a winter coat to photograph fellow subway passengers; Helen Levitt fixed a right-angle finder to her 35mm Leica to record kids at play in Spanish Harlem. Leon Levinstein and Louis Faurer found more subtle ways to hide in plain sight. Friedlander, in an ironic sleight of hand, manages to disappear by making himself or his doppelgänger the subject. Both William Klein and Winogrand use the force of their physical presence as the invisible center of their pictures, while in Robert Frank's work, a lyrical absence resonates at the heart of the matter.

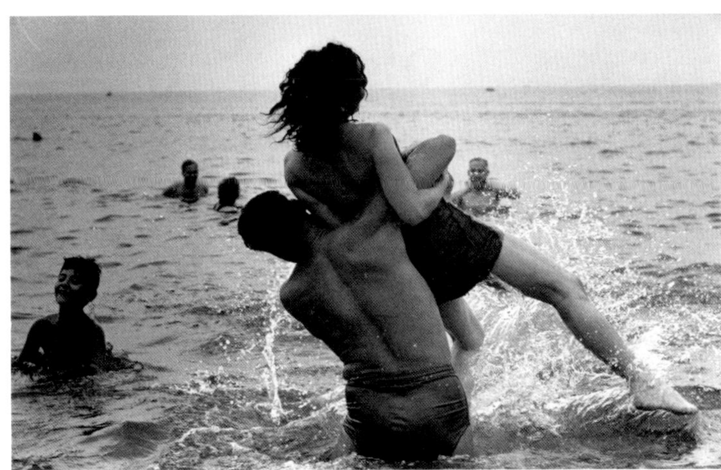

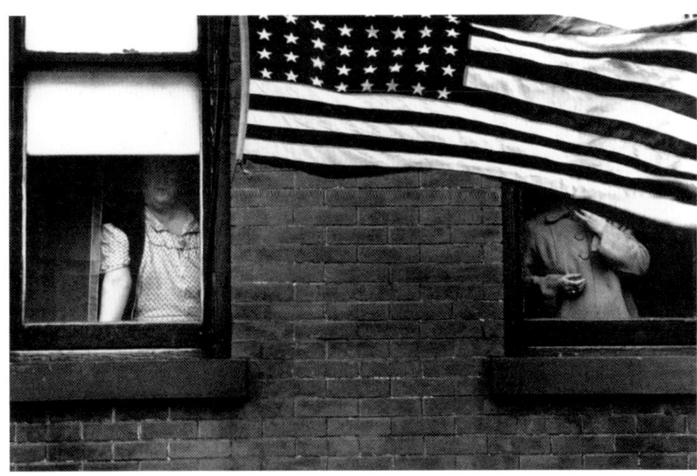

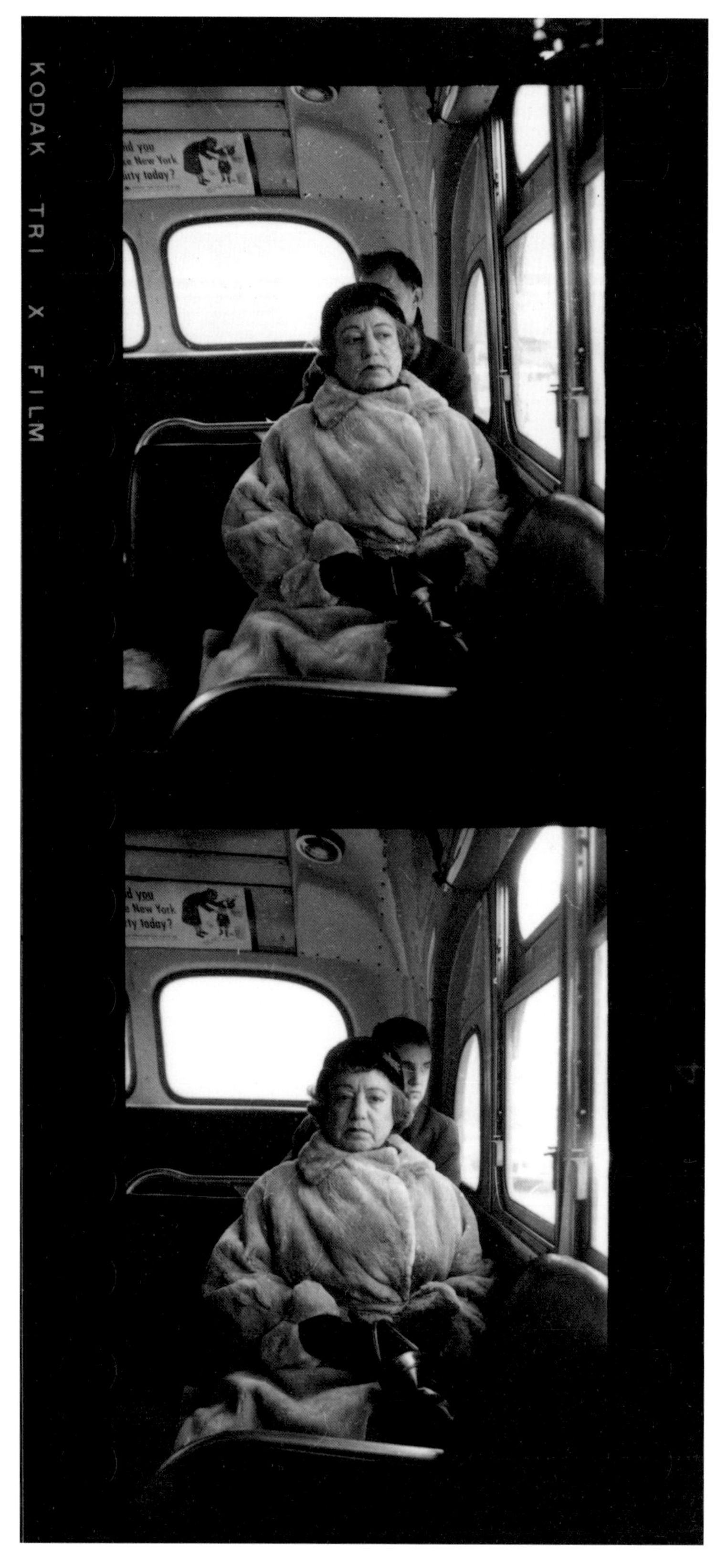

DIANE ARBUS
Lady on a bus, N.Y.C. 1957. Contact sheet, roll 93 #3–4

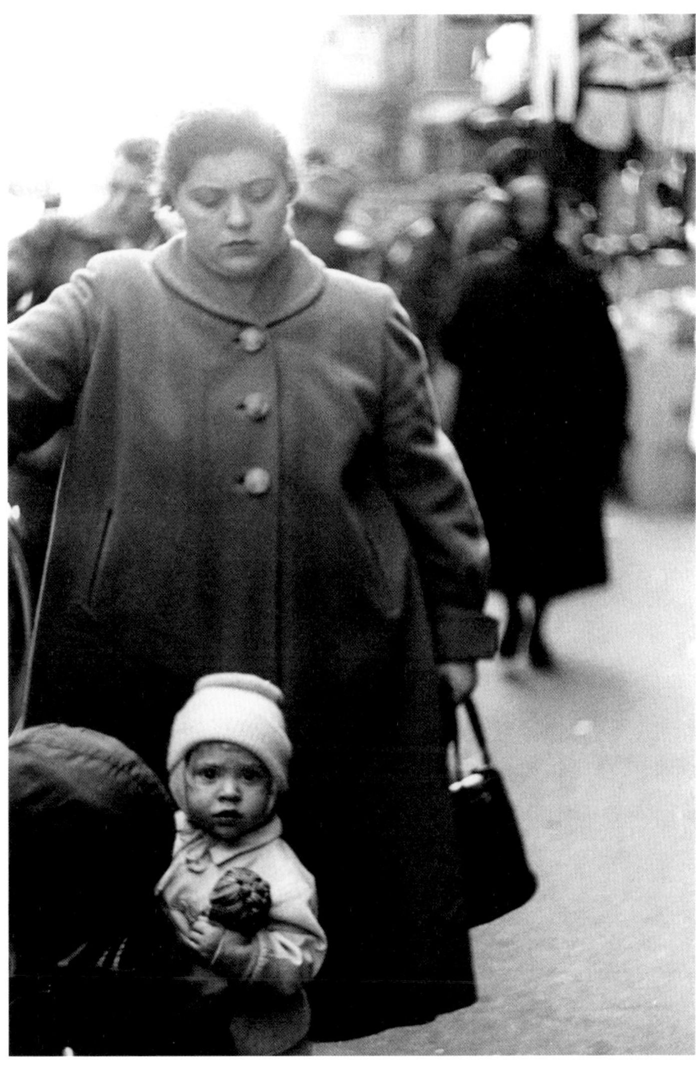

All these photographers developed strategies to remain personally disengaged and largely detached from their subjects, convinced that as documentarians the only legitimate record was one in which they themselves appear to play little or no role. By contrast, Arbus was looking for the poignancy of a direct personal encounter (see *opposite* and *above*): "For me the subject of the picture is always more important than the picture. And more complicated."[2] This longing to know, this curiosity about the hidden nature of who or what she was photographing, coupled with her belief in the power of the camera to make that visible, is, above all, what sets her apart.

---

2. Arbus, quoted in *Diane Arbus* (Millerton, N.Y.: Aperture, 1972), p. 15.

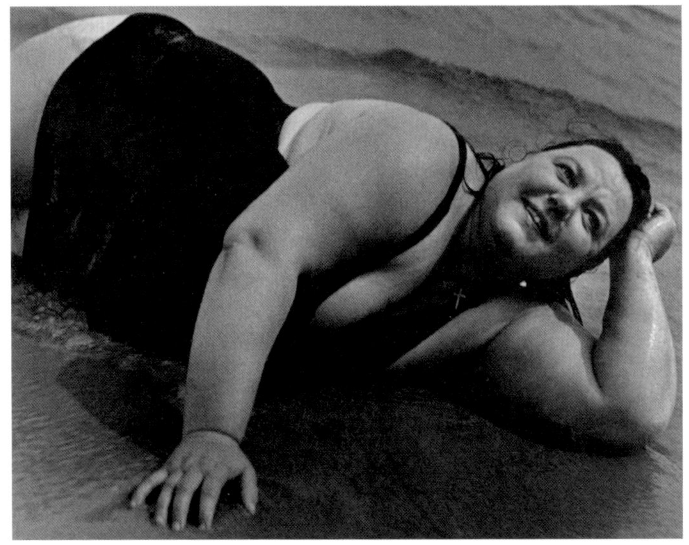

The two photographers who meant the most to Arbus at this stage in her career were Europeans: Lisette Model, the iconoclastic Austrian émigré and teacher, and August Sander, the German typological portraitist. In the fall of 1956, Arbus enrolled in Model's Greenwich Village photography class.[3] By all accounts, the experience almost immediately transformed Arbus's confidence in the pursuit of her own vision. In Model's words, "I've never in my life seen anybody—not listening to me but suddenly listening to herself through what was said."[4] The source of Model's influence lay not in her own photography—of which Arbus saw little until years later—but as a spiritual mentor and lifelong friend.[5] Curiously enough, however, it is with the classical photographs of Sander that Arbus's early street pictures seem to have the greatest affinity.[6] While Sander's photographs are deliberately

---

3. Jacob Deschin listed the class in his *New York Times* column on September 23, 1956: "Lisette Model offers a course in 'The Function of the Small Camera' to be given in twelve weekly evening sessions at 8 o'clock at 247 West Thirteenth Street. The course fee is $60. Phone CHelsea 2-4626 at noon and 7–8 P.M." Arbus had previously taken photography classes at the New School for Social Research, New York, with Berenice Abbott in 1941 and Alexey Brodovitch in 1955.
4. Lisette Model, quoted in *Revelations*, p. 141. Further, Allan Arbus recalled: "After three weeks [in the class] she felt totally freed and able to photograph." Ibid.
5. In 1968, Model gave Arbus a print of *Coney Island Bather, New York*, now in the Diane Arbus Archive, The Metropolitan Museum of Art, New York.
6. Arbus probably first saw Sander's photographs in Edward Steichen's 1955 Museum of Modern Art exhibition and accompanying publication, *The Family of Man* (which also included a photograph by "Diane & Allan Arbus"), and in MoMA's 1956 exhibition, "Diogenes with a Camera III." Most significantly, prior to the spring of 1960, she received from her friend Marvin Israel a copy of the November 1959 issue of *Du* magazine that featured fifty photographs by Sander. Her copy of *Du*, as well as *Deutschenspiegel: Menschen Des 20. Jahrhunderts* (1962) is in the Diane Arbus Archive.

posed and these Arbus works generally are not; while his subjects are expressly conscious of representing their roles in society and hers represent only their idiosyncratic selves, all share a dignity and solemnity in the way they confront the camera.

From the start, Arbus saw the street as a place full of secrets waiting to be fathomed. Even in her earliest studies of pedestrians, her subjects seem magically, if just momentarily, freed from the flux and turmoil of their surroundings. This isolation is at times the effect of selective focus, at times due to the photographer's patience or persistence, at times merely happenstance. Regardless of origin, the result is a singular look of introspection. In reacting to Arbus and her camera, her subjects are revealed almost as if they were alone, catching a brief glimpse of themselves in a shop window or a mirror (see *following page*). The exchange on both sides of the camera — of seeing and being seen — raises existential questions in the subject, questions that ultimately transmit themselves to the viewer.

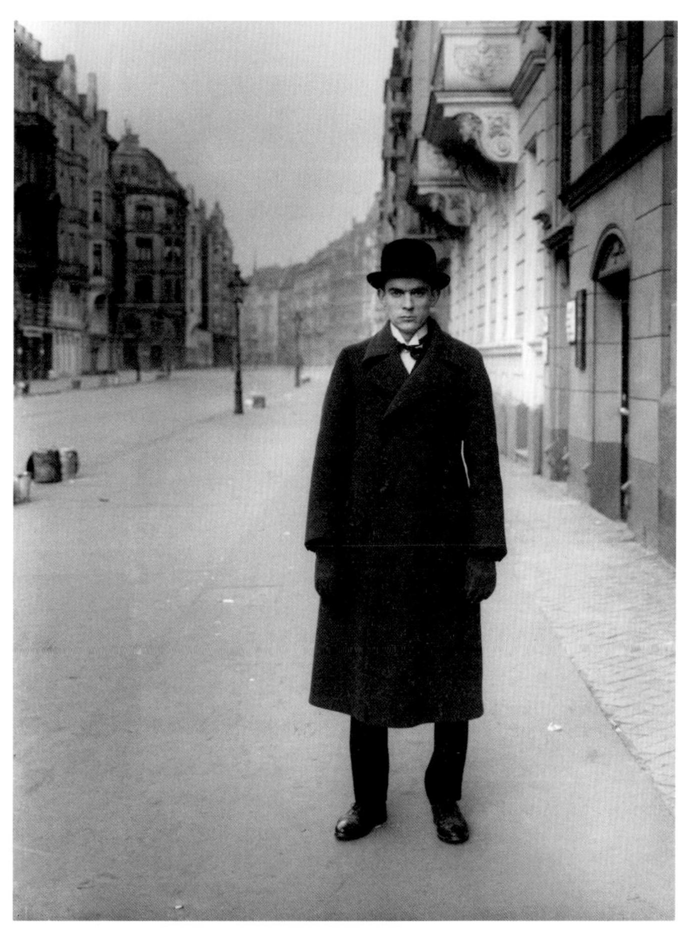

AUGUST SANDER
The Painter Anton Räderscheidt, 1927

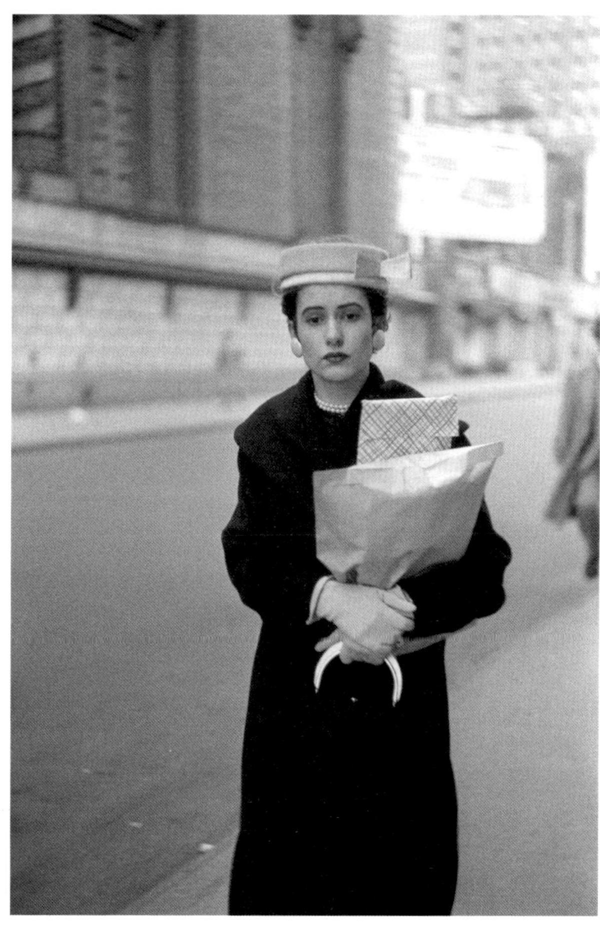

DIANE ARBUS
Woman on the street with parcels, N.Y.C. 1957

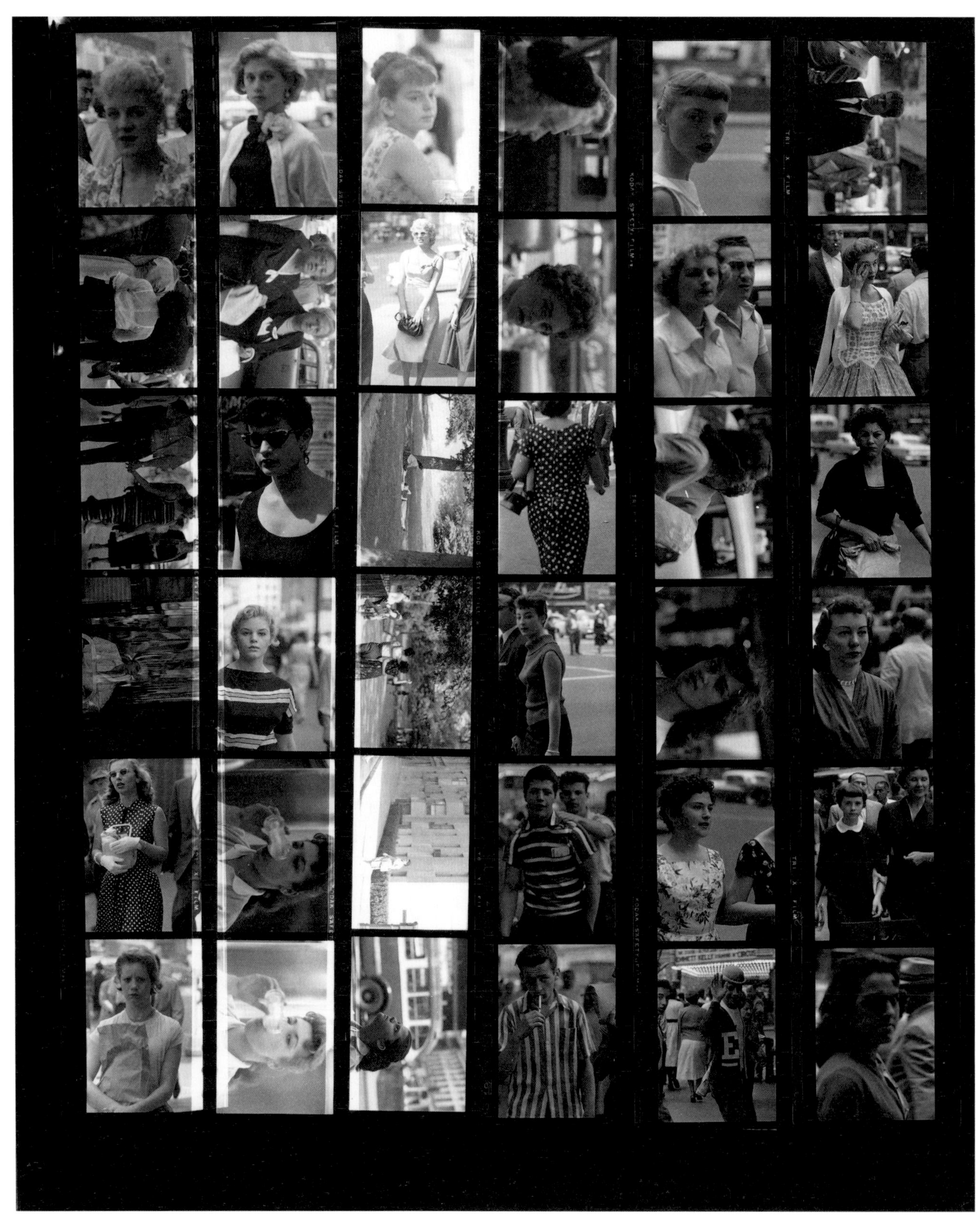

DIANE ARBUS
Contact sheet, roll 50B, 1956

This phenomenon, however, is not solely a matter of personal chemistry. Many of the early photographs involve no direct interaction and depend not on where and with whom Arbus found herself, but rather on what happened when she looked. In her hands, the camera acted like a divining rod, and Arbus became the medium through which the process worked. The specter of *Windblown headline on a dark pavement, N.Y.C. 1956* (p. 3) is echoed in the gravity of *Boy stepping off the curb, N.Y.C. 1957–58* (p. 87) and in the riddle of *Clouds on screen at a drive-in movie, N.J. 1961* (p. 183) as well as in Arbus's haunting pietà, *Woman carrying a child in Central Park, N.Y.C. 1956* (p. 37). In the same spirit, her photographs through doorways or shop windows or past the heads of audience members to what is on the other side seem like glimpses of secret worlds, souvenirs brought back by an enchanted stranger in a strange land. To look at this body of work as a whole — even those photographs that could have been taken by someone else — is to encounter, over and over again, a particular aesthetic imperative, the moment of recognition that compelled Arbus to make the picture. As she wrote to a friend in 1960, "I don't press the shutter. The image does. And it's like being gently clobbered."[7]

Of course, Arbus was not only an agent of mysterious forces beyond her control. Much of what she wanted to photograph could not be found by simply stepping out the door but required considerable research and tenacity. Her working method was in many ways like that of an urban anthropologist. As early as 1958, she kept notebooks in which she recorded what she had gleaned from books, newspapers, including the tabloids, the telephone directory, radio talk shows, her own mind, and even conversations with friends and acquaintances. Her notes often took the form of lists of potential subjects or general topics:

morgue; freak at home; jewel box revue; roller derby women;
dressing rm; womans prison; weird women; paddy wagon;
meat slaughterhouse; tattoo parlor; taxi dance hall-before hrs;
lonelyhearts club; Happinesss Exch.; lady wrestling;
beggars-blind; place-waterfr. hotel;
ladies room-coney-subway; daughters of J[acob] dying.[8]

crime; despair; sin; madness; death; fame; wealth; innocence.[9]

---

7. Diane Arbus, postcard to Marvin Israel, February 4, 1960, quoted in *Revelations*, p. 127.
8. Diane Arbus, Notebook 3 (1959), p. [49]. All of the artist's notebooks are in the Diane Arbus Archive. The Jewel Box Revue was a touring company of female impersonators that started in 1939. A "taxi dance hall" was a popular venue where male patrons paid women to dance with them, using a ticketed system. *Big Joe's Happiness Exchange* was a WABC call-in radio program that began in 1959. The Daughters of Jacob is a private Jewish nursing home in the Bronx.
9. Notebook 3, p. [59].

Interspersed with these jottings are extracts from a wide range of ancient and modern sources: Plato, Zen literature, Bram Stoker, Jean Cocteau (on Pablo Picasso), Fyodor Dostoyevsky, and Allen Ginsberg, among many others.

> To a mind that is still the whole universe surrenders. —Lao Tzu

> Faith is that faculty which enables us to believe things
> which we know to be untrue. —*Dracula*

> The event comes in through the door you haven't opened.

> Does existence occur or does occurrence exist?

> People are a trap for circumstance to fall into.

> Every single work of art is the fulfillment of a prophecy: for every work of
> art is the conversion of an idea into an image. —Oscar Wilde [10]

While it is not remarkable for an artist to be preoccupied by philosophical paradoxes, it is astonishing to see them revealed as plain facts (among all the other indisputable facts) by a single photographer in picture after picture. One only has to consider *The Backwards Man in his hotel room, N.Y.C. 1961* (p. 17) about which Arbus wrote, "[He] is a metaphor for human destiny — walking blind into the future with an eye on the past."[11] *The Backwards Man* is, of course, just a contortionist in a hotel room, *Female impersonator holding long gloves, Hempstead, L.I. 1959* (p. 13) is just a man getting dressed, and *Child with a toy hand grenade in Central Park, N.Y.C. 1962* (p. 257) is just a kid playing in a park; but they are simultaneously Arbus's unapologetic documents of the mythic as a manifestation of the ordinary.

Progress or change is never as steady or hierarchical as a chronological survey such as *in the beginning* might encourage us to believe. Anything that seems to emerge from this body of work — whether suddenly or gradually — turns out to have always been there, lurking in what came before. Over the course of the seven years (1956–62) in which these photographs were made, an evolution takes place, from pictures of individuals that spring

---

10. Diane Arbus, Notebook 1 (1958–59), p. [13]: Lao Tzu, quoted in Arthur Waley, *The Way and Its Power: A Study of the Tao Te Ching and Its Place in Chinese Thought* (London: Allen & Unwin, 1934), p. 58. Diane Arbus, Notebook 2 (1959), p. [201]: Bram Stoker, *Dracula* (New York: Modern Library, 1897), p. 211. The original volume is in the archive. Notebook 2, pp. [273, 273, 283]: three unattributed quotations. Notebook 2, p. [327]: Oscar Wilde, *De Profundis* (New York: Modern Library, 1905).

11. Diane Arbus, 1961 Appointment Book, July 6, Diane Arbus Archive. See p. 173 in this volume.

out of fortuitous chance encounters to portraits in which the chosen subjects become engaged participants, with as much stake in the outcome as the photographer. The street portraiture of *Woman in a mink stole and bow shoes, N.Y.C. 1956* (p. 35) and *Man in hat, trunks, socks and shoes, Coney Island, N.Y. 1960* (p. 161) gives way to the increasing authority of photographs such as *Jack Dracula at a bar, New London, Conn. 1961* (p. 175) and *Stripper with bare breasts sitting in her dressing room, Atlantic City, N.J. 1961* (p. 185) in which the merely incidental and extraneous details are overwhelmed by the encounter between photographer and subject, leaving the viewer with nowhere else to look. Behind a carnival tent, backstage, or in a bedroom, Arbus's role as a curious outsider receded over time in favor of that of a privileged—if only provisional—insider. This was an ongoing process. As late as 1965

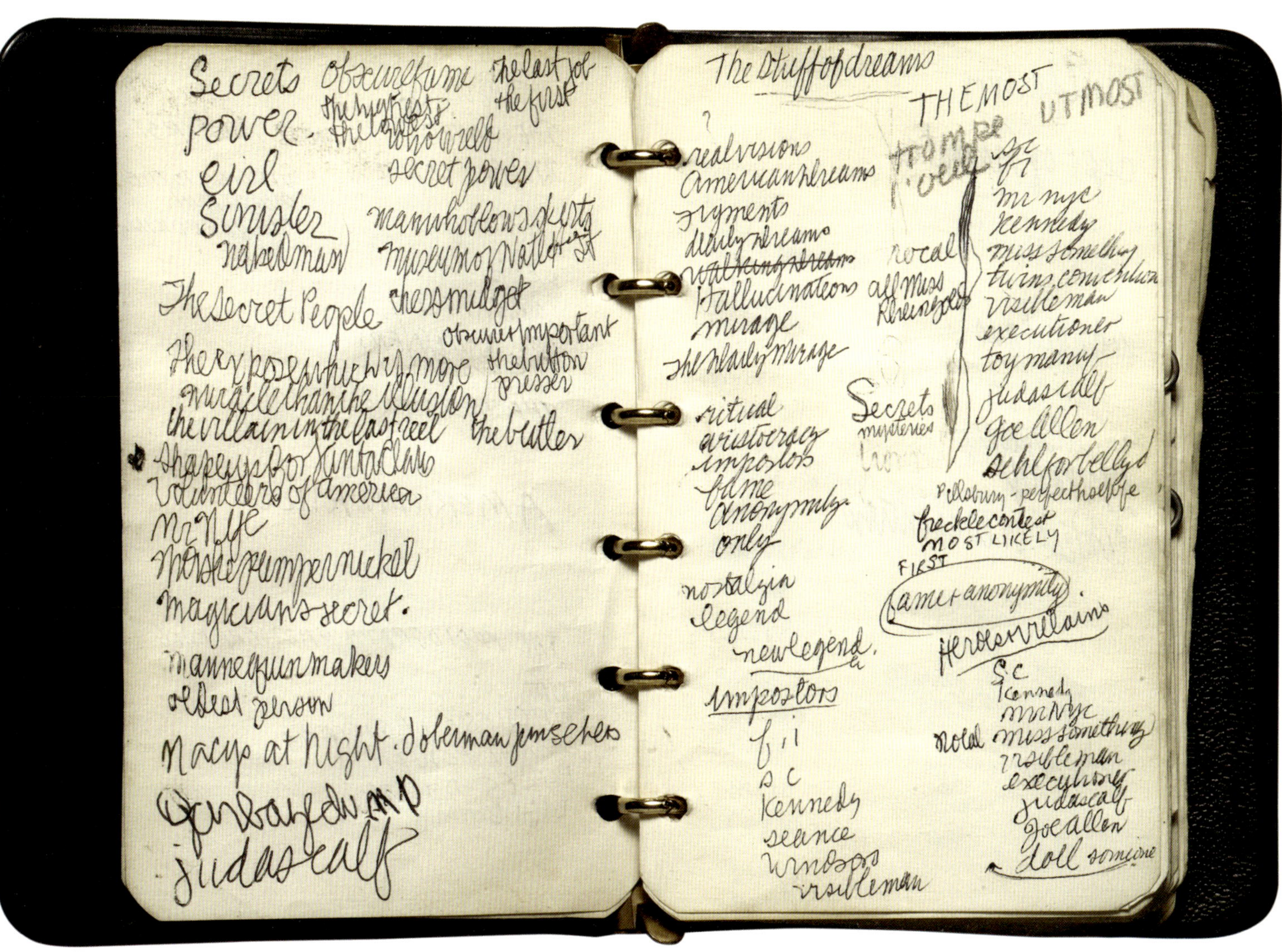

DIANE ARBUS
Notebook 9 (1962), pp. [4–5]

in her second Guggenheim Foundation application, she wrote: "I have learned to get past the door, from the outside to the inside. One milieu leads to another. I want to be able to follow."[12]

During this early period Arbus used a variety of 35mm rangefinder and single-lens-reflex format cameras (either owned or borrowed), including a Contax D, a Nikon S3, and a Nikon F, but in 1962 she purchased a Wide-Angle Rolleiflex twin-lens reflex camera. In hindsight the change from the spontaneity afforded by the 35mm camera to the formality demanded by the precision of the bulkier 2 ¼ inch square-format camera — which took place over the course of that entire year — appears almost inevitable. All of the salient attributes of the legendary square-format pictures from 1962 and later in her career — their centrality, boldness, intimacy, and apparent artlessness — turn out to have been present in the work all along. They inform *Woman with white gloves and a pocket book, N.Y.C. 1956* (p. 41) as clearly as they do *Tall partygoer in a taffeta dress, N.Y.C. 1962* (p. 197). The new camera did not generate these qualities; it just clarified them, making them easier for us to recognize.

From the beginning and throughout Arbus's work, individuals momentarily confronting their own singularity challenge us to do the same. The photographs call into question what we thought we knew about identity, gender, race, appearance, and the distinctions between artifice and reality. At the same time, without embellishment or fanfare, Arbus brings us face to face with what she had first glimpsed at the age of sixteen, "the divineness in ordinary things," and through her photographs we begin to see it too.

---

12. Diane Arbus, Guggenheim Foundation Fellowship application for a project that she titled "The Interior Landscape" (1965), quoted in *Revelations*, p. 176.

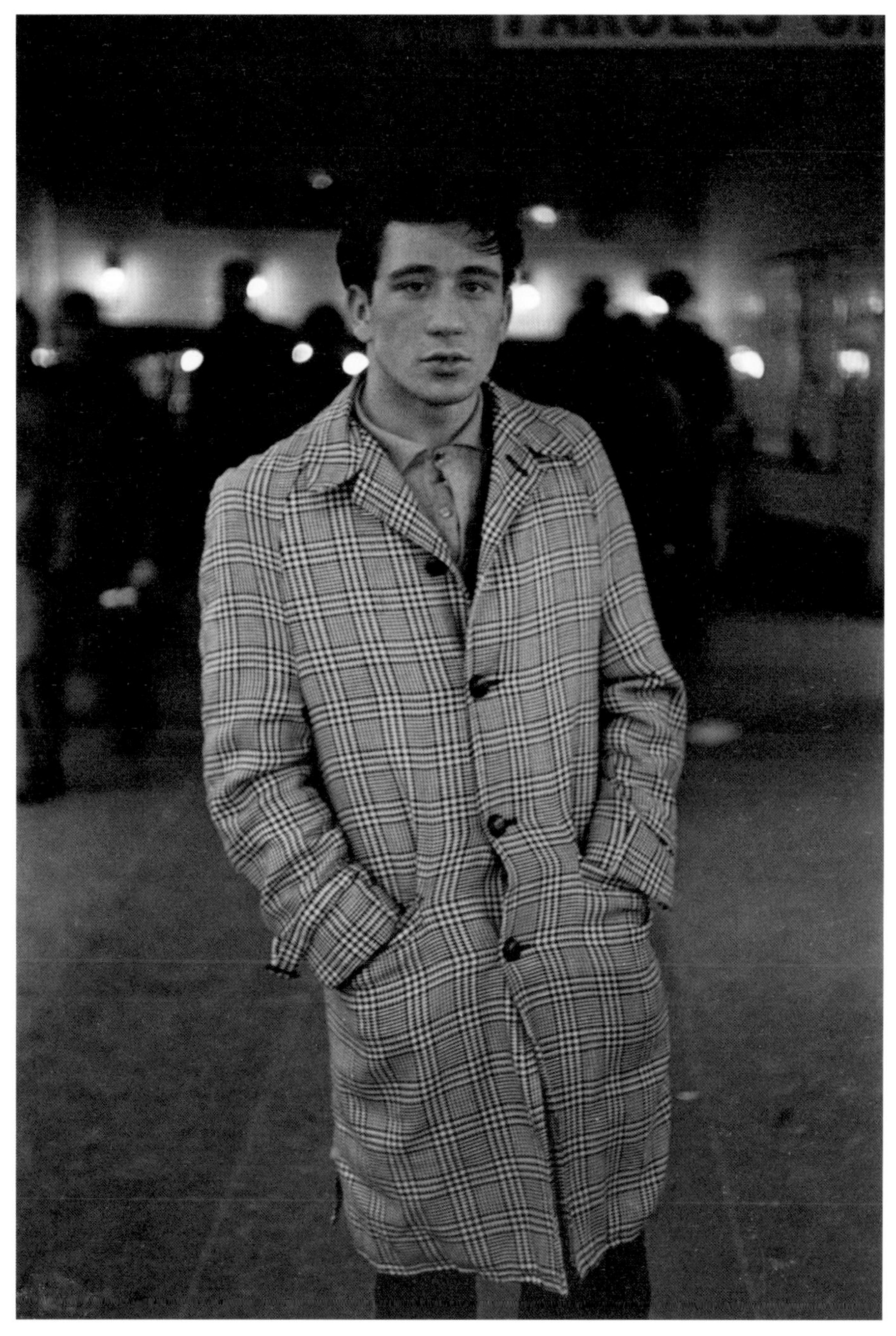

DIANE ARBUS
Young man in a plaid coat with a toothpick, N.Y.C. 1961

DIANE ARBUS
American, 1923–1971
202 Self-portrait with 35mm Contax D
camera, 1959
Contact sheet, roll 614 #34
Gelatin silver print
Promised Gift of Doon Arbus and Amy Arbus
L.2008.63.451b

PAUL STRAND
American, 1890–1976
204 *Portrait—New York*, 1916
Photogravure
9 × 6 3/4 in. (22.8 × 17.1 cm)
From *Camera Work*, nos. 49–50
Alfred Stieglitz Collection,
by exchange, 1953
53.701.50

WALKER EVANS
American, 1903–1975
204 *Subway Passengers*, 1938
Gelatin silver print
4 13/16 × 5 15/16 in. (12.2 × 15 cm)
Gift of Arnold H. Crane, 1971
1971.646.18

HELEN LEVITT
American, 1913–2009
204 *New York*, ca. 1940
Gelatin silver print
11 3/4 × 8 in. (29.9 × 20.4 cm)
Purchase, Lila Acheson Wallace Gift,
and Gift of William and Mimi Levitt,
by exchange, 1996
1996.2.5

LEON LEVINSTEIN
American, 1910–1988
204 *New York*, 1955
Gelatin silver print
14 × 12 15/16 in. (35.5 × 32.9 cm)
Gift of Gary Davis, 2008
2008.664.18

LOUIS FAURER
American, 1916–2001
204 *Times Square, NYC*, 1947
Gelatin silver print
12 7/8 × 8 3/8 in. (32.7 × 21.3 cm)
Courtesy Howard Greenberg Gallery,
New York

LEE FRIEDLANDER
American, born 1934
205 *Shadow, New York City*, 1966
Gelatin silver print
6 5/16 × 9 1/2 in. (16 × 24.1 cm)
Purchase, The Horace W. Goldsmith
Foundation Gift, through Joyce and
Robert Menschel, 1990
1990.1009.7

WILLIAM KLEIN
American, born 1928
205 *Christmas Shopping, Macy's, New York*, 1954
Gelatin silver print
11 × 13 7/8 in. (27.9 × 35.3 cm)
Purchase, The Horace W. Goldsmith
Foundation Gift, through Joyce and
Robert Menschel, 1989
1989.1037.1

GARRY WINOGRAND
American, 1928–1984
205 *Coney Island, New York*, ca. 1952
Gelatin silver print
8 11/16 × 12 15/16 in. (22 × 33 cm)
Museum of Modern Art, New York,
Purchase and gift of Barbara Schwartz in
memory of Eugene M. Schwartz

ROBERT FRANK
American, born Switzerland, 1924
205 *Parade, Hoboken, New Jersey*, 1955–56
Gelatin silver print
9 1/16 × 13 3/4 in. (23 × 34.9 cm)
Purchase, Anonymous Gifts, 1986
1986.1198.26

DIANE ARBUS
American, 1923–1971
206 *Lady on a bus, N.Y.C. 1957*
Contact sheet, roll 93 #3–4
Gelatin silver print
Promised Gift of Doon Arbus and Amy Arbus
L.2008.63.77

DIANE ARBUS
American, 1923–1971
207 *Mother contemplating her toddler,*
N.Y.C. 1956
Gelatin silver print
8 $^{13}/_{16}$ × 5 $^{11}/_{16}$ in. (22.4 × 14.5 cm)
Gift of Doon Arbus and Amy Arbus, 2007
2007.501.52

LISETTE MODEL
American, born Austria, 1901–1983
208 *Coney Island Bather, New York*, ca. 1939
Gelatin silver print
15 $^{1}/_{4}$ × 19 $^{1}/_{4}$ in. (38.7 × 48.9 cm)
Promised Gift of Doon Arbus and Amy Arbus
L.2008.82.3.9

AUGUST SANDER
German, 1876–1964
209 *The Painter Anton Räderscheidt*, 1927
Gelatin silver print
11 $^{15}/_{16}$ × 9 $^{3}/_{8}$ in. (30.3 × 23.8 cm)
Warner Communications Inc. Purchase
Fund, 1979
1979.521.4

DIANE ARBUS
American, 1923–1971
209 *Woman on the street with parcels, N.Y.C. 1957*
Gelatin silver print by Neil Selkirk
9 × 5 $^{7}/_{8}$ in. (22.8 × 15 cm)
Private collection

DIANE ARBUS
American, 1923–1971
210 Contact sheet, roll 50B, 1956
Gelatin silver print
10 × 8 in. (25.4 × 20.3 cm)
Promised Gift of Doon Arbus and Amy Arbus
L.2008.63.41

DIANE ARBUS
American, 1923–1971
213 Notebook 9 (1962), pp. [4–5]
Ink on paper
Promised Gift of Doon Arbus and Amy Arbus
L.2008.77.2.9

DIANE ARBUS
American, 1923–1971
215 *Young man in a plaid coat with a toothpick,*
N.Y.C. 1961
Gelatin silver print by Neil Selkirk
9 × 5 $^{7}/_{8}$ in. (22.8 × 15 cm)
Gift of Neil Selkirk, 2012
2012.552.48

11 × 14 inch glassine print sleeves annotated by Diane Arbus
Top to bottom: 2007.505.1.7, 2007.505.1.19, 2007.505.1.13, 2007.505.1.20, 2007.505.1.37, 2007.505.1.46, 2007.505.1.125

notes from the archive
titles, locations, and dates

KARAN RINALDO

The Diane Arbus Archive is housed in the Department of Photographs at The Metropolitan Museum of Art and comprises the artist's negatives, including over 6,200 rolls of black-and-white film and their corresponding contact sheets and annotated glassine film sleeves. The archive also preserves over 600 vintage prints and numerous annotated glassine print sleeves as well as the artist's notebooks (starting in late 1958), appointment books (beginning in January 1959), correspondence, business records, and other photographic and manuscript objects. The Estate of Diane Arbus maintained these materials from 1971 until 2007, when they were deposited at the Museum.[1] Beyond illuminating the artist's working methods and enriching the overall understanding of her work, the breadth of the archive has enabled the Metropolitan to cross-reference a variety of resources in an effort to identify subjects and events throughout Arbus's career. This now eight-year study has revealed certain discrepancies among the titles, locations, and dates of some of the photographs presented in this publication.[2] The following are highlights of the discoveries that led to selected revisions noted in the list of works (p. 240). Given the extent of the archive, this research is ongoing and reaches well beyond the photographs published in this volume.

Boy stepping off the curb, N.Y.C. 1957–58
Blurry woman gazing up smiling, N.Y.C. 1957–58

Although the archive preserves the source negatives for all but a few photographic prints by Arbus, it includes neither the rolls of film from which these two prints were made nor any prints from related negatives that could assist in determining a likely date or date range for

1. Unless otherwise noted, all items reproduced in this essay are from the Diane Arbus Archive at The Metropolitan Museum of Art and are gifts or promised gifts of Doon Arbus and Amy Arbus. All photographs and contact sheets are gelatin silver prints; all notebooks and appointment books have inscriptions and writings by the artist in ink or graphite.
2. All title, location, and date revisions have been made in consultation with The Estate of Diane Arbus. The print sleeves inscribed by Arbus on the facing page illustrate several title and date variations.

these photographs. Based on the subject matter, general composition, and 35mm format, the date for both works is probably 1957 or 1958. *Boy stepping off the curb, N.Y.C.* (p. 87) was dated 1957 in the 1972 retrospective at the Museum of Modern Art, New York, and ca. 1956 in *Diane Arbus Revelations* (2003).[3] This is the first publication of *Blurry woman gazing up smiling, N.Y.C.* (p. 109).

Lady on a bus, N.Y.C. 1957

Lady on a bus, N.Y.C. (p. 55) appears in *Revelations* with the date 1956. The print is from a negative on roll 93 for which "1956" is marked on the film sleeve in an Estate hand.[4] However, the original contact sheet in this case includes a divergent date inscription, "Jan. 1957," also in an Estate hand.[5] Among the sixteen rolls of film from roll 83 to roll 98, twelve have original film sleeves annotated by the artist and inscribed "Jan 57." Moreover, the roll that immediately follows this sequence, roll 101, is inscribed "2/57."[6] Although the distinction between

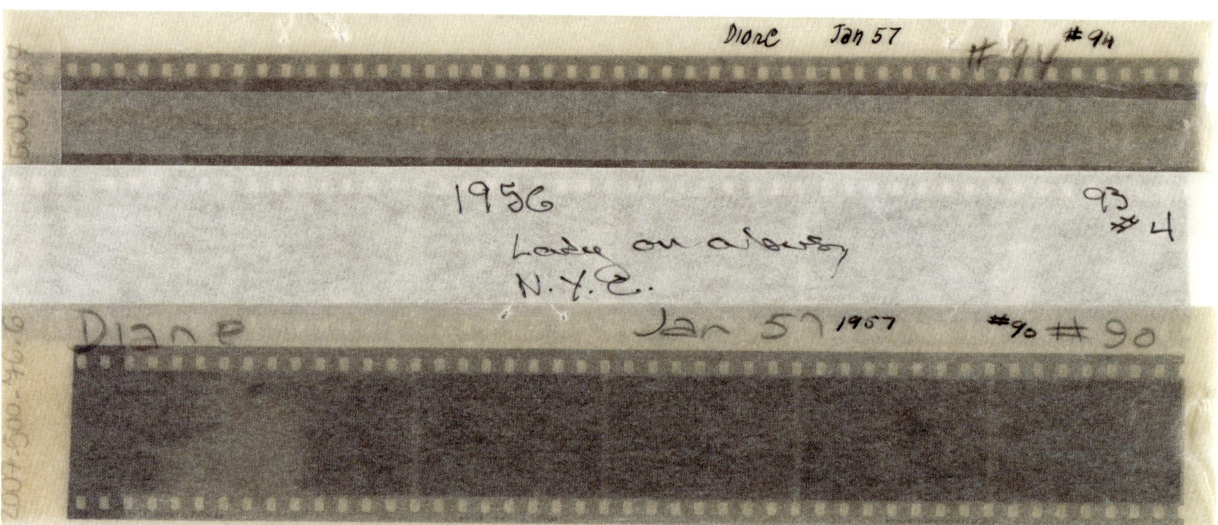

35mm negatives and glassine film sleeves annotated by Arbus and others
Top to bottom: 2007.500.78, 2007.500.77, 2007.500.76

---

3. Although the 1972 MoMA exhibition, "Diane Arbus," featured ten 35mm photographs dating from 1956 to 1962, the Aperture monograph that accompanied the show included square-format photographs only and as a result did not contain any 35mm photographs or any work prior to 1962.

4. Diane Arbus began numbering her rolls of film in 1956, inscribing roll numbers on the film sleeves and contact sheets. She maintained this numbering system throughout her life. The phrase "Estate hand" designates posthumous inscriptions that were made under the auspices of The Estate of Diane Arbus.

5. While Arbus's film sleeves frequently include a date, contact sheets generally do not. The few dates inscribed on contact sheets are in an Estate hand.

6. The periodic gaps in the artist's negative numbering sequence may or may not indicate missing rolls of film.

December 1956 and January 1957 may seem minor, most archival evidence suggests a date of 1957. As indicated in the list of works, several other prints in this publication that were previously dated 1956 have been revised to 1957.

Boy above a crowd, N.Y.C. 1957

Boy above a crowd, N.Y.C. (p. 77) is among those prints previously dated 1956 and was published in *Revelations* with this date. The film sleeve for roll 174 and the majority of the numerically contiguous sleeves are dated 1957 by the Estate. The numerical placement of the roll further suggests that it dates from mid-1957, a fact confirmed by a leaflet pictured in an adjacent frame on the same roll that shows that the event depicted was an I Am an American Day rally, held in Central Park on May 12, 1957.[7]

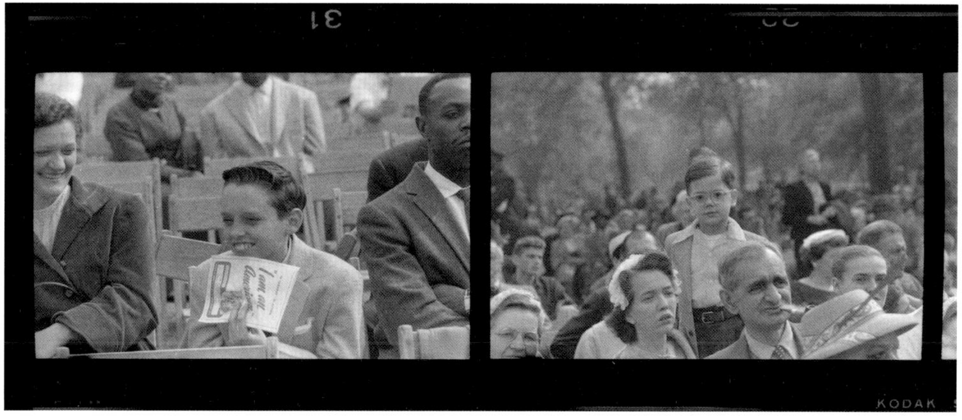

Roll 174 #31–32
2007.500.145

Clown in a fedora, Palisades Park, N.J. 1957

This photograph was previously titled *Clown in a fedora backstage, N.Y.C.* (p. 79). Roll 169, however, depicts a tent and fairgrounds, suggesting that the subject's location is not in New York City. While the archive does not have notebooks or appointment books to confirm events in 1957, Arbus included Palisades Park in the titles of prints from neighboring rolls of film, notably *Fire Eater at a carnival, Palisades Park, N.J. 1957* (p. 67) and *Sunny South Syncopaters*

---

7. "80,000 at I Am an American Day Rally In Central Park Hear Mayor and Baruch," *New York Times*, May 13, 1957. Although Congress moved I Am an American Day in 1952 from May to September and renamed it Citizenship Day, New York City rallies for I Am an American Day continued to be held in May through the mid-1960s.

and other sideshow banners at night, Palisades Park, N.J. 1957 (p. 71). Also, roll 160, which features views of the same tent and setting as roll 169, includes one frame showing a Hunt Bros. Circus tent with a sign for another circus, Hamid-Morton, and an additional frame of a roller coaster that appears to be the Cyclone at Palisades Park.[8]

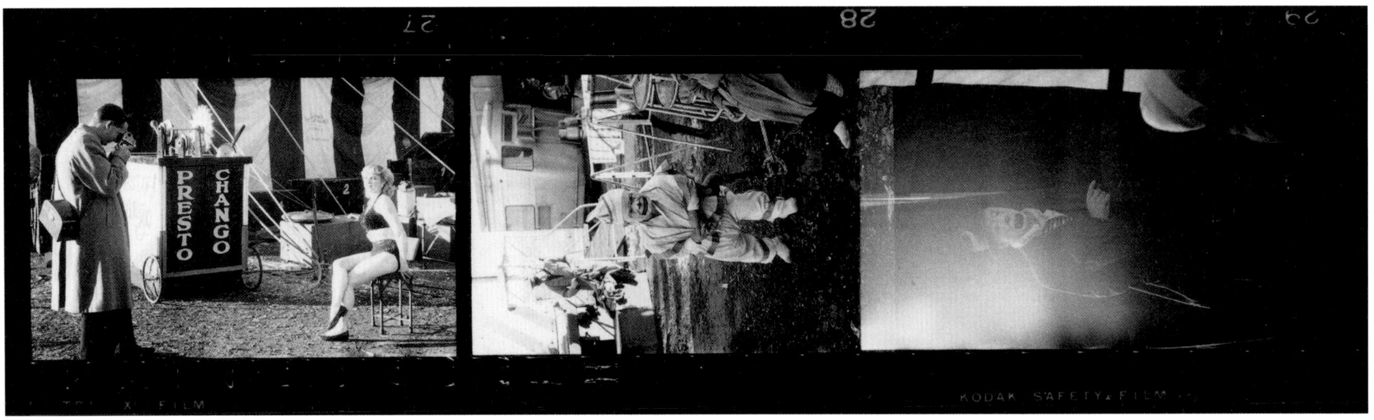

Contact sheet, roll 169 #27–29
L.2008.63.140

The *New York Times* and *Billboard* newspapers confirm that the combined Hamid-Morton and Hunt Bros. Circus performed in Palisades Park from April 12 to 28, 1957. The three-ring circus was touted in the press as "the first old fashioned tent circus in the metropolitan area in forty years" and as competition for the Ringling Bros. and Barnum & Bailey Circus at Madison Square Garden from April 3 to May 12, 1957, which Arbus also photographed.[9] Related location changes in this volume include *Girl in her circus costume backstage, Palisades Park, N.J. 1960* (p. 156) and *Headless woman, Palisades Park, N.J. 1961* (p. 187).

Young man with a paper bag at night, Coney Island, N.Y. 1957

This photograph was previously titled *Young man with a paper bag at night, N.Y.C.* (p. 81). While this is a seemingly trivial location correction, it is one that offers the opportunity to discuss Arbus's use of the designation "N.Y.C." Other frames from roll 222 reveal that Arbus made

---

8. Arbus always made the prints from her negatives, but until 1969 studio assistants processed her rolls of film, often in bulk. Thus, the rolls of film are not consistently numbered in the order in which they were exposed. Two rolls from a particular event may be separated by ten or more rolls from a completely unrelated event or set of events. For example, rolls 160 and 169 are interspersed with rolls of Easter Sunday in Central Park. Given how Arbus's early rolls were processed, they may have been numbered out of order or she may have visited the circus in Palisades Park more than once in April 1957.
9. "Circus Opens in Jersey," *New York Times*, April 13, 1957; "Hunt Top Bulging with Big H-M Unit" and "Hamid Snares TV, But R-B Cops Press," *Billboard*, April 20, 1957.

the photograph in Coney Island. Among the boardwalk attractions pictured is the Gyroscope or Gyro Globe, a lighted sphere ride that operated until 1964.[10] While some might argue that Coney Island is a part of New York City, including "N.Y.C." in the photograph's title differs from the artist's standard practice. Arbus's titles consistently use "N.Y.C." to refer to locations in Manhattan only, not those in the other boroughs, in this case, Brooklyn. Coney Island is a prime example of this careful treatment, as it is one of Arbus's most frequented outer-borough destinations. This designation is illustrated among the annotated print sleeves in the archive that are inscribed either "Coney Island" or "Coney Island, N.Y.," with none noting "Coney Island, N.Y.C."

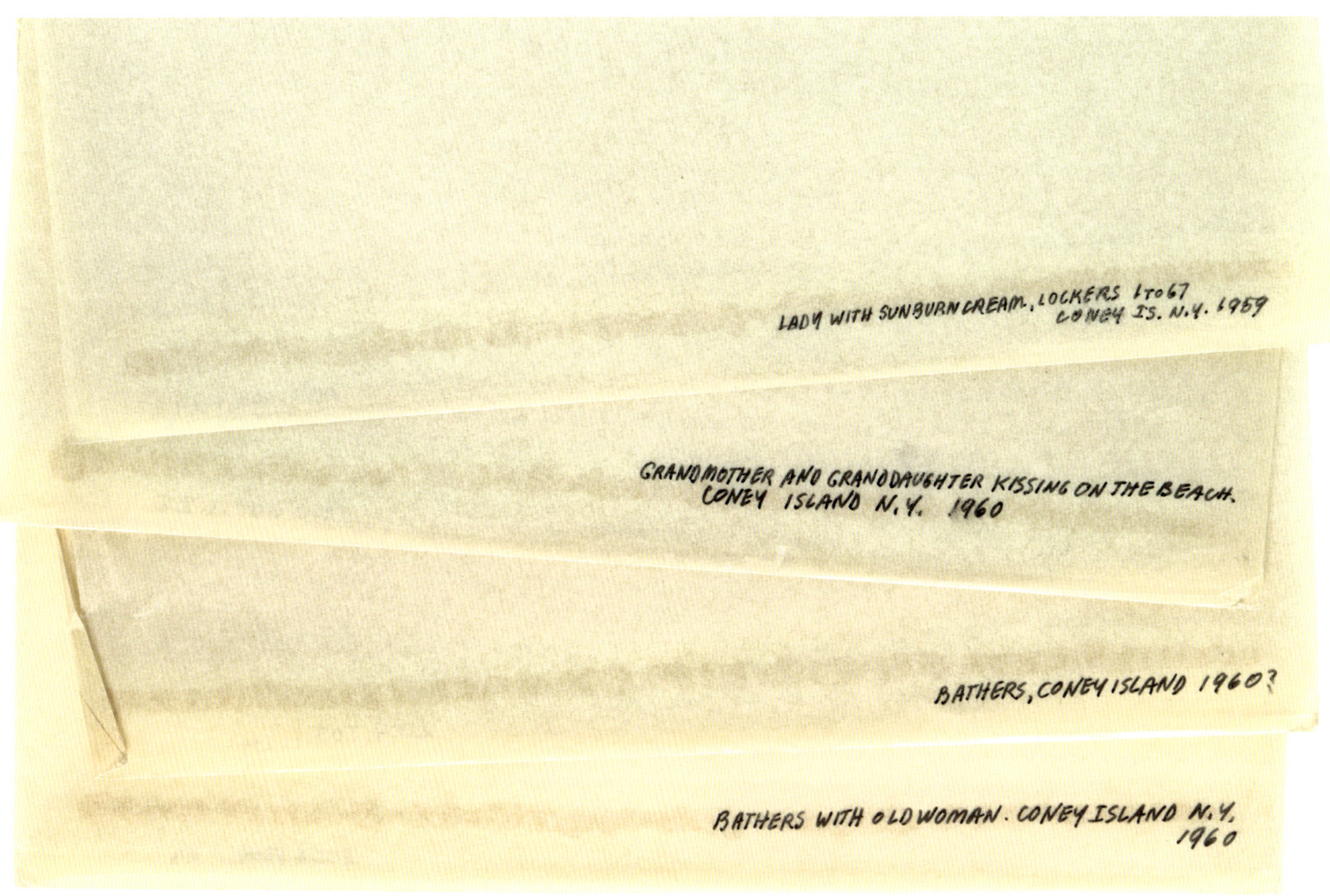

11 × 14 inch glassine print sleeves annotated by Arbus
Top to bottom: 2007.505.1.14, 2007.505.1.22, 2007.505.1.24, 2007.505.1.23

10. "Coney Island Undergoing Face-Lifting in Anticipation of a Record Throng," *New York Times*, April 6, 1947; "Coney Workers Ending a Season: But Lure of Sand Lingers On and Many Will Return," *New York Times*, October 3, 1964.

Lady in the shower, Coney Island, N.Y. 1959
Norma and Gallo, members of a Brooklyn teen gang, N.Y.C. 1960
Contestant in a physique contest, N.Y.C. 1960

Woman showering in a bathhouse, Coney Island, N.Y. has been retitled *Lady in the shower, Coney Island, N.Y.* (p. 121) based on an alternate title on a glassine sleeve in the archive. Similarly, *Norma and Gallo, members of a Brooklyn teen gang, N.Y.C.* (p. 153) was revised per the inscription, "Norma and Gallo, members of a Bklyn teen gang," on another print from the same negative. "Brooklyn" was added to the title, but "N.Y.C." was retained because there is no confirmation that the photograph was made in Brooklyn. *Contestant in a physique contest, N.Y.C.* (p. 155) was also revised from *Young man in a physique contest, N.Y.C.* based on another print from the same negative that is inscribed "contestant in a physique contest for young men at the McBurney Y."

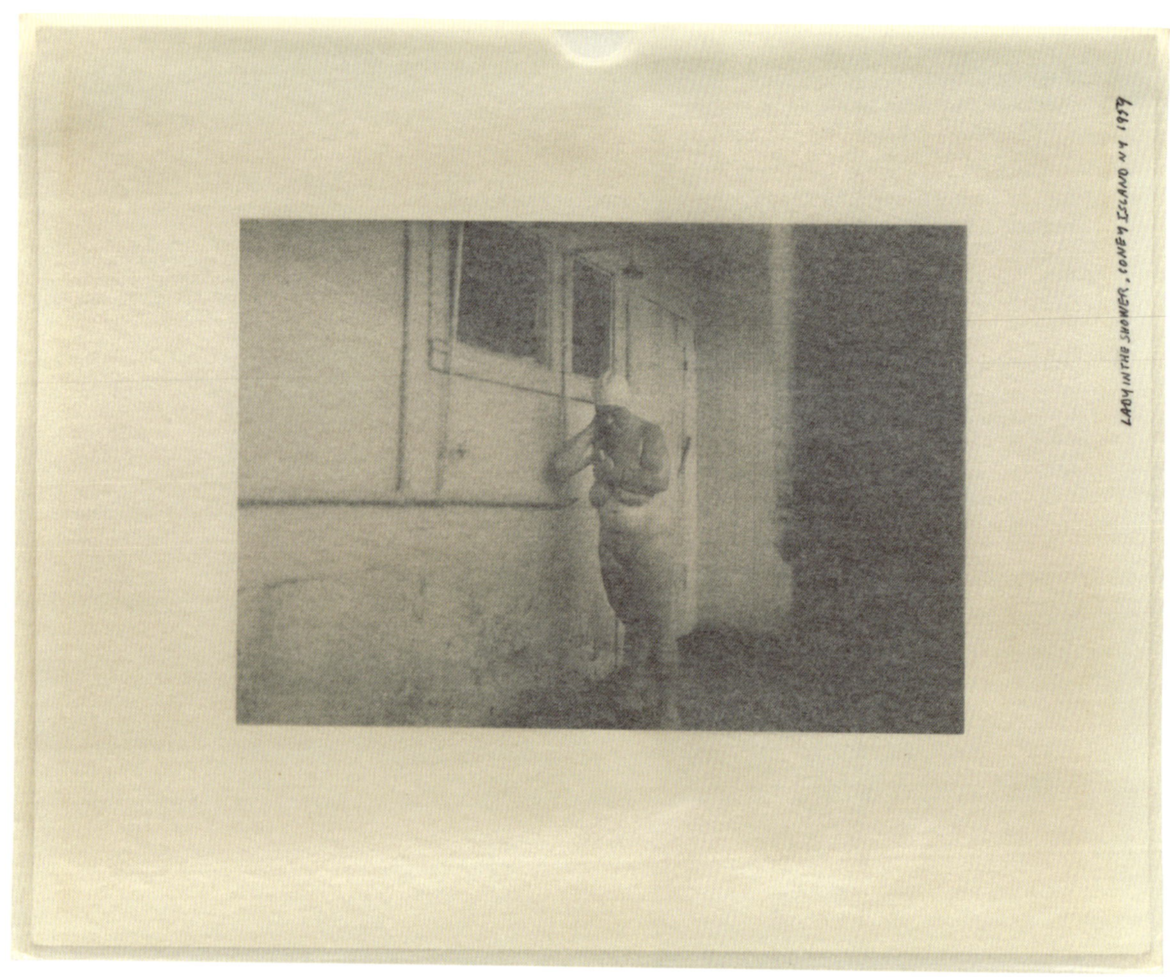

Lady in the shower, Coney Island, N.Y. 1959. 2015.133
11 × 14 inch glassine print sleeve annotated by Arbus. 2007.505.1.13

Female impersonator holding long gloves, Hempstead, L.I. 1959
Blonde female impersonator standing by a dressing table, Hempstead, L.I. 1959
Seated female impersonator in an open kimono, Hempstead, L.I. 1959
Female impersonator putting on lipstick, Hempstead, L.I. 1959

Female impersonator with a garter belt has been retitled *Female impersonator holding long gloves* (p. 13) to acknowledge that adjacent frames confirm that the subject is holding a pair of evening gloves, not a garter belt. All of Arbus's photographs of female impersonators in dressing rooms previously used "N.Y.C." as the location. Most feature members of the Jewel Box Revue, a national touring company frequently performing in New York; others were made at Club 82 on East Fourth Street. *Female impersonator holding long gloves, Blonde female impersonator standing by a dressing table* (p. 123), *Seated female impersonator in an open kimono* (p. 129), and *Female impersonator putting on lipstick* (p. 251) appear to have been made in November 1959 at the Hempstead Theater in Long Island,

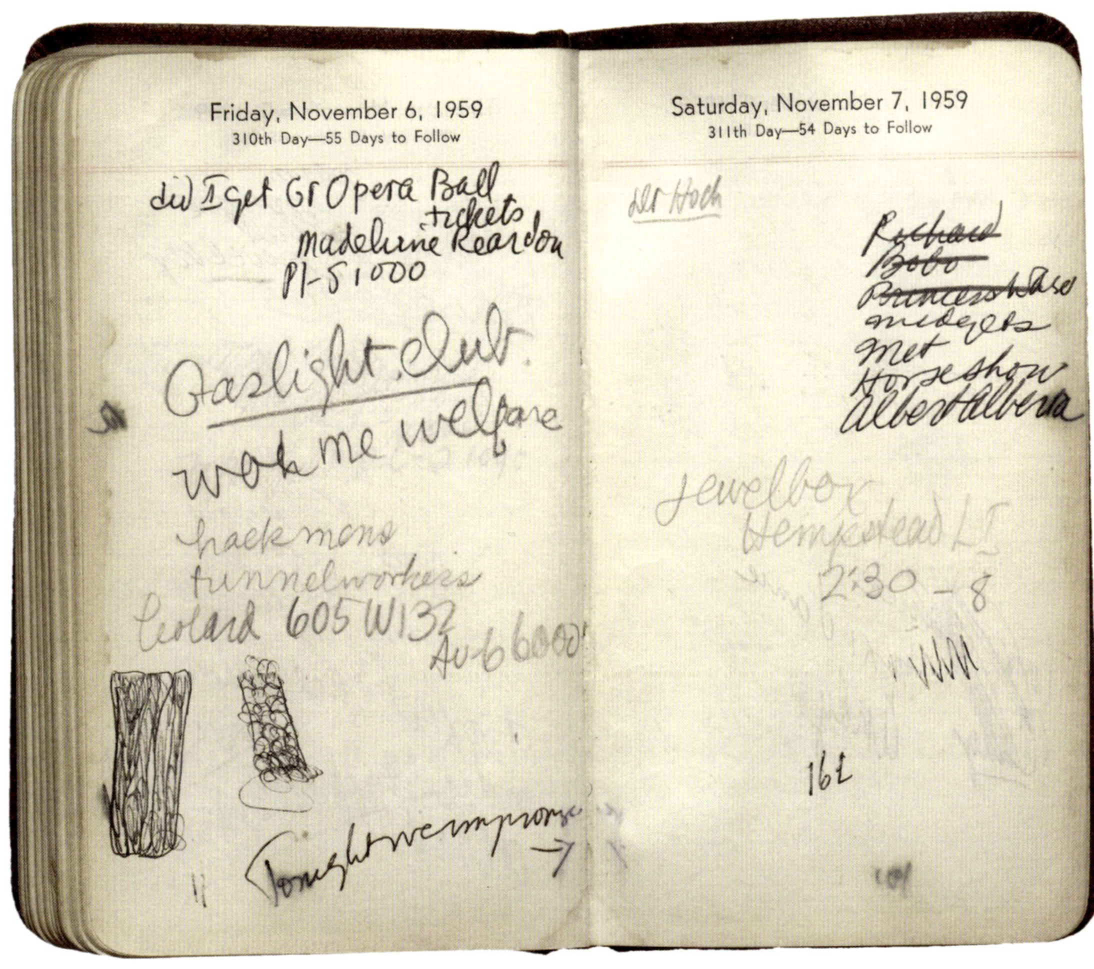

1959 Appointment Book
L.2008.77.1.1

New York.[11] Earlier rolls of film indicate that this was Arbus's second visit to see the Jewel Box Revue performers and her first primarily backstage. She made her first rolls of the Jewel Box Revue in late 1958, probably at the Loew's State Theater in Times Square.

These four prints are from negatives on rolls 650 and 668. Roll 650 is dated "11/59" by the artist on an original film sleeve. Although roll 668 does not retain an original film sleeve, it was evidently made in the same setting as roll 650. The artist's appointment book for November 7, 1959, notes "jewel-box; Hempstead LI; 2:30–8" (see *previous page*). This location is corroborated by a notebook entry from the time, "jewel box; Hempstead Thea; LI rail," as well as the item "Female Impersonators–Hempstead N.J. [*sic*] Nov. 7" on Arbus's expense list submitted to *Esquire* magazine on May 4, 1960, for her picture story, "The Vertical Journey: Six Movements of a Moment Within the Heart of the City" (*Esquire*, July 1960).[12] The expense list also includes a November 9 entry, "Morgue," which is pictured on the latter portion of roll 668, frames 20–31.

35mm negatives in glassine film sleeve annotated by Arbus
2007.500.484

Elderly woman whispering to her dinner partner, Grand Opera Ball, N.Y.C. 1959
Miss Marian Seymour dancing with Baron Theo Von Roth at
the Grand Opera Ball, N.Y.C. 1959

The Grand Opera Ball was a fund-raising dinner held on November 10, 1959, in the Grand Ballroom of the Sheraton-East. Arbus photographed the ball as part of "The Vertical Journey" project (in which a related image, *Mrs. Dagmar Patino at the Grand Opera Ball, N.Y.C. 1959*, was published). Previously dated 1960, *Elderly woman whispering to her dinner partner* (p. 253) did not originally include "Grand Opera Ball" in the title. *Miss Marian Seymour dancing with Baron Theo Von Roth at the Grand Opera Ball, N.Y.C.* (p. 131) was revised to correct the spelling of the baron's name.

---

11. Arbus used the abbreviation "L.I." to refer to locations in Long Island but generally did not add the state as was her convention for most other locations outside New York City. See *Xmas tree in a living room in Levittown, L.I. 1962* (pp. 199, 238–39).
12. The "1950" date in the subject line of the *Esquire* expense list is a typo for "1959."

May 4, 1960

Esquire Magazine
488 Madison Avenue
New York City
ATT: Harold Hayes

Expenses for The Vertical Journey; October 1950-February 1960:

```
I24 rolls Film @ $.77                                             95.48
49 Complimentary Prints (to starred people)                      98.00
*Armory Carnival-2 visits                                         3.00
 Coney Island Waxworks and Side-show                              4.65
*I4 Visits Hubert's Museum (Midget, Half-Man, Creep)             II.35
*Two trips to Andy and Midget friends                             6.25
*Female Impersonators-Hempstead N.J. Nov. 7                       6.48
 Morgue-Nov. 9                                                    I.65
 Grand Opera Ball-Nov. IO                                         3.45
 Horse Show Opening-Nov. 3                                        6.55
 Metropolitan Opera Opening                                       3.20
 Stock Yards-Dec.9                                                2.20
 Sewer-Dec. IO ($5.00 tip)                                        7.30
*Mrs. deRham's Dance Classes at the Colony                        3.80
*D.A.R. Meeting in Washington Heights-Dec.I2                       .30
 River Club, Mrs. deRham-Dec. I2                                  4.35
 Debutante Ball-Dec. 27                                           4.55
 Big Joe's Happiness Exchange-Jan. II ($3.00 contribution)        6.40
 Subway Track Cleaner-Jan. I3                                     I.35
 Boy Scout Luncheree-Jan.I4                                       3.40
 2 Trips to Mother Cabrini                                         .60
*3 Nights on the Bowery with Harry Baronian                       5.40
* 2 Trips to the Tall Peoples Club                                4.30
 4 Trips to the Marie Antoinette Hotel                            3.40
*Boy Scout Meeting-Jan. I9                                         .30
 Accident Investigation Unit-Jan. I6 (accident chasing)          14.65
*Progessive Gents Fraternity-Jan. I9 (Gang Meeting)              3.50
 Bowery Mission Tour-Jan. 2I                                      2.65
*Empire Health Club-Jan 22 (Physique Posing)                     2.30
*Weight Lifting Tournament-Jan.23                                 3.40
 Vogue School of Beauty Culture                                  3.60
 Animal Crematory-Jan. 26                                         .30
 D.A.R. Lady at home in Riverdale                                 .30
 2 Trips to Animal Cremetery, Wantagh L.I.-Jan.30, Feb.2
                                       (tips $2.00)              II.40
 Municipal Shelter-Feb.3                                          2.IO
*Prisons-Women's N.Y.C. and Men's Brooklyn                        .30
 Pool Room-Feb.5                                                  2.40
*Florence Squassi-Feb. 6 (rich child)                            3.IO
*Mr. New York City Contest                                       6.35
 Gang Dance                                                      2.I5
 Slaughter House-Feb. 9                                           2.25
 Cathy Hart-Feb. 9                                                3.60
```

Diane & Allan Arbus 71 Washington Place, New York 11, N. Y. GR 7-1848

Expense list for "The Vertical Journey: Six Movements of a Moment Within the Heart of the City"
L.2008.78.1.1

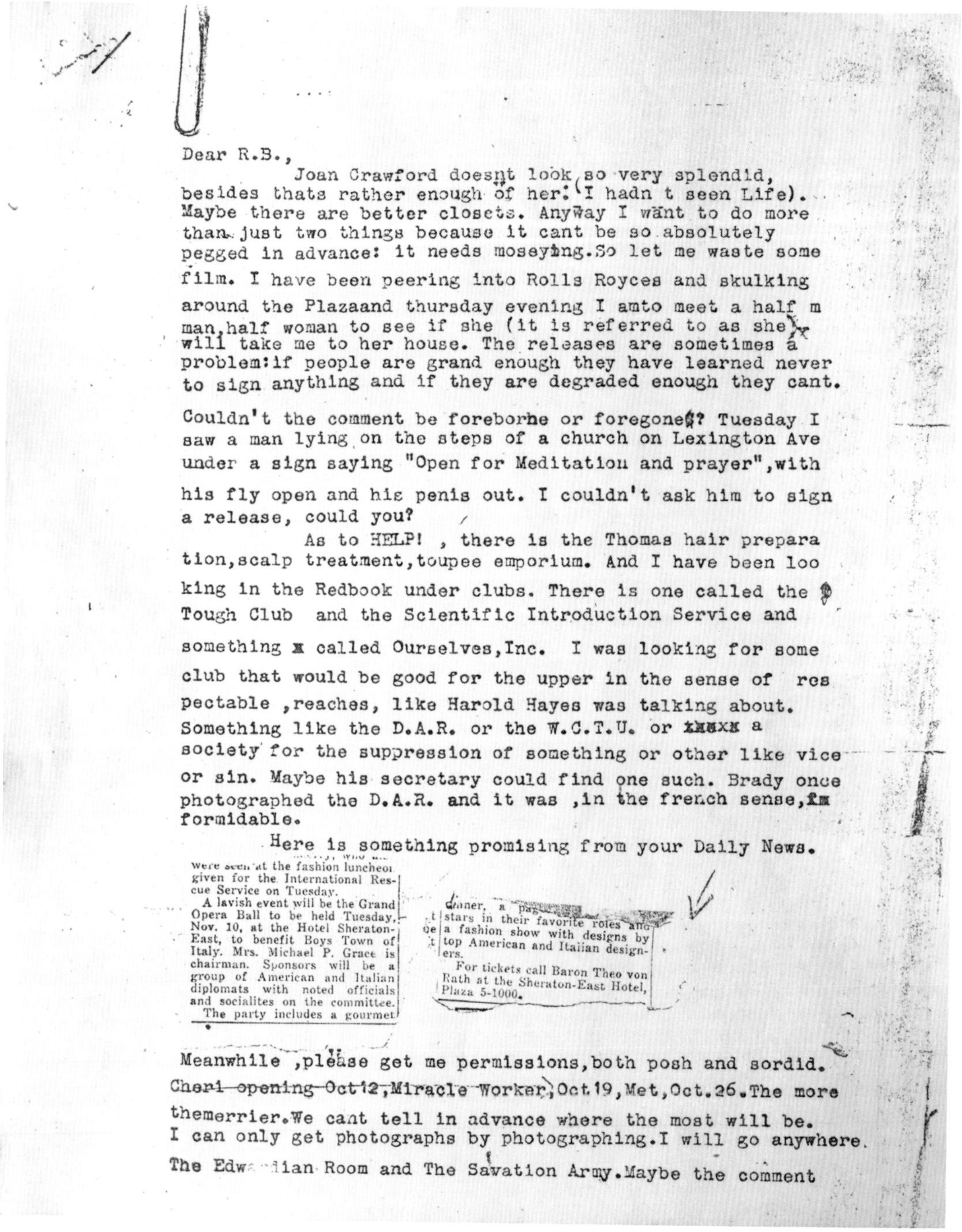

Dear R.B.,

Joan Crawford doesnt look so very splendid, besides thats rather enough of her.(I hadn t seen Life). Maybe there are better closets. Anyway I want to do more than just two things because it cant be so absolutely pegged in advance: it needs moseying.So let me waste some film. I have been peering into Rolls Royces and skulking around the Plazaand thursday evening I amto meet a half m man,half woman to see if she (it is referred to as she) will take me to her house. The releases are sometimes a problem:if people are grand enough they have learned never to sign anything and if they are degraded enough they cant.

Couldn't the comment be foreborne or foregone? Tuesday I saw a man lying on the steps of a church on Lexington Ave under a sign saying "Open for Meditation and prayer",with his fly open and his penis out. I couldn't ask him to sign a release, could you?
              As to HELP! , there is the Thomas hair prepara tion,scalp treatment,toupee emporium. And I have been loo king in the Redbook under clubs. There is one called the Tough Club and the Scientific Introduction Service and something called Ourselves,Inc. I was looking for some club that would be good for the upper in the sense of res pectable ,reaches, like Harold Hayes was talking about. Something like the D.A.R. or the W.C.T.U. or a society for the suppression of something or other like vice or sin. Maybe his secretary could find one such. Brady once photographed the D.A.R. and it was ,in the french sense, formidable.
              Here is something promising from your Daily News.

were seen at the fashion luncheon given for the International Res- cue Service on Tuesday.
 A lavish event will be the Grand Opera Ball to be held Tuesday, Nov. 10, at the Hotel Sheraton- East, to benefit Boys Town of Italy. Mrs. Michael P. Grace is chairman. Sponsors will be a group of American and Italian diplomats with noted officials and socialites on the committee. The party includes a gourmet

dinner, a pag... stars in their favorite roles and a fashion show with designs by top American and Italian design- ers.
 For tickets call Baron Theo von Rath at the Sheraton-East Hotel, Plaza 5-1000.

Meanwhile ,please get me permissions,both posh and sordid. Cheri opening Oct 12,Miracle Worker,Oct 19,Met,Oct.26.The more themerrier.We cant tell in advance where the most will be. I can only get photographs by photographing.I will go anywhere. The Edwardian Room and The Savation Army.Maybe the comment

Photocopy of a letter from Arbus to Robert Benton at *Esquire*, October 1959
L.2008.77.3.14

A letter in the archive from Arbus to Robert Benton, an art director at *Esquire*, reveals the origin of the misnomer "von Rath": Arbus included with the letter a clipping from the *Daily News* that identified the event organizer as "Theo von Rath." Publications such as *Jet*, *Life*, and the *New York Times* as well as Social Security records confirm that his name was Von Roth.

Previously titled *Boy in a cap at a pool hall, N.Y.C.*, this photograph (p. 133) was made during the first months of 1960 when Arbus noted "pool room" several times in her appointment book and made multiple prints of young men in a pool hall (see *Boy at a pool hall, N.Y.C. 1960*, roll 699, p. 127). However, roll 700, from which this print was made, does not depict a pool hall, but rather teenagers dressed up and assembled in a social hall.

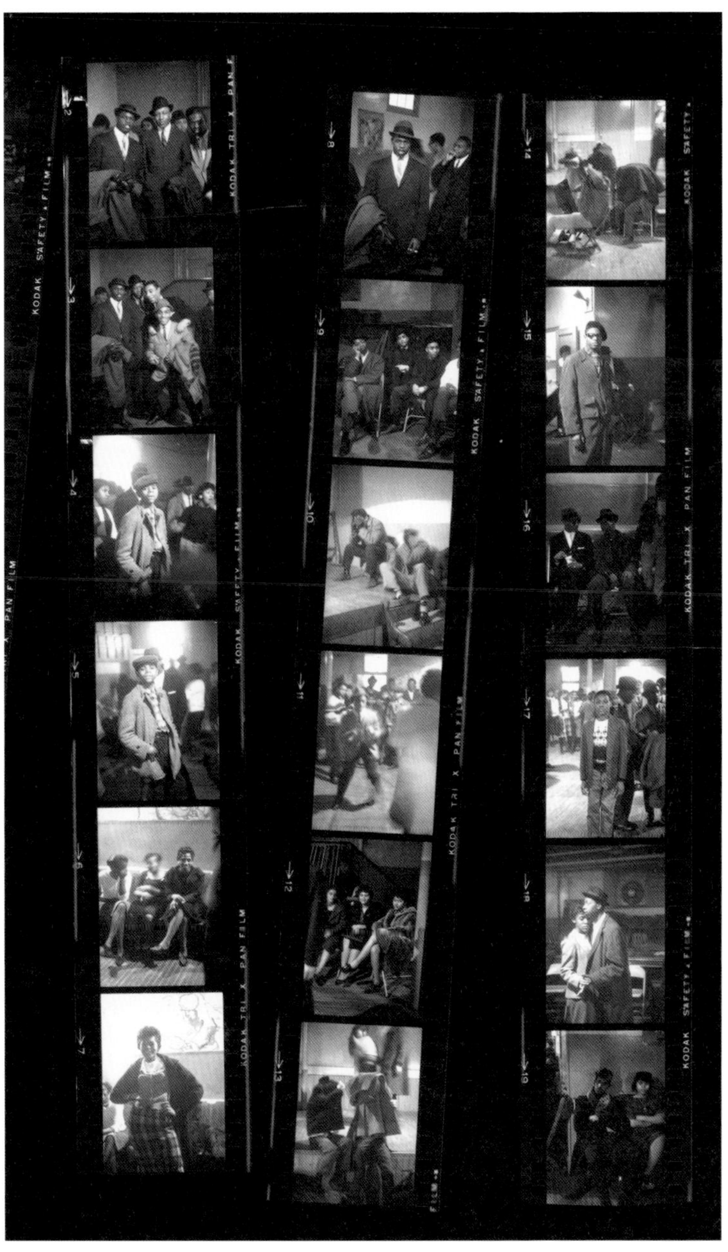

Contact sheet, roll 700 #2–19
L.2008.63.538

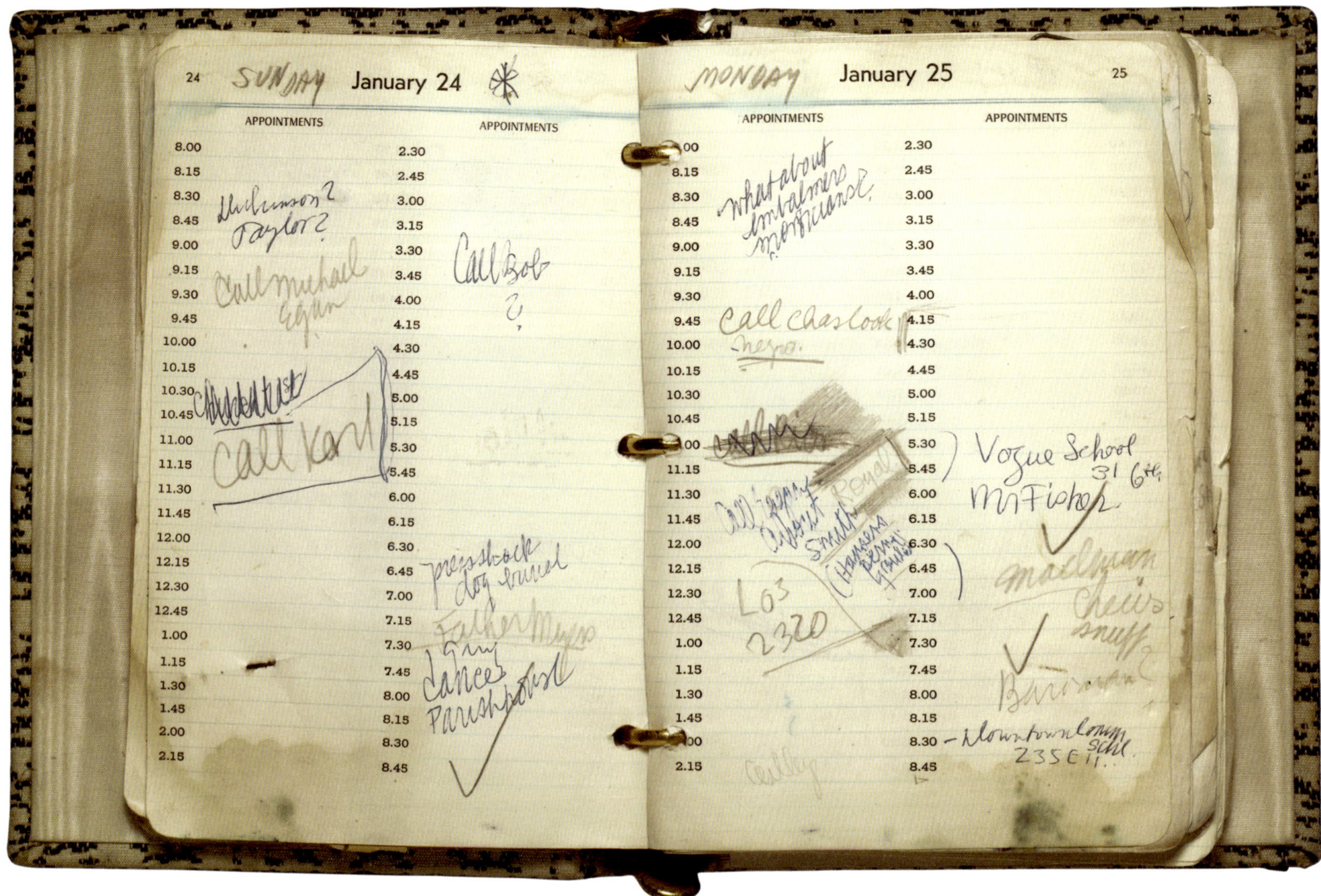

1960 Appointment Book
L.2008.77.1.2

Arbus's appointment book records dances on Sundays, January 24 and February 7, 1960. The January 24 entry notes "Father Myers; [gang?]; dance; Parish house."[13] On her expense list for "The Vertical Journey," the corresponding item "Gang Dance" is listed between February 6 and 9 but without a specific date (p. 227). It follows "Mr. New York City Contest," which appears in Arbus's appointment book and is verified in contemporaneous publications as having taken place on February 6, 1960.

---

13. Reverend C. Kilmer Myers, vicar of St. Augustine's Chapel on Henry Street from 1952 to 1960, was known for his efforts to alleviate gang violence on the Lower East Side through youth-focused programs. In a memoir, he tells the story of his work with one "street club" and references their attendance at "our Sunday night dances." See C. Kilmer Myers, *Light the Dark Streets* (Greenwich, Conn.: Seabury Press, 1957), p. [27].

Miss Katheryn Lambert with her dogs in the backyard, Brooklyn, N.Y. 1960

Previously *Backyard from above, Brooklyn, N.Y.C.*, the title of this photograph (p. 141) was revised based on the title of a related work from the same roll (695). *Miss Cecilia Lange and Miss Katheryn Lambert with some of their forty dogs, Brooklyn, N.Y. 1960* confirms that the woman in the backyard is Katheryn Lambert. The related print verso offers further information: "Mrs [*sic*] Cecilia Lange and Miss Katheryn Lambert her daughter, who live with; 40 derelict, neglected, abused, deformed or maladjusted dogs in a house; in Bklyn which they call The Helping Hand Haven, but which is a mess." Arbus wrote "Lambert" and "Helping Hand Haven" numerous times in February 1960 in her appointment book and made notes on their meeting in Notebook 3 (1960). The location was also revised from "Brooklyn, N.Y.C." to "Brooklyn, N.Y." to conform to the artist's standard usage.

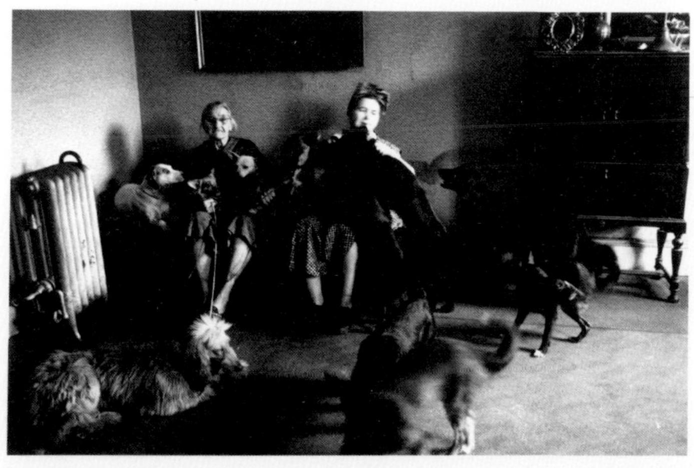

Miss Cecilia Lange and Miss Katheryn Lambert with some of their forty dogs, Brooklyn, N.Y. 1960
L.2008.62.427

Clouds on screen at a drive-in movie, N.J. 1961

Clouds on screen at a drive-in movie, N.J. (p. 183) was previously dated and published as 1960. However, the roll of film — though inscribed "1960" in an Estate hand—dates from 1961, as do the adjacent rolls. Additionally, Arbus's appointment book for July 18, 1961, notes "Curse of the Werewolf; Shadow of the Cat; Drive-in, MA-4.2330; what; time; where; 9:01; Newark under; the; Route 1." Movie listings found online confirm the phone number and location of the Newark Drive-In in New Jersey. Both horror films, *Curse of the Werewolf* and *The Shadow of the Cat* were released in 1961 and shown as a double feature. The photograph was made at a moment in *Curse of the Werewolf* when the clouds move to expose a full moon, provoking the werewolf's transformation.

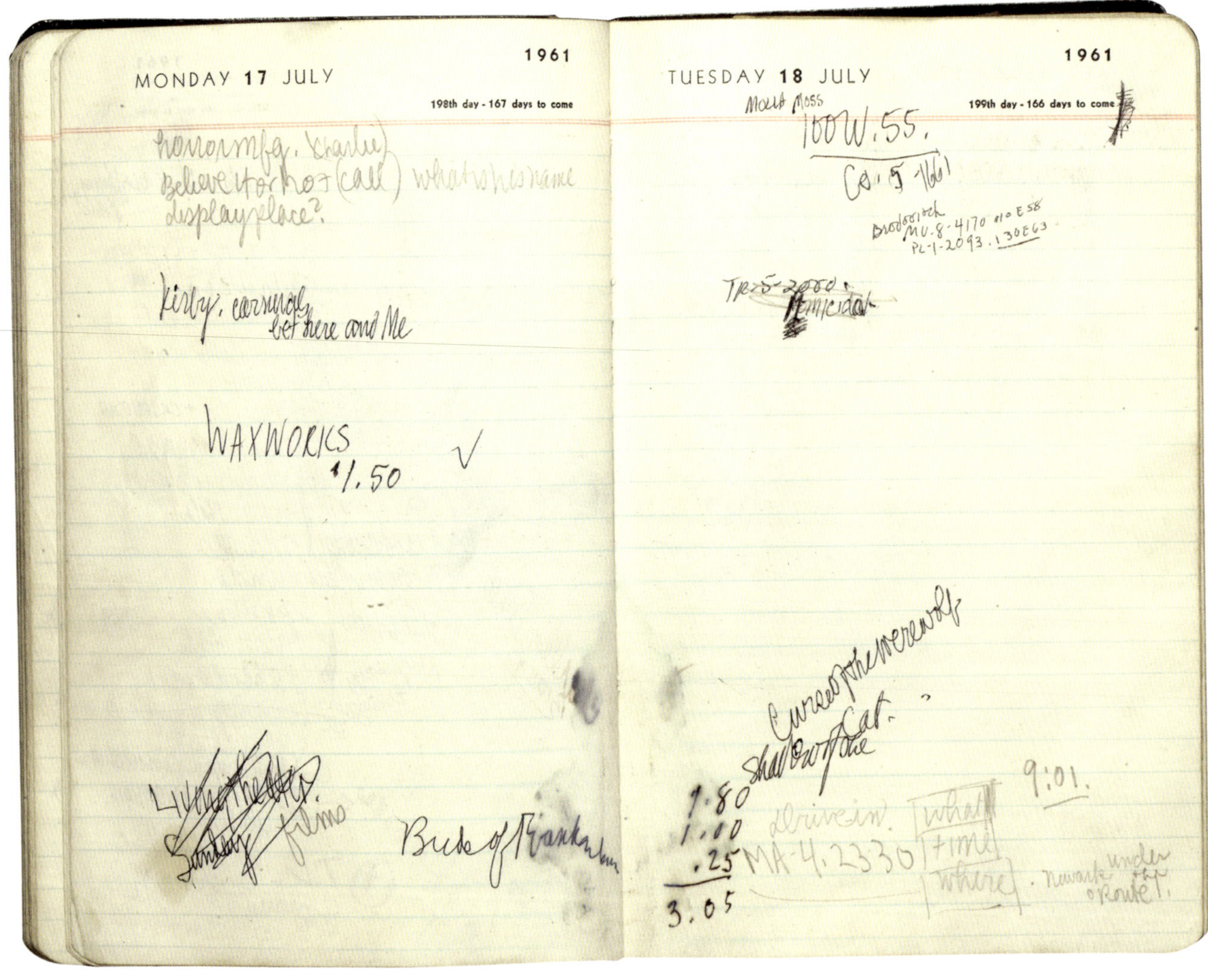

1961 Appointment Book
L.2008.77.1.3

The Human Pincushion, Ronald C. Harrison, N.J. 1961
Stripper with bare breasts sitting in her dressing room, Atlantic City, N.J. 1961

The Human Pincushion, Ronald C. Harrison, N.J. (p. 186) was also published with an incorrect date, 1962. Again, the surrounding rolls of film are dated 1961, and in this case, the original film sleeve for roll 1131 is inscribed "1961." This date is substantiated by an appointment-book entry for September 19, 1961, that notes "Trenton Fair," "pincushion," and "Ronald C Harrison." *Stripper with bare breasts sitting in her dressing room, Atlantic City, N.J.* (p. 185) was also revised from 1962 to 1961 based on the original film-sleeve inscriptions and roll placement.

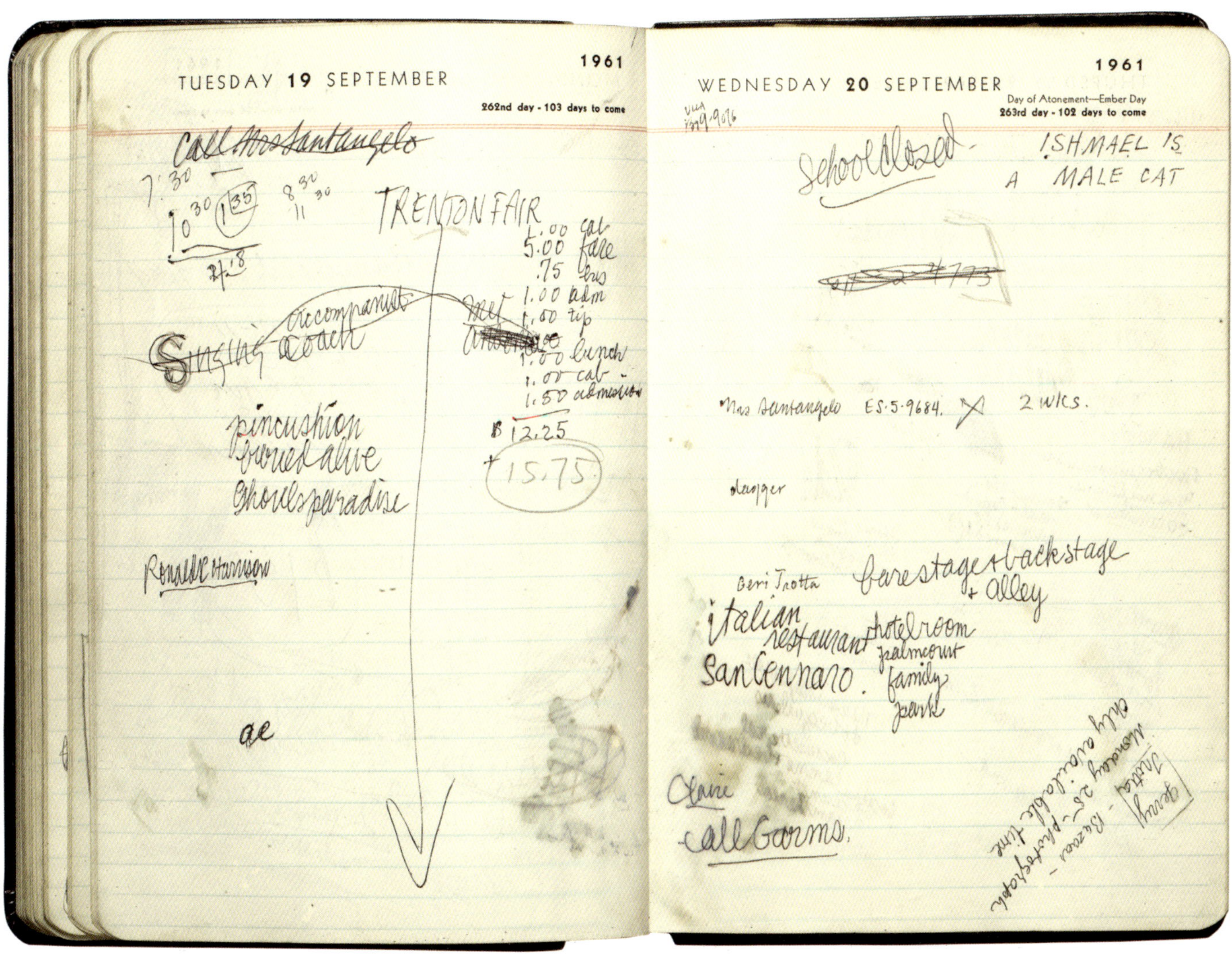

1961 Appointment Book
L.2008.77.1.3

Screaming woman with blood on her hands 1961

This photograph (p. 189) was difficult to date because the original roll of film is not in the archive. However, rolls 1122 and 1124 from 1961 include variant frames of the same scene in *Horrors of the Black Museum* (1959) depicted in the photograph. In the film, a woman has just unwittingly tested a pair of booby-trapped binoculars spring-loaded with spikes. Appointment-book entries for September 1 and 2, 1961, note that *Horrors of the Black Museum* was playing at the Empire Theater. While it is possible that Arbus photographed this film when it was originally released in 1959, it is far more likely that this picture is from 1961 at the time when rolls 1122 and 1124 were made and while she was at work photographing horror movies and other subjects related to an unpublished story on the genre that she had proposed to *Esquire* and *Show* magazines. The archive does not include a roll numbered 1123, which raises the possibility that the missing negative was on that roll.

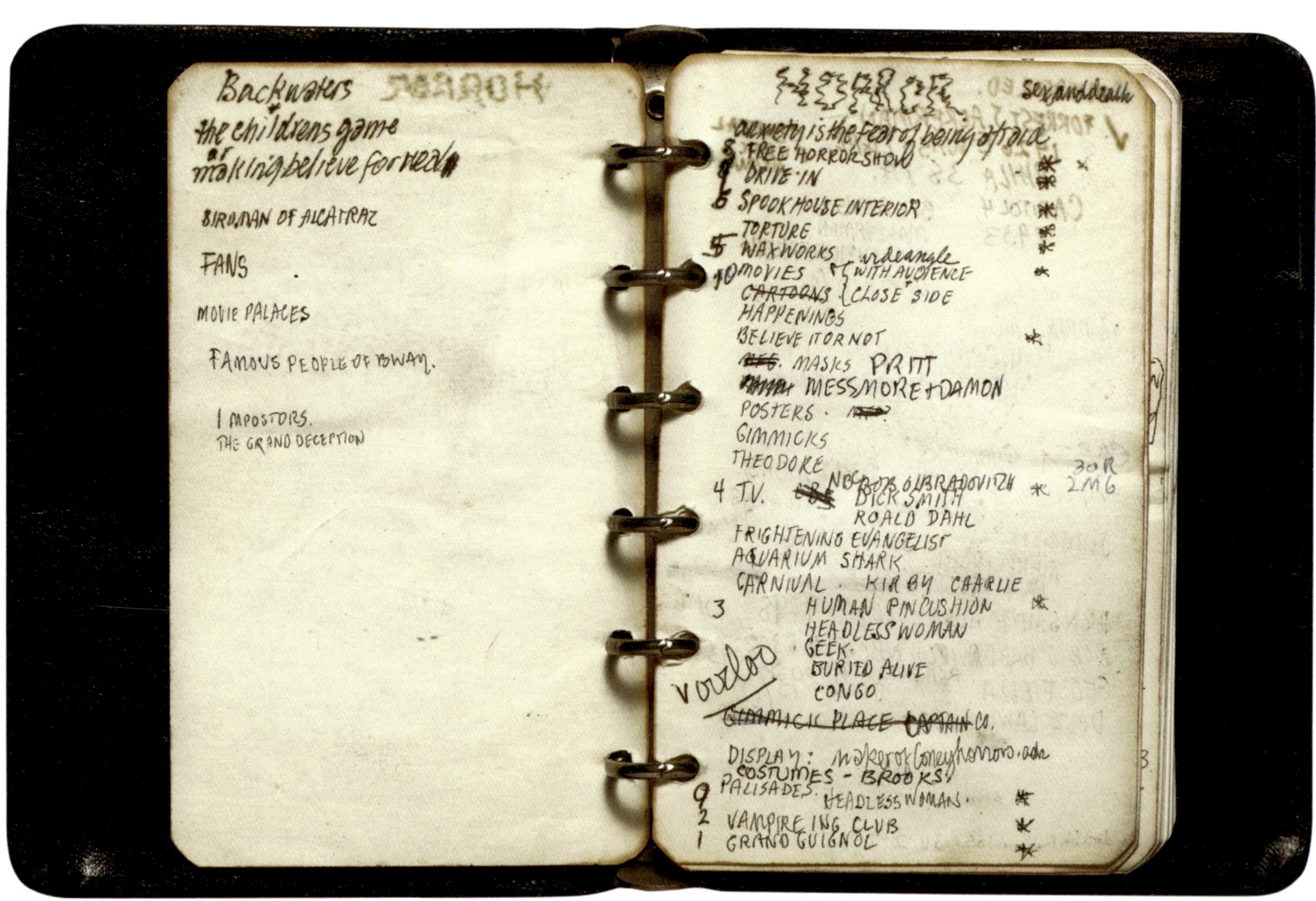

Notebook 7 (1961), pp. [2–3]
L.2008.77.1.7

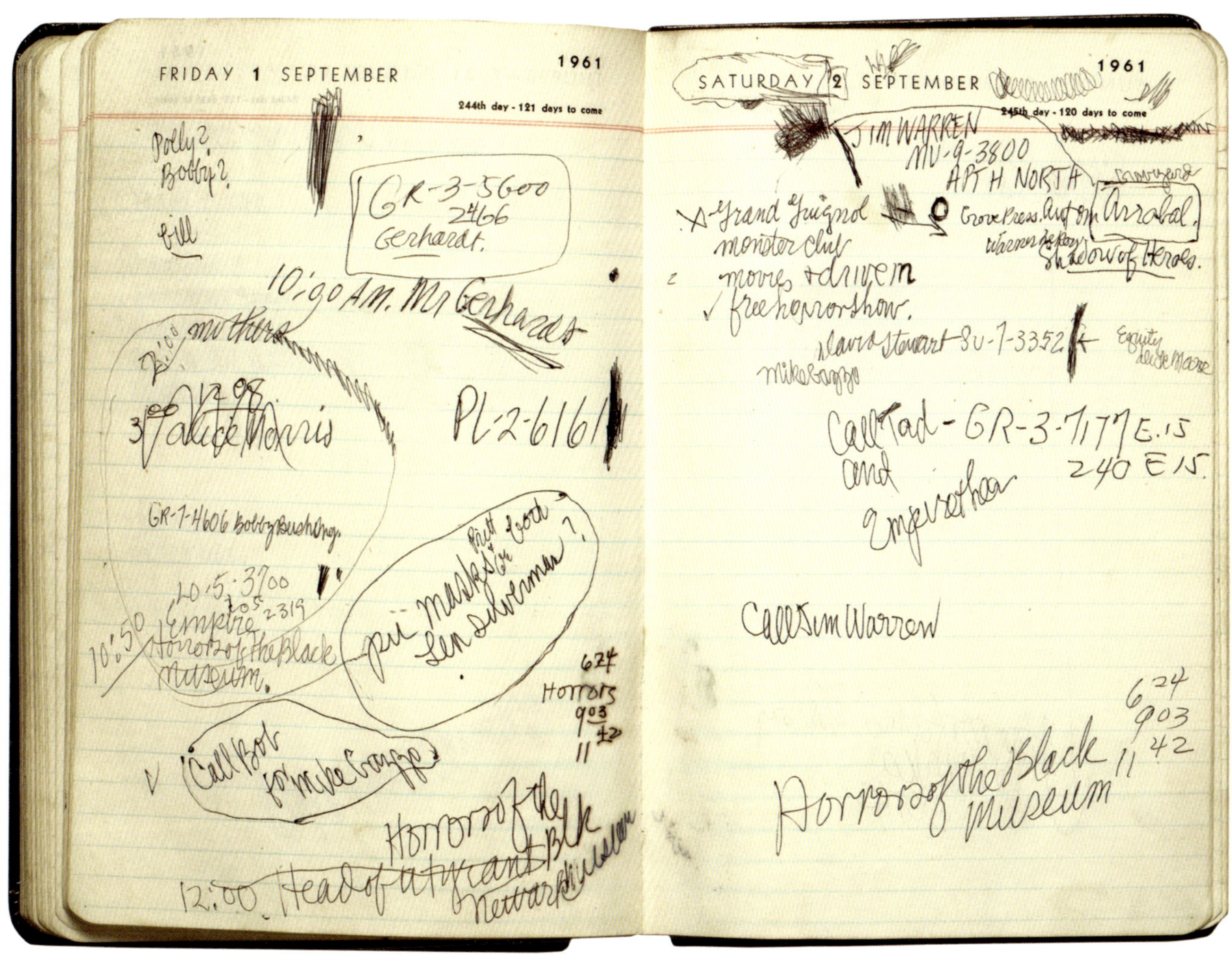

1961 Appointment Book
L.2008.77.1.3

Jack Dracula at a bar, New London, Conn. 1961

Previously titled *Jack Dracula at a bar, N.Y.C.*, this photograph (p. 175) was made on a day trip to New London, Connecticut. The location change is established by numerous appointment-book and notebook references to visiting Jack Dracula in New London. Arbus's contact sheets confirm that she first encountered Jack Dracula at Hubert's Museum in New York as early as August 1959, but the first mention of him in her appointment book is not until May 9, 1961.[14]

---

14. The entry reads "Gay Talese; Jack Dracula; Dick Hylan; tattoo parlor; Stanley Moskowitz." Arbus was already acquainted with Talese, a pioneer of New Journalism, and subsequent notes in her appointment book suggest that she may have contacted him and others after reading his article on tattooing that features Jack Dracula. Gay Talese, "Twenty Million Tattooed: Why?," *New York Times*, November 22, 1959.

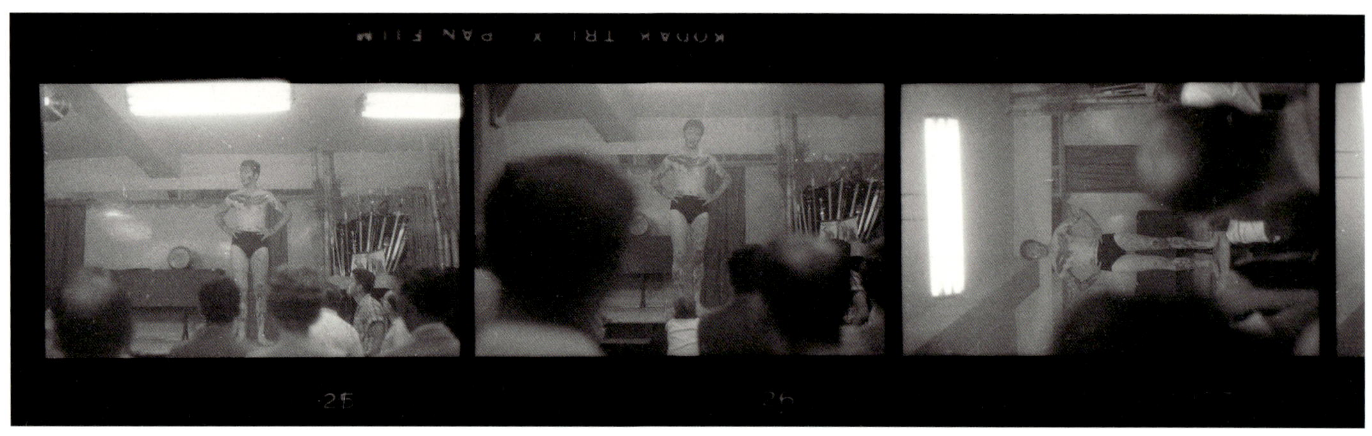

Contact sheet, roll 639 #25–27
L.2008.63.474

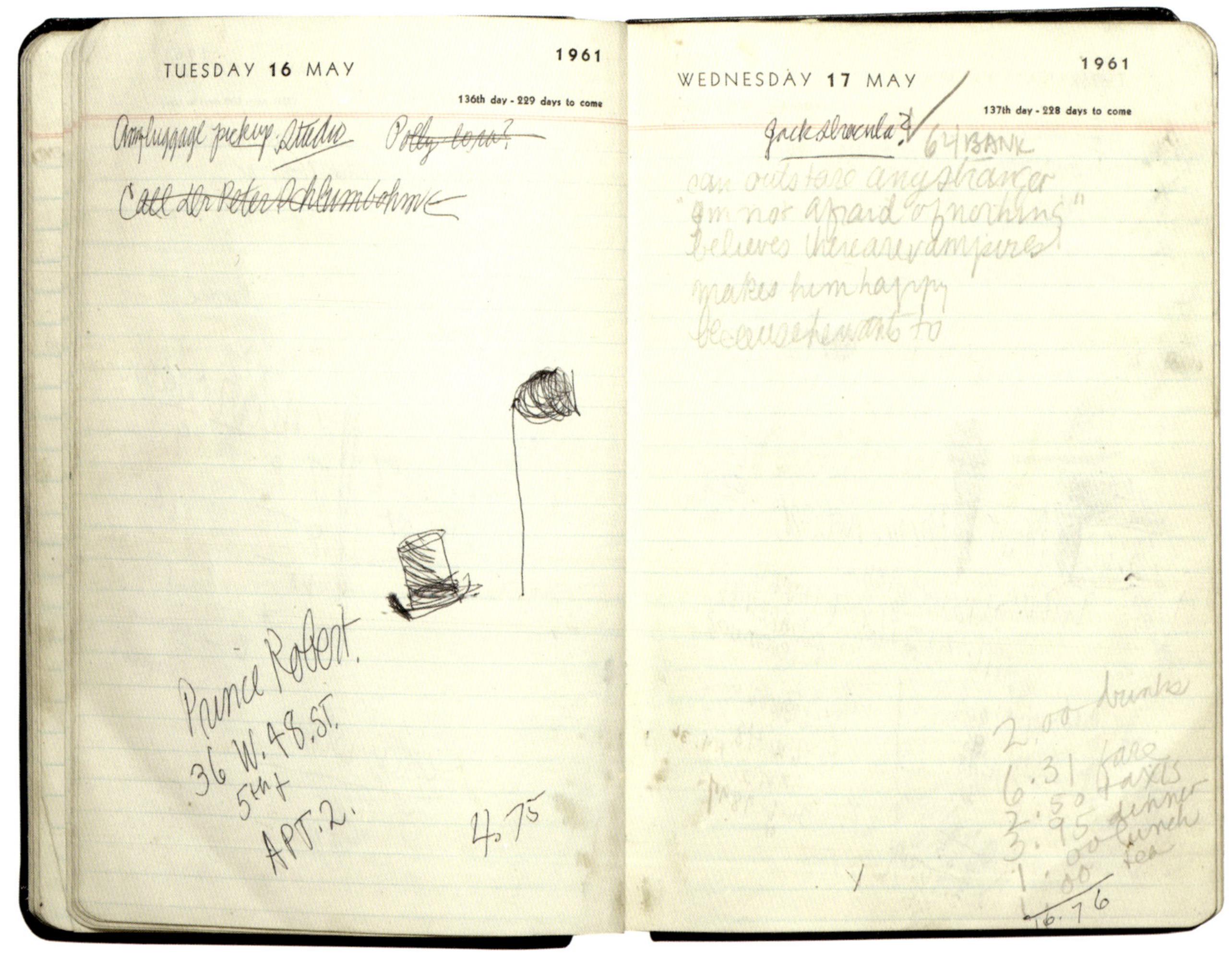

1961 Appointment Book
L.2008.77.1.3

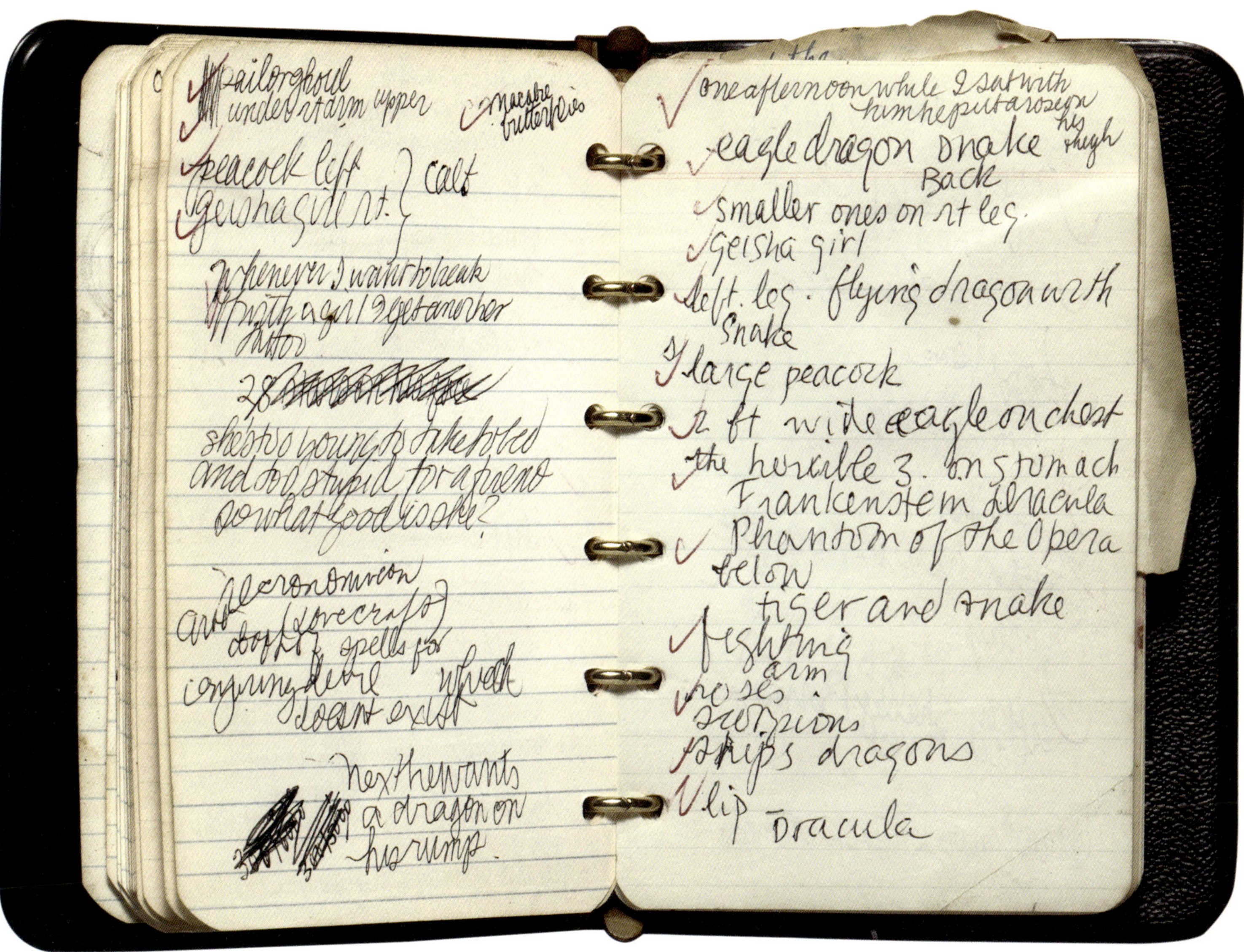

Notebook 6 (1961), pp. [48–49]
L.2008.77.1.6

On May 15, Arbus recorded the train schedule to and from New London, and on May 17
"Jack Dracula," "64 BANK," along with several quotes and expenses for the trip. Notebook 6
(1961) provides more information about her visit to New London, including extensive quotes
from her conversation with Jack Dracula, lists of his 306 tattoos—"left leg. flying dragon
with snake; large peacock; 2 ft wide eagle on chest; the horrible 3 on stomach; Frankenstein
Dracula; Phantom of the Opera"—and his shop address "64 Bank Street, N.L., Conn." Jack
Dracula, also known as the Marked Man, had moved to Connecticut earlier in 1961, the year
New York City would ban tattoo parlors after a hepatitis outbreak.

Xmas tree in a living room in Levittown, L.I. 1962

In the artist's own inscriptions on her prints, the photograph *Xmas tree in a living room in Levittown, L.I.* (p. 199) has been variously dated 1962 and 1963. The Metropolitan's 16 × 20 inch print features the inscription "Xmas tree in a living room, Levittown, Long Island N.Y. 1962" while an annotated 11 × 14 inch print sleeve in the archive is inscribed "Parlor, Levittown, L.I. Christmas 1963." Although the 1963 date was published in both the 1972 monograph and in *Revelations*, materials in the archive indicate that the correct date is probably 1962. Among general ideas and to-do lists, Arbus wrote "Levittown" on four dates in her appointment book from December 19 to December 30, 1962, and none in 1963. Furthermore, the unopened presents around the tree strongly suggest that the picture was made before Christmas Day 1962.

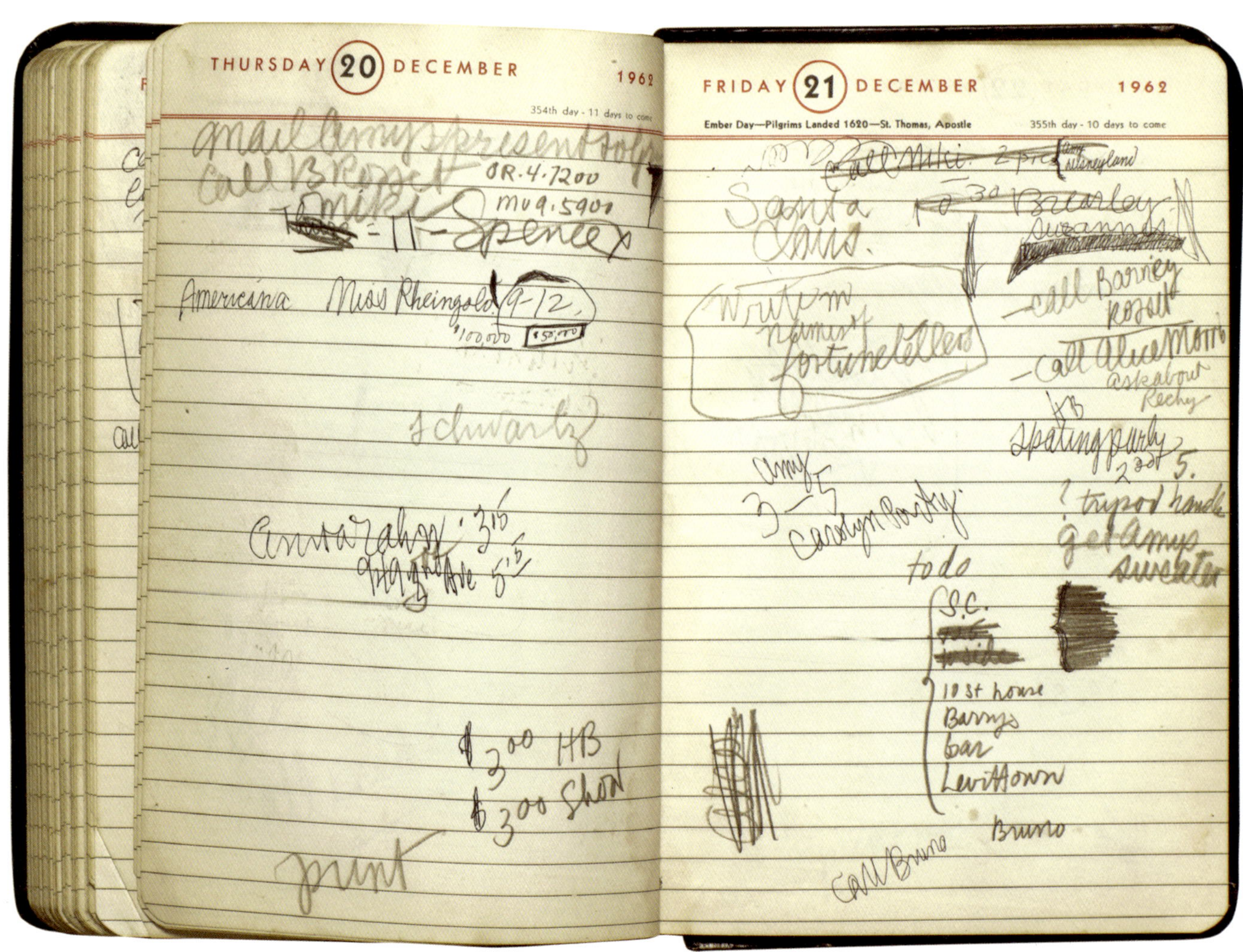

1962 Appointment Book
L.2008.77.1.4

11 × 14 inch glassine print sleeve annotated by Arbus. 2007.505.1.57
16 × 20 inch print signed and inscribed on the verso by Arbus. 69.546.2

Diane Arbus customarily titled her photographs, often by writing them on the back of the print. She also frequently inscribed titles on the glassine sleeves in which she stored her early finished prints. Photographs in the collection of the artist at the time of her death that had no known titles were given titles by Doon Arbus on behalf of the Estate of Diane Arbus in a style and format faithful to the artist's own titles. It has become evident that a number of photographs had, over time, been given two or more different titles, either by the artist or by the Estate. After an eight-year study, this publication is a first attempt to correct many inconsistencies or inaccuracies relating to photographs from the period 1956 to 1962. All title, location, and date revisions have been made in consultation with the Estate.

All photographs in the exhibition are gelatin silver prints made by Diane Arbus. Dimensions refer to the image, not the sheet. Unless otherwise noted, all works are in the collection of The Metropolitan Museum of Art. An asterisk designates photographs whose titles and/or dates have been revised.

---

3   *Windblown headline on a dark pavement,*
N.Y.C. 1956
6 × 8 3/4 in. (15.2 × 22.3 cm)
Promised Gift of Doon Arbus and Amy Arbus
L.2008.62.256

7   *Lady in front of a portrait,*
N.Y.C. 1956
5 5/8 × 8 9/16 in. (14.3 × 21.8 cm)
Gift of Doon Arbus and Amy Arbus, 2007
2007.501.57

9   *Girl with schoolbooks stepping onto the curb,*
N.Y.C. 1957 *
Previous date: 1956
8 7/8 × 5 3/4 in. (22.6 × 14.6 cm)
Gift of Doon Arbus and Amy Arbus, 2007
2007.501.80

11   *Blonde on screen about to be kissed 1958* *
Previous date: 1957
5 15/16 × 8 7/8 in. (15.1 × 22.5 cm)
Promised Gift of Doon Arbus and Amy Arbus
L.2008.62.265

13   *Female impersonator holding long gloves,*
Hempstead, L.I. 1959 *
Previous title and date: *Female impersonator*
with a garter belt, N.Y.C. 1958
9 3/4 × 5 7/8 in. (24.8 × 14.9 cm)
Purchase, The Robert and Joyce Menschel
Family Foundation Gift, 2015
2015.136

15   *Child teasing another, N.Y.C. 1960*
9 × 6 1/8 in. (22.8 × 15.5 cm)
Private collection, San Francisco

17 *The Backwards Man in his hotel room,*
N.Y.C. 1961
9 $^{15}/_{16}$ × 7 $^{1}/_{16}$ in. (25.2 × 18 cm)
Purchase, Joyce Frank Menschel, and Ann
Tenenbaum and Thomas H. Lee Gifts;
Louis V. Bell, Harris Brisbane Dick, Fletcher,
and Rogers Funds and Joseph Pulitzer
Bequest; and Marlene Nathan Meyerson
Family Foundation, Twentieth-Century
Photography Fund, Diana Barrett and
Robert Vila, Elizabeth S. and Robert J.
Fisher, Charlotte and Bill Ford, Lita
Annenberg Hazen Charitable Trust and
Hazen Polsky Foundation Inc., Jennifer
and Joseph Duke, Jennifer and Philip
Maritz, Saundra B. Lane, The Jerry and
Emily Spiegel Family Foundation and
Pamela and Arthur Sanders, Anonymous,
and The Judith Rothschild Foundation
Gifts, 2007
2007.523

27 *Woman on the street with her eyes closed,*
N.Y.C. 1956
5 $^{3}/_{8}$ × 6 $^{3}/_{4}$ in. (13.6 × 17.1 cm)
Promised Gift of Doon Arbus and Amy Arbus
L.2008.62.81

29 *Girl in profile looking up, N.Y.C. 1956*
4 $^{5}/_{8}$ × 7 $^{5}/_{8}$ in. (11.8 × 19.3 cm)
Promised Gift of Doon Arbus and Amy Arbus
L.2008.62.75

31 *Mannequin in evening gown, N.Y.C. 1956*
6 $^{1}/_{2}$ × 5 $^{1}/_{2}$ in. (16.5 × 13.9 cm)
Promised Gift of Doon Arbus and Amy Arbus
L.2008.62.82

33 *Woman in a black hat with a pearl choker,*
N.Y.C. 1956
9 $^{3}/_{4}$ × 6 $^{5}/_{8}$ in. (24.7 × 16.9 cm)
Gift of Doon Arbus and Amy Arbus, 2007
2007.501.44

34 *Santa Claus on the street with a lady passing,*
N.Y.C. 1956
8 $^{7}/_{16}$ × 5 $^{13}/_{16}$ in. (21.4 × 14.8 cm)
Gift of Doon Arbus and Amy Arbus, 2007
2007.501.30

35 *Woman in a mink stole and bow shoes,*
N.Y.C. 1956
8 $^{7}/_{8}$ × 5 $^{11}/_{16}$ in. (22.5 × 14.5 cm)
Gift of Doon Arbus and Amy Arbus, 2007
2007.501.46

37 *Woman carrying a child in Central Park,*
N.Y.C. 1956
6 $^{5}/_{8}$ × 9 $^{7}/_{8}$ in. (16.9 × 25.1 cm)
Private collection, San Francisco

39 *Movie theater usher standing by the box*
office, N.Y.C. 1956
9 $^{13}/_{16}$ × 6 $^{3}/_{4}$ in. (24.9 × 17.1 cm)
Courtesy Fraenkel Gallery,
San Francisco

41 *Woman with white gloves and a pocket*
book, N.Y.C. 1956
9 $^{7}/_{8}$ × 6 $^{1}/_{2}$ in. (25.1 × 16.5 cm)
Collection of Jennifer and Philip Maritz

43 *Man with a curious baby on the subway,*
N.Y.C. 1956
9 × 5 $^{11}/_{16}$ in. (22.8 × 14.4 cm)
Gift of Doon Arbus and Amy Arbus, 2007
2007.501.81

45 *Taxicab driver at the wheel with two passengers,*
N.Y.C. 1956
6 $^{3}/_{16}$ × 8 $^{13}/_{16}$ in. (15.7 × 22.4 cm)
Gift of Doon Arbus and Amy Arbus, 2007
2007.501.32

47 *Kiss from "Baby Doll," N.Y.C. 1956*
6 $^{3}/_{16}$ × 9 in. (15.7 × 22.8 cm)
Collection of John Cheim, New York

49 *Puddle on the sidewalk, N.Y.C. 1957* *
Previous date: 1956
5 $^{11}/_{16}$ × 8 $^9/_{16}$ in. (14.5 × 21.8 cm)
Promised Gift of Doon Arbus and Amy Arbus
L.2008.62.122

51 *Kid in a hooded jacket aiming a gun,
N.Y.C. 1957*
8 $^1/_2$ × 5 $^{13}/_{16}$ in. (21.6 × 14.7 cm)
Gift of Doon Arbus and Amy Arbus, 2007
2007.501.84

53 *Barbershop interior through a glass door,
N.Y.C. 1957* *
Previous date: 1956
8 $^9/_{16}$ × 5 $^5/_8$ in. (21.7 × 14.3 cm)
Promised Gift of Doon Arbus and Amy Arbus
L.2008.62.116

55 *Lady on a bus, N.Y.C. 1957* *
Previous date: 1956
8 $^1/_2$ × 5 $^3/_4$ in. (21.6 × 14.6 cm)
Gift of Danielle and David Ganek, 2005
2005.493.11

56 *Girl with a pointy hood and white schoolbag
at the curb, N.Y.C. 1957* *
Previous date: 1956
5 $^5/_{16}$ × 8 $^1/_8$ in. (13.5 × 20.7 cm)
Promised Gift of Doon Arbus and Amy Arbus
L.2008.62.217

57 *Man holding a sleeping child, N.Y.C. 1957* *
Previous date: 1956
8 $^3/_4$ × 4 $^{15}/_{16}$ in. (22.2 × 12.5 cm)
Gift of Doon Arbus and Amy Arbus, 2007
2007.501.76

59 *Trapeze act, N.Y.C. 1957* ^{k}
Previous date: 1956
8 × 5 $^3/_8$ in. (20.3 × 13.7 cm)
Promised Gift of Doon Arbus and Amy Arbus
L.2008.62.311

61 *Bedroom in a store window, N.Y.C. 1957* *
Previous date: 1956
5 $^{11}/_{16}$ × 8 $^1/_2$ in. (14.5 × 21.6 cm)
Gift of Doon Arbus and Amy Arbus, 2007
2007.501.72

63 *Woman with a crescent rhinestone brooch,
N.Y.C. 1957* *
Previous date: 1956
8 $^7/_{16}$ × 5 $^7/_8$ in. (21.5 × 14.9 cm)
Gift of Doon Arbus and Amy Arbus, 2007
2007.501.14

65 *Mood meter machine, N.Y.C. 1957*
7 $^5/_8$ × 4 $^{15}/_{16}$ in. (19.3 × 12.5 cm)
Gift of Doon Arbus and Amy Arbus, 2007
2007.501.73

67 *Fire Eater at a carnival, Palisades Park,
N.J. 1957* *
Previous date: 1956
7 $^{11}/_{16}$ × 5 $^3/_{16}$ in. (19.5 × 13.1 cm)
Gift of Danielle and David Ganek, 2005
2005.493.12

69 *Kid in black face, N.Y.C. 1957*
9 × 5 $^{13}/_{16}$ in. (22.8 × 14.7 cm)
Gift of Doon Arbus and Amy Arbus, 2007
2007.501.79

71 *Sunny South Syncopaters and other sideshow
banners at night, Palisades Park, N.J. 1957* *
Previous date: 1956
5 $^7/_8$ × 8 $^7/_{16}$ in. (15 × 21.4 cm)
Gift of Doon Arbus and Amy Arbus, 2007
2007.501.112

73 *Father and child at Italian Street Festival,
N.Y.C. 1957* *
Previous date: 1959
8 $^3/_8$ × 5 $^{15}/_{16}$ in. (21.3 × 15.1 cm)
Promised Gift of Doon Arbus and Amy Arbus
L.2008.62.28

75 *Masked boy with friends, Coney Island,
N.Y. 1957* *
Previous date: 1956
9 × 5 $^{13}/_{16}$ in. (22.8 × 14.8 cm)
Purchase, Joyce Frank Menschel, and Ann
Tenenbaum and Thomas H. Lee Gifts;
Louis V. Bell, Harris Brisbane Dick, Fletcher,
and Rogers Funds and Joseph Pulitzer
Bequest; and Marlene Nathan Meyerson
Family Foundation, Twentieth-Century
Photography Fund, Diana Barrett and

Robert Vila, Elizabeth S. and Robert J.
Fisher, Charlotte and Bill Ford, Lita
Annenberg Hazen Charitable Trust and
Hazen Polsky Foundation Inc., Jennifer
and Joseph Duke, Jennifer and Philip
Maritz, Saundra B. Lane, The Jerry and
Emily Spiegel Family Foundation and
Pamela and Arthur Sanders, Anonymous,
and The Judith Rothschild Foundation
Gifts, 2007
2007.525

77 *Boy above a crowd, N.Y.C. 1957**
Previous date: 1956
5 7/8 × 8 13/16 in. (15 × 22.4 cm)
Collection of Roger Mooney and
Donald Steele

79 *Clown in a fedora, Palisades Park, N.J. 1957**
Previous title: *Clown in a fedora backstage,
N.Y.C. 1957*
7 7/8 × 5 1/16 in. (20 × 12.9 cm)
Promised Gift of Doon Arbus and Amy Arbus
L.2008.62.310

81 *Young man with a paper bag at night,
Coney Island, N.Y. 1957**
Previous title: *Young man with a paper bag at
night, N.Y.C. 1957*
8 15/16 × 6 1/8 in. (22.7 × 15.5 cm)
Promised Gift of Doon Arbus and Amy Arbus
L.2008.62.50

83 *Empty snack bar, N.Y.C. 1957**
Previous date: 1958
5 15/16 × 8 7/8 in. (15.1 × 22.6 cm)
Promised Gift of Doon Arbus and Amy Arbus
L.2008.62.107

87 *Boy stepping off the curb, N.Y.C. 1957–58**
Previous date: ca. 1956
10 × 6 7/8 in. (25.4 × 17.4 cm)
Collection of Jeffrey Fraenkel and Alan Mark

88 *Man yelling in Times Square, N.Y.C. 1958*
10 1/16 × 5 1/2 in. (25.5 × 14 cm)
Gift of Doon Arbus and Amy Arbus, 2007
2007.501.33

89 *Wrestlers in the ring, N.Y.C. 1958*
5 13/16 × 8 5/8 in. (14.8 × 21.9 cm)
Gift of Doon Arbus and Amy Arbus, 2007
2007.501.27

91 *Two Cha-Cha dancers performing for an
audience, N.Y.C. 1958*
5 7/8 × 8 3/8 in. (14.9 × 21.3 cm)
Promised Gift of Doon Arbus and Amy Arbus
L.2008.62.58

93 *Woman in white fur with a cigarette,
Mulberry Street, N.Y.C. 1958*
8 13/16 × 6 in. (22.4 × 15.3 cm)
Gift of Doon Arbus and Amy Arbus, 2007
2007.501.21

95 *Contortionist Lydia Suarez performing
for an audience, Hubert's Museum, N.Y.C. 1958*
6 3/8 × 9 3/8 in. (16.2 × 23.8 cm)
Purchase, Jade Lau Gift, 2015
2015.132

97 *Woman with a change purse at a pastry counter,
N.Y.C. 1958*
5 7/8 × 9 in. (14.9 × 22.8 cm)
Promised Gift of Doon Arbus and Amy Arbus
L.2008.62.113

99 *Little man biting woman's breast,
N.Y.C. 1958*
8 3/4 × 5 7/8 in. (22.3 × 14.9 cm)
Gift of Doon Arbus and Amy Arbus, 2007
2007.501.13

101 *Old couple on a park bench, N.Y.C. 1958*
5 7/8 × 8 3/4 in. (14.9 × 22.2 cm)
Gift of Doon Arbus and Amy Arbus, 2007
2007.501.25

103 *Audience with projection booth,
N.Y.C. 1958*
6 5/8 × 9 15/16 in. (16.8 × 25.3 cm)
Private collection

104 *Mighty Mouse western cartoon 1958*
6 5/8 × 9 15/16 in. (16.9 × 25.2 cm)
Gift of Doon Arbus and Amy Arbus, 2007
2007.501.100

105 *Man on screen being choked 1958*
6 1/4 × 9 7/16 in. (15.9 × 24 cm)
Promised Gift of Doon Arbus and Amy Arbus
L.2008.62.473

107 *42nd Street movie theater audience,*
N.Y.C. 1958
6 5/8 × 10 in. (16.8 × 25.4 cm)
Pier 24 Photography, San Francisco

109 *Blurry woman gazing up smiling,*
N.Y.C. 1957–58
9 1/8 × 6 1/8 in. (23.1 × 15.6 cm)
Promised Gift of Doon Arbus and Amy Arbus
L.2008.62.23

111 *Bela Lugosi as Dracula*
*on television 1958 ***
Previous title: *Bela Lugosi as "Dracula,"*
close-up 1958
6 5/16 × 9 7/16 in. (16 × 24 cm)
Promised Gift of Doon Arbus and Amy Arbus
L.2008.62.268

113 *Old woman in a hospital bed,*
N.Y.C. 1958
8 1/8 × 5 11/16 in. (20.7 × 14.4 cm)
Promised Gift of Doon Arbus and Amy Arbus
L.2008.62.87

115 *Corpse with receding hairline*
and a toe tag, N.Y.C. 1959
9 1/2 × 6 5/16 in. (24.2 × 16 cm)
Promised Gift of Doon Arbus and Amy Arbus
L.2008.62.259

117 *James Dean in the wax museum,*
*Coney Island, N.Y. 1959 ***
Previous date: 1960
8 5/8 × 5 15/16 in. (21.9 × 15.1 cm)
Promised Gift of Doon Arbus and Amy Arbus
L.2008.62.461

119 *Wax museum axe murderer,*
*Coney Island, N.Y. 1959 ***
Previous date: 1960
9 5/8 × 6 3/8 in. (24.4 × 16.2 cm)
Promised Gift of Doon Arbus and Amy Arbus
L.2008.62.463

121 *Lady in the shower, Coney Island, N.Y. 1959 ***
Previous title: *Woman showering in*
a bathhouse, Coney Island, N.Y. 1959
6 × 9 1/8 in. (15.2 × 23.2 cm)
Purchase, Jade Lau Gift, 2015
2015.133

123 *Blonde female impersonator standing by a dressing*
*table, Hempstead, L.I. 1959 ***
Previous title and date: *Blonde female imperson-*
ator standing by a dressing table, N.Y.C. 1958
9 1/16 × 5 15/16 in. (23 × 15.1 cm)
Promised Gift of Andrea Krantz and
Harvey Sawikin

125 *Andy "Potato Chips" Ratoucheff doing his*
Maurice Chevalier impersonation, Hubert's
Museum, N.Y.C. 1959
8 7/8 × 5 7/8 in. (22.6 × 15 cm)
Promised Gift of Doon Arbus and Amy Arbus
L.2008.62.322

126 *Miss Makrina, a Russian midget, in her kitchen,*
*N.Y.C. 1959 ***
Previous date: 1960
8 1/2 × 5 1/2 in. (21.6 × 14 cm)
Purchase, Jade Lau Gift, 2015
2015.134

127 *Boy at a pool hall, N.Y.C. 1960 ***
Previous date: 1959
9 × 5 7/8 in. (22.8 × 14.9 cm)
Promised Gift of Doon Arbus and Amy Arbus
L.2008.62.441

129 *Seated female impersonator in an open kimono,*
*Hempstead, L.I. 1959 ***
Previous title: *Seated female impersonator in*
an open kimono, N.Y.C. 1959
8 7/8 × 5 5/8 in. (22.5 × 14.3 cm)
Purchase, Jade Lau Gift, 2015
2015.131

131 *Miss Marian Seymour dancing with Baron Theo*
*Von Roth at the Grand Opera Ball, N.Y.C. 1959 ***
Previous title and date: *Miss Marian Seymour*
dancing with Baron Theo von Rath at the
Grand Opera Ball, N.Y.C. 1960
8 11/16 × 5 13/16 in. (22.1 × 14.7 cm)
Promised Gift of Doon Arbus and Amy Arbus
L.2008.62.450

133 *Boy in a cap at a dance, N.Y.C. 1960* *
Previous title: *Boy in a cap at a pool hall,
N.Y.C. 1960*
9 × 5 7/8 in. (22.8 × 14.9 cm)
Courtesy Fraenkel Gallery, San Francisco

135 *Flora Knapp Dickinson, Honorary Regent of
the Washington Heights Chapter of the Daughters
of the American Revolution, N.Y.C. 1960*
9 × 6 in. (22.8 × 15.3 cm)
Promised Gift of Doon Arbus and Amy Arbus
L.2008.62.482

137 *Man at the Municipal Shelter, holding up
a dollar bill, N.Y.C. 1960*
9 1/8 × 6 1/4 in. (23.1 × 15.9 cm)
Promised Gift of Doon Arbus and Amy Arbus
L.2008.62.435

139 *A boy practicing physique posing at the Empire
Gym, N.Y.C. 1960*
8 7/8 × 5 7/8 in. (22.5 × 14.9 cm)
Promised Gift of Doon Arbus and Amy Arbus
L.2008.62.43

141 *Miss Katheryn Lambert with her dogs in the
backyard, Brooklyn, N.Y. 1960* *
Previous title: *Backyard from above, Brooklyn,
N.Y.C. 1960*
8 7/8 × 5 7/8 in. (22.6 × 14.9 cm)
Promised Gift of Doon Arbus and Amy Arbus
L.2008.62.426

143 *Headstone for "Killer" at Bide a Wee Cemetery,
Wantagh, N.Y. 1960*
8 7/8 × 5 15/16 in. (22.6 × 15.1 cm)
Promised Gift of Doon Arbus and Amy Arbus
L.2008.62.460

145 *Dead pigs hanging, N.Y.C. 1960*
8 7/8 × 5 7/8 in. (22.6 × 15 cm)
Promised Gift of Doon Arbus and Amy Arbus
L.2008.62.453

147 *Mother Cabrini, a disinterred saint in her glass
and gold casket, N.Y.C. 1960* *
Previous title: *A disinterred saint in her glass
and gold casket, N.Y.C. 1960*
5 15/16 × 8 3/4 in. (15.1 × 22.2 cm)
Promised Gift of Doon Arbus and Amy Arbus
L.2008.62.455

149 *The Madman from Massachusetts in an empty
bar, N.Y.C. 1960*
8 15/16 × 5 7/8 in. (22.7 × 14.9 cm)
Promised Gift of Doon Arbus and Amy Arbus
L.2008.62.434

151 *Patti, a resident of the New Holland Hotel seated
on her bed, N.Y.C. 1960*
9 × 6 1/8 in. (22.8 × 15.5 cm)
Gift of Doon Arbus and Amy Arbus, 2007
2007.501.125

153 *Norma and Gallo, members of a Brooklyn teen
gang, N.Y.C. 1960* *
Previous title: *Norma and Gallo, members of
a teen gang, N.Y.C. 1960*
8 7/8 × 5 7/8 in. (22.6 × 14.9 cm)
Promised Gift of Doon Arbus and Amy Arbus
L.2008.62.37

155 *Contestant in a physique contest,
N.Y.C. 1960* *
Previous title: *Young man in a physique contest,
N.Y.C. 1960*
8 × 5 11/16 in. (20.3 × 14.5 cm)
Promised Gift of Doon Arbus and Amy Arbus
L.2008.62.48

156 *Girl in her circus costume backstage, Palisades
Park, N.J. 1960* *
Previous title: *Girl in her circus costume
backstage, N.Y.C. 1960*
9 × 6 1/8 in. (22.8 × 15.5 cm)
Promised Gift of Doon Arbus and Amy Arbus
L.2008.62.352

157 *Hezekiah Trambles, "The Jungle Creep," on stage
at Hubert's Museum, N.Y.C. 1960* *
Previous title: *Hezekiah Trambles, "The Jungle
Creep," N.Y.C. 1960*
8 3/4 × 5 15/16 in. (22.2 × 15.1 cm)
Promised Gift of Doon Arbus and Amy Arbus
L.2008.62.414

159 *Couple arguing, Coney Island,
N.Y. 1960*
8 9/16 × 5 5/8 in. (21.8 × 14.3 cm)
Collection of Thomas H. Lee and
Ann Tenenbaum, New York

161 *Man in hat, trunks, socks and shoes,
Coney Island, N.Y. 1960*
9 1/16 × 5 11/16 in. (23 × 14.5 cm)
Promised Gift of Doon Arbus and Amy Arbus
L.2008.62.3

163 *Old woman with hands raised in the ocean,
Coney Island, N.Y. 1960*
5 15/16 × 8 15/16 in. (15.1 × 22.7 cm)
Gift of Doon Arbus and Amy Arbus, 2007
2007.501.9

165 *The Man Who Swallows Razor Blades,
Hagerstown, Md. 1960**
Previous date: 1961
9 1/8 × 5 13/16 in. (23.2 × 14.8 cm)
Purchase, Joyce Frank Menschel, and Ann
Tenenbaum and Thomas H. Lee Gifts;
Louis V. Bell, Harris Brisbane Dick, Fletcher,
and Rogers Funds and Joseph Pulitzer
Bequest; and Marlene Nathan Meyerson
Family Foundation, Twentieth-Century
Photography Fund, Diana Barrett and
Robert Vila, Elizabeth S. and Robert J.
Fisher, Charlotte and Bill Ford, Lita
Annenberg Hazen Charitable Trust and
Hazen Polsky Foundation Inc., Jennifer
and Joseph Duke, Jennifer and Philip
Maritz, Saundra B. Lane, The Jerry and
Emily Spiegel Family Foundation and
Pamela and Arthur Sanders, Anonymous,
and The Judith Rothschild Foundation
Gifts, 2007
2007.524

167 *Siamese twins in a carnival tent,
N.J. 1960**
Previous date: 1961
6 1/8 × 9 1/8 in. (15.6 × 23.1 cm)
Purchase, The Horace W. Goldsmith
Foundation Gift, through Joyce and
Robert Menschel, 1987
1987.1127

169 *Uncle Sam leaning on a cot at home,
N.Y.C. 1960**
Previous date: 1961
8 13/16 × 5 13/16 in. (22.4 × 14.7 cm)
Promised Gift of Doon Arbus and Amy Arbus
L.2008.62.356

171 *Seated female impersonator with arms crossed on
her bare chest, N.Y.C. 1960*
8 × 6 in. (20.3 × 15.3 cm)
Promised Gift of Andrea Krantz and
Harvey Sawikin

175 *Jack Dracula at a bar, New London,
Conn. 1961**
Previous title: *Jack Dracula at a bar,
N.Y.C. 1961*
9 3/4 × 6 5/8 in. (24.8 × 16.9 cm)
Promised Gift of Doon Arbus and Amy Arbus
L.2008.62.371

177 *Two girls by a brick wall, N.Y.C. 1961*
9 × 6 1/8 in. (22.9 × 15.6 cm)
Gift of Doon Arbus and Amy Arbus, 2007
2007.501.15

179 *Miss Stormé de Larverie, the Lady Who Appears
to be a Gentleman, N.Y.C. 1961*
9 7/8 × 6 3/4 in. (25.1 × 17.2 cm)
Promised Gift of Doon Arbus and Amy Arbus
L.2008.62.366

181 *Five members of The Monster Fan Club,
N.Y.C. 1961*
8 7/8 × 5 13/16 in. (22.5 × 14.7 cm)
Promised Gift of Doon Arbus and Amy Arbus
L.2008.62.213

183 *Clouds on screen at a drive-in movie,
N.J. 1961**
Previous date: 1960
6 1/4 × 9 1/2 in. (15.9 × 24.1 cm)
Collection of Kathy and Steve Kloves,
Los Angeles

185 *Stripper with bare breasts sitting in her dressing
room, Atlantic City, N.J. 1961**
Previous date: 1962
9 1/2 × 6 1/2 in. (24.1 × 16.5 cm)
Purchase, Jade Lau Gift, 2015
2015.135

186 *The Human Pincushion, Ronald C. Harrison,
N.J. 1961**
Previous date: 1962
10 × 6 3/4 in. (25.4 × 17.1 cm)
Collection of Joyce F. Menschel

187 *Headless woman, Palisades Park,*
*N.J. 1961**
Previous title: *Headless woman,*
N.Y.C. 1961
8 5/8 × 6 in. (21.9 × 15.3 cm)
Purchase, The Horace W. Goldsmith
Foundation Gift, through Joyce and
Robert Menschel, 1998
1998.357

189 *Screaming woman with blood on her*
*hands 1961**
Previous date: ca. 1958
7 1/16 × 10 1/2 in. (18 × 26.6 cm)
Purchase, Henry Buhl Gift, 1996
1996.299

191 *Blonde receptionist behind a picture window,*
N.Y.C. 1962
8 1/8 × 7 3/4 in. (20.6 × 19.7 cm)
Gift of Doon Arbus and Amy Arbus, 2007
2007.501.102

193 *A castle in Disneyland, Cal. 1962*
9 1/2 × 9 7/16 in. (24.2 × 23.9 cm)
Purchase, Joyce Frank Menschel, and Ann
Tenenbaum and Thomas H. Lee Gifts;
Louis V. Bell, Harris Brisbane Dick, Fletcher,
and Rogers Funds and Joseph Pulitzer
Bequest; and Marlene Nathan Meyerson
Family Foundation, Twentieth-Century
Photography Fund, Diana Barrett and
Robert Vila, Elizabeth S. and Robert J.
Fisher, Charlotte and Bill Ford, Lita
Annenberg Hazen Charitable Trust and
Hazen Polsky Foundation Inc., Jennifer
and Joseph Duke, Jennifer and Philip
Maritz, Saundra B. Lane, The Jerry and
Emily Spiegel Family Foundation and
Pamela and Arthur Sanders, Anonymous,
and The Judith Rothschild Foundation
Gifts, 2007
2007.511

195 *Girl and governess with baby carriage,*
N.Y.C. 1962
8 3/8 × 8 1/8 in. (21.3 × 20.7 cm)
Promised Gift of Doon Arbus and Amy Arbus
L.2008.62.285

197 *Tall partygoer in a taffeta dress,*
N.Y.C. 1962
8 3/8 × 8 1/8 in. (21.3 × 20.7 cm)
Gift of Doon Arbus and Amy Arbus, 2007
2007.501.103

199 *Xmas tree in a living room in Levittown,*
*L.I. 1962**
Previous date: 1963
14 5/8 × 14 15/16 in. (37.1 × 37.9 cm)
Purchase, Dorothy Levitt Beskind Gift, 1969
69.546.2

249 *A Dominant Picture 1958*
6 × 8 7/8 in. (15.2 × 22.5 cm)
Collection of Jeffrey Fraenkel and Alan Mark

251 *Female impersonator putting on lipstick,*
*Hempstead, L.I. 1959**
Previous title: *Female impersonator putting on*
lipstick, N.Y.C. 1959
8 7/8 × 6 in. (22.5 × 15.2 cm)
Purchase, The Robert and Joyce Menschel
Family Foundation Gift, 2015
2015.137

253 *Elderly woman whispering to her dinner partner,*
*Grand Opera Ball, N.Y.C. 1959**
Previous date: 1960
8 3/4 × 5 13/16 in. (22.2 × 14.7 cm)
Gift of Doon Arbus and Amy Arbus, 2007
2007.501.128

255 *Girl with a white handbag, N.Y.C. 1960**
Previous date: 1961
8 7/8 × 5 7/8 in. (22.6 × 14.9 cm)
Promised Gift of Doon Arbus and Amy Arbus
L.2008.62.419

257 *Child with a toy hand grenade in Central Park,*
N.Y.C. 1962
15 9/16 × 15 1/16 in. (39.5 × 38.3 cm)
Purchase, Jennifer and Joseph Duke
Gift, 2001
2001.474

269 *Rocks on wheels, Disneyland, Cal. 1962*
6 5/16 × 9 1/2 in. (16 × 24.1 cm)
Collection of Eileen and Michael Cohen

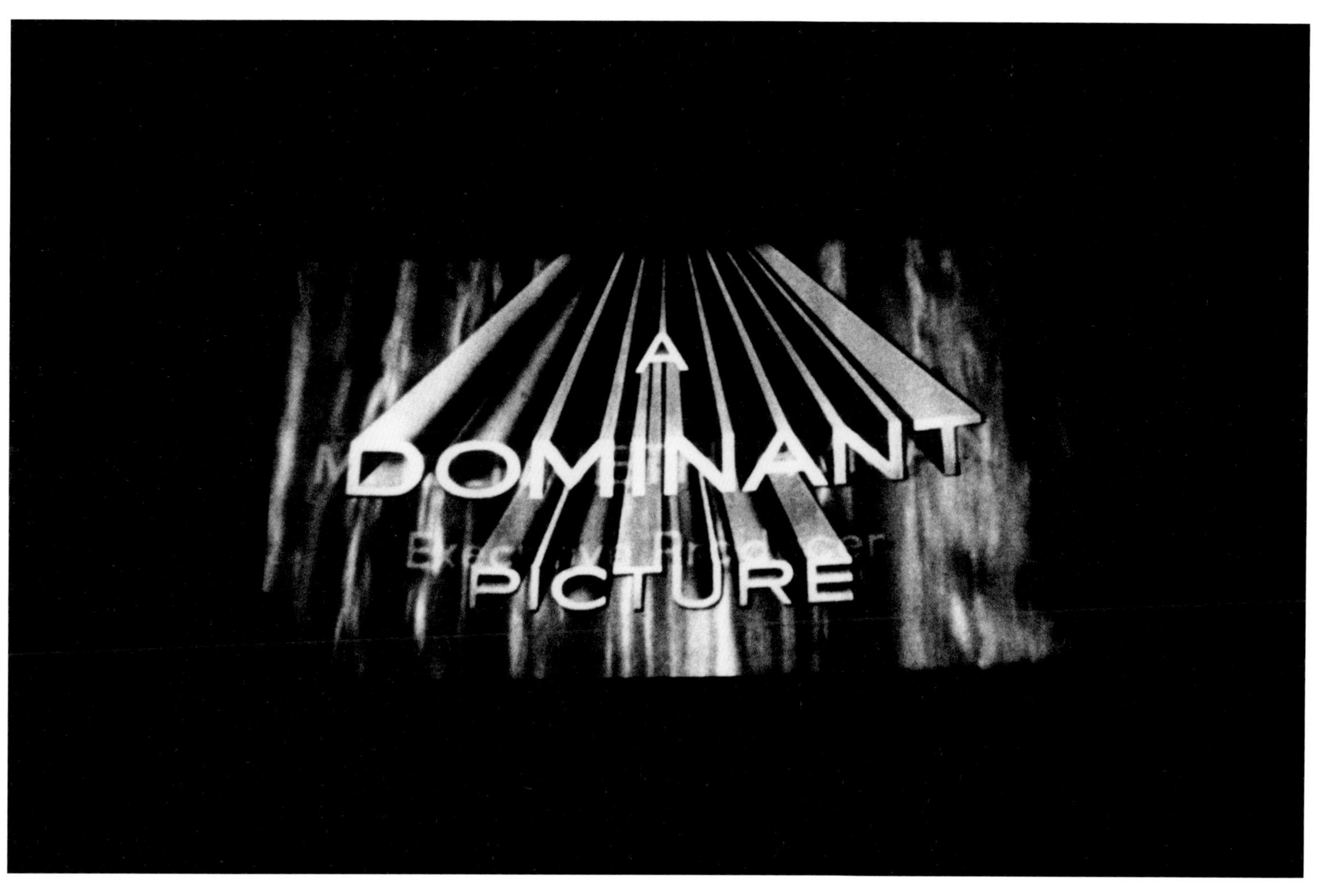

A Dominant Picture 1958

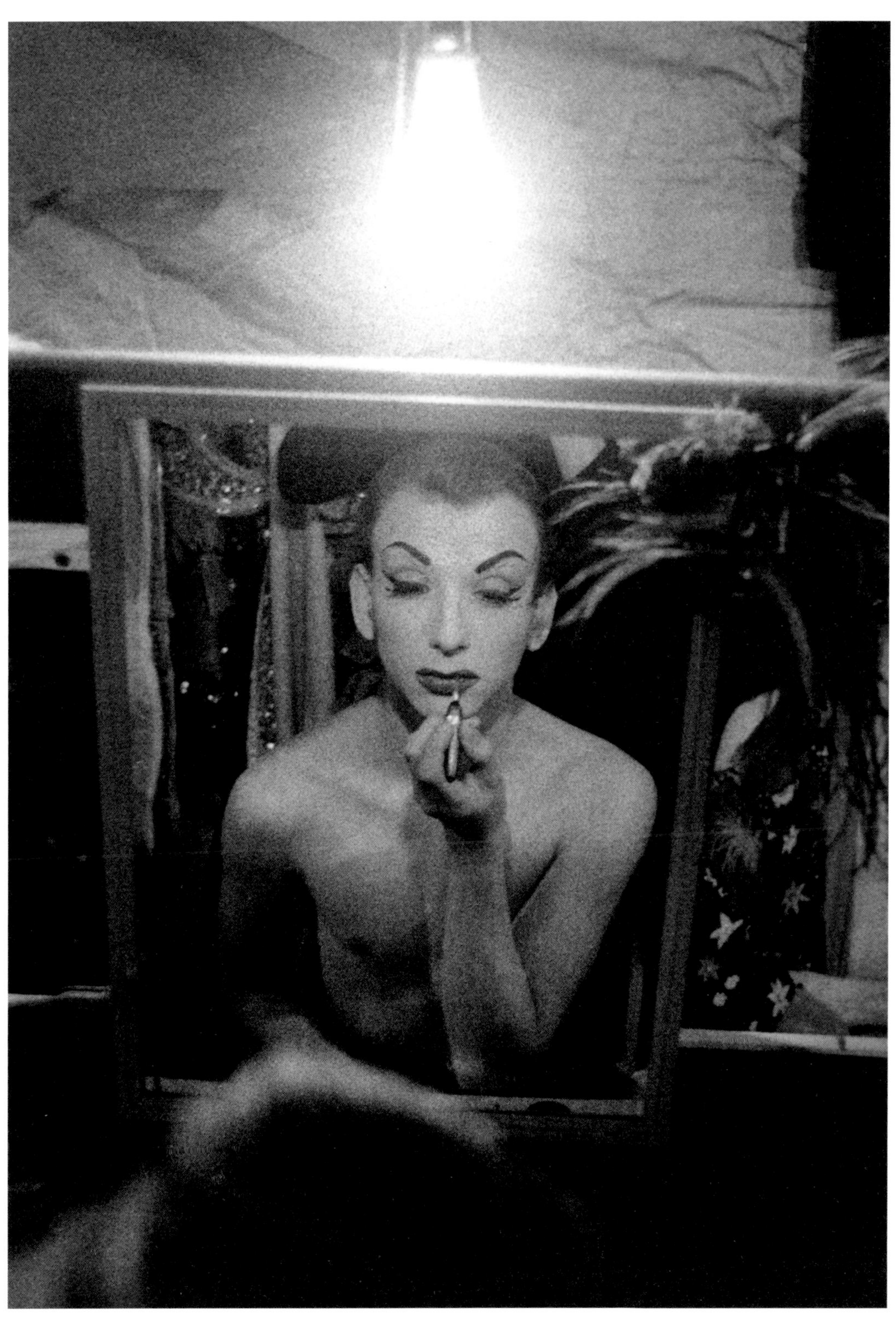

Female impersonator putting on lipstick, Hempstead, L.I. 1959

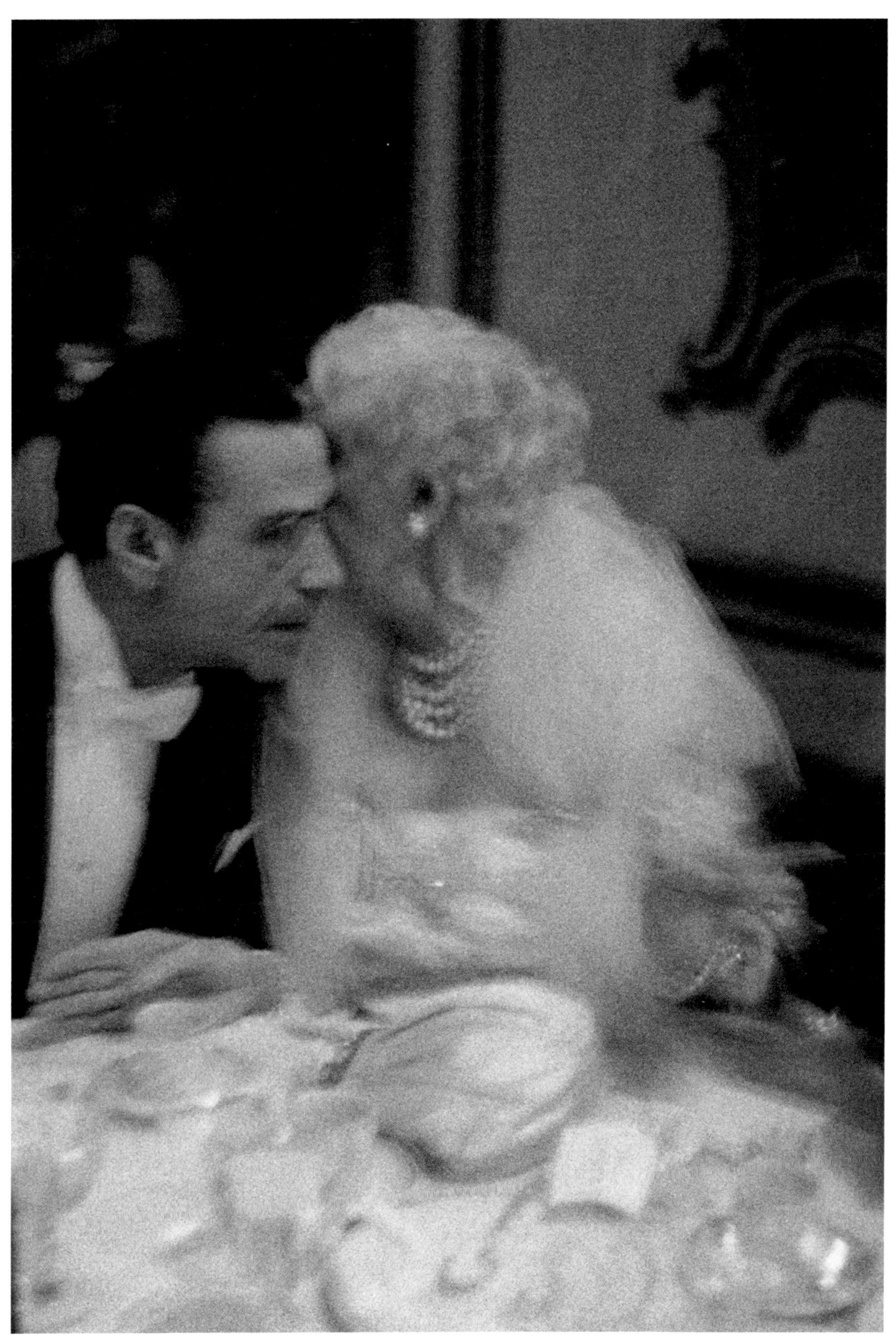

Elderly woman whispering to her dinner partner, Grand Opera Ball, N.Y.C. 1959

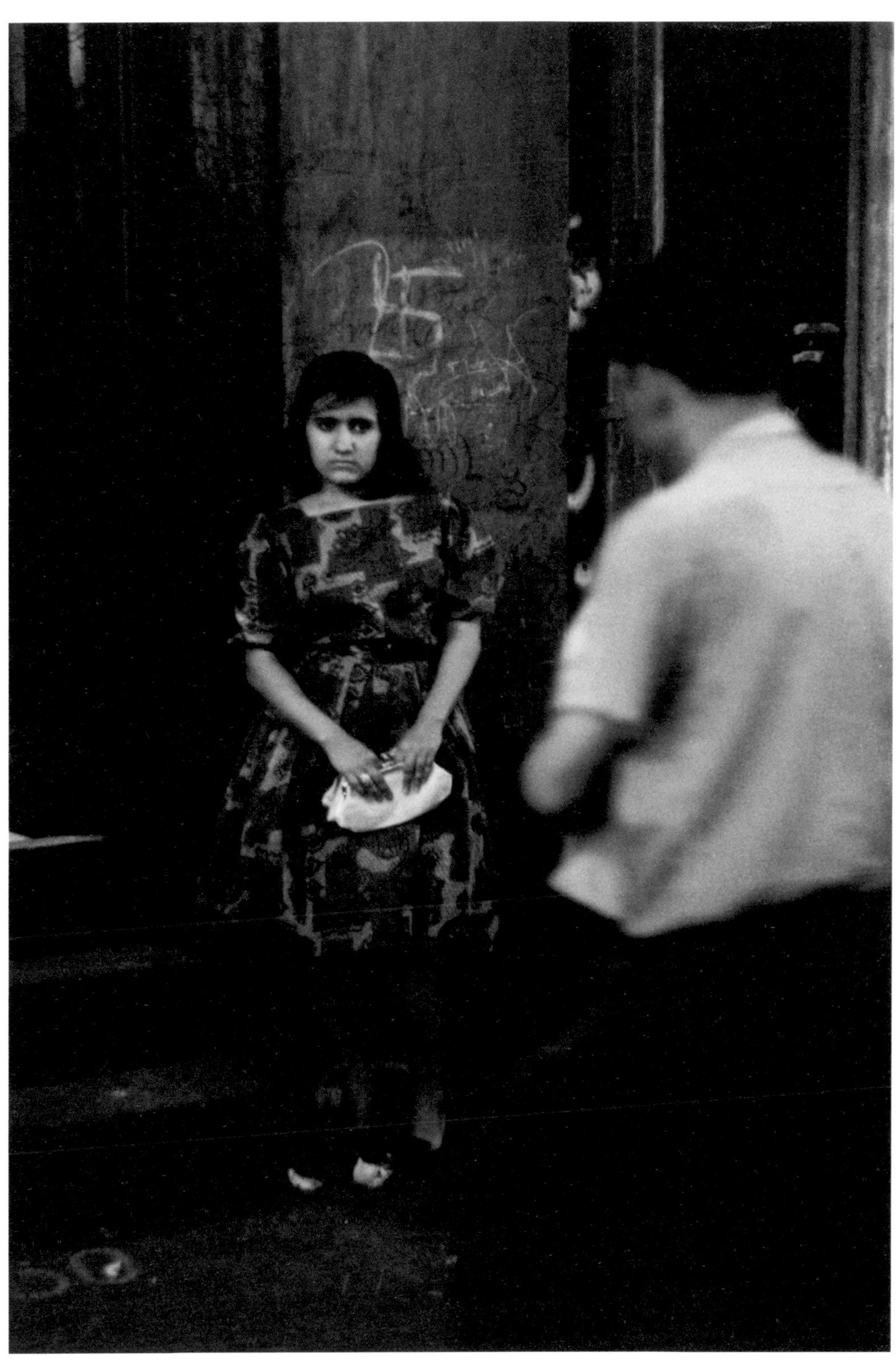

Girl with a white handbag, N.Y.C. 1960

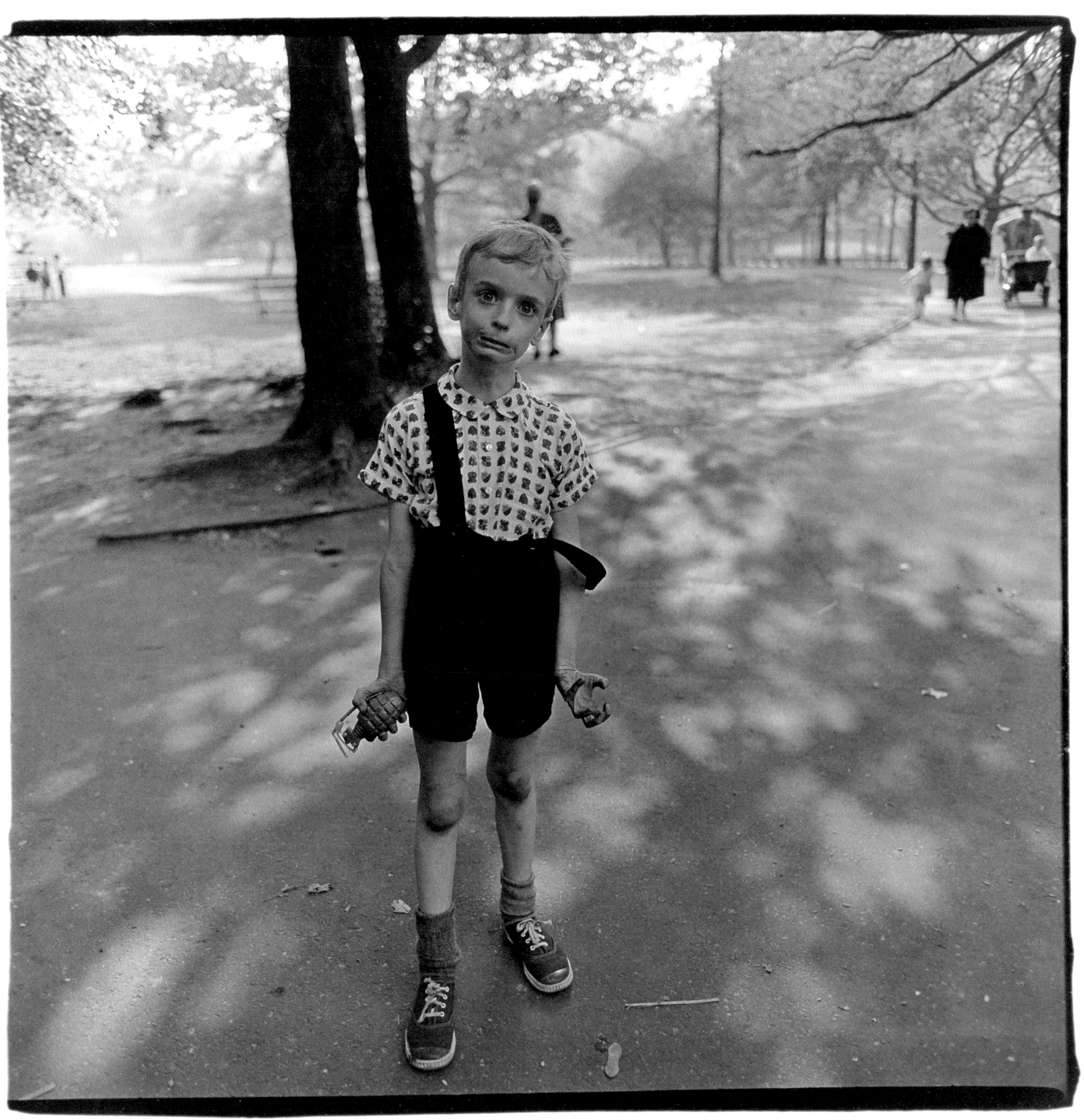

Child with a toy hand grenade in Central Park, N.Y.C. 1962

acknowledgments

One evening in 2003 or 2004 during the national run of the exhibition "Diane Arbus Revelations," I asked Doon Arbus if she had any plans for the institutional preservation of her mother's negatives, papers, and collections. Thus began a multiyear conversation with Doon and Amy Arbus that culminated in December 2007 with their gift and promised gift of the Diane Arbus Archive to The Metropolitan Museum of Art. I offer my heartfelt thanks to Doon and Amy for entrusting The Met with this extraordinary archive and for their long-lasting friendship.

The acquisition of the archive and the unique requirements it demanded rest on the spectacular generosity of the Arbuses and the support of three other dear colleagues: Jeffrey Fraenkel, Neil Selkirk, and John Pelosi. Without the attention and intelligence of this terrific trio, there would likely have been no gift, no show, no book, and very little fun over the last fifteen years. Thank you for bringing me along on this wonderful journey.

The preservation and cataloguing that began in early 2008 and continues today has been led from the start by Karan Rinaldo, Senior Research Assistant, Department of Photographs, an indefatigable scholar who came to the Museum expressly to work on the archive. Karan's position has been funded by Trustee Joyce Frank Menschel, Jennifer Johnson Duke, Hideyuki Osawa, Mary Ann and Frank B. Arisman, and Susan Unterberg, whose generous gifts supported the research that is the foundation of this catalogue and the exhibition it accompanies. Karan authored the "notes from the archive" published here and has supervised dedicated academic interns and volunteers: Cole Maritz, Will Patterson, Kerri Sullivan, Sean O'Hanlan, Samantha Anderson, Joy Kerveillant, Lizzie Zelter, Lila Murphy, Michelle Gingras, Lauren Wright, Rachel Andrews, Becca Gray, Virginia McBride, and, most recently, Emma Fisher. Russell Isaacs, Liz Garofano, and Lowell Pettit helped The Estate of Diane Arbus to prepare the archive for its new home at The Met. Long-term volunteer Jeanne Savitt deserves special mention for her acuity and camaraderie on this project and so many others.

The Met's team of conservators, headed by Nora Kennedy, Sherman Fairchild Conservator in Charge of the Department of Photograph Conservation, has spent hundreds of hours working on the original materials in the archive, managing with Karan the proper storage of the artist's negatives and prints, her collection of photographs by other artists, and her papers and library. For the exhibition itself, conservators Katherine C. Sanderson, Lisa Barro, Nancy Reinhold, Jana Krizanova, and Georgia Southworth worked on the conservation of more than seventy vintage gelatin silver prints that have never before been exhibited or published.

Under the direction of Mark Polizzotti, Publisher and Editor in Chief, the Museum produced a book as idiosyncratic as its subject, a volume edited by Kamilah Foreman and designed by Daphne Geismar. Peter Antony and Lauren Knighton oversaw the physical printing of the volume, and Elizabeth De Mase secured all image rights for photographs outside The Met's collection. Eileen Travell, in the Museum's Photograph Studio, created the image files from which Martin Senn in his atelier in Switzerland made the tritone separations.

While The Met has unparalleled holdings of vintage prints by Arbus, the shape of the artist's achievement in the years 1956–62 could not be fully understood without important loans of rare works. The following generous art lovers as well as several others who wish to remain anonymous lent photographs to the exhibition: Trustees Joyce Frank Menschel, Ann Tenenbaum, and Philip Maritz; Andrea Krantz and Harvey Sawikin; Eileen and Michael Cohen; John Cheim; Mary and Andy Pilara, Pier 24 Photography, San Francisco; Roger Mooney and Donald Steele; Kathy and Steve Kloves; Jeffrey Fraenkel and Alan Mark; Fraenkel Gallery, San Francisco; and of course Doon Arbus and Amy Arbus. These loans were managed by Karan Rinaldo with the assistance of Anna Wall and Beth Saunders in the Department of Photographs and Allison E. Barone in the Registrars Office.

The exhibition design at The Met Breuer was executed by Brian Oliver Butterfield, Senior Exhibition Designer, who worked from a series of provisional sketches I conceived years ago; the graphics were by Anna Rieger. Allison Barone and Katy Uravitch in the Exhibitions Office, Ellium Roberts in Buildings, and Patrick Paine at The Met Breuer all helped to bring the show to life in the galleries. Jed Bark of Bark Frameworks designed and manufactured the frames; at the Museum, Predrag Dimitrijevic cut the mats, fitted the photographs, and with Ryan Franklin, installed the show with classic finesse, efficiency, and their renowned attention to detail.

Jennifer Russell, former Associate Director for Exhibitions; Aileen Chuk, Chief Registrar; and their staffs including Linda Sylling, Martha Deese, and Allison Barone orchestrated the exhibition tour. Sharon H. Cott, Senior Vice President, Secretary, and General Counsel, and her team including Cristina Del Valle coordinated all legal matters with John Pelosi, counsel to The Estate of Diane Arbus. Clyde B. Jones III, Senior Vice President for Institutional Advancement, and the entire Development team, including Nina McN. Diefenbach, Jason Herrick, Sarah Higby, and Elizabeth A. Burke, found the necessary resources. Sandra Jackson-Dumont, Frederick P. and Sandra P. Rose Chairman of Education, and her colleagues conceived and executed all the educational activities including symposia, talks, and teen workshops. The successful promotion of the exhibition worldwide was coordinated by Alexandra Kozlakowski, Senior Press Officer, and Jennifer Oetting, Senior Manager for Advertising and Marketing, under the supervision of Cynthia L. Round and Elyse Topalian, all in Communications.

Additional expertise and advice came from numerous individuals near and far, all of whom merit my grateful acknowledgment: Carrie Rebora Barratt and Christine Coulson in the Office of the Director; Jeffrey Fraenkel, Frish Brandt, Amy Whiteside, and Tiffany Harker at Fraenkel Gallery, San Francisco; Bonnie Briant in New York; Robert Rubin and Mark Lyon in Paris; Anthony d'Offay and Marie-Louise Laband in London; Maria Morris Hambourg in Providence; Eddie Rosenheim in Saint Louis; and Phoebe, Julia, and Kellye Rosenheim on West End Avenue.

Lastly, I am profoundly indebted to Philippe de Montebello and Thomas P. Campbell, the two museum directors I have had the great pleasure to serve under at The Met for the last twenty-eight years. The former challenged me personally to make sure that the Museum would always offer the world's most important works of art; he signed the acquisition papers for the Diane Arbus Archive in 2007. The latter approved this foundational exhibition and gave it pride of place in the inaugural season of The Met Breuer. I sincerely appreciate their support as well as that of my other talented colleagues in the Department of Photographs: Douglas Eklund, Mia Fineman, Stephen Pinson, Meredith Reiss, and Myriam Rocconi.

JEFF L. ROSENHEIM

monographs

Diane Arbus. With texts by Arbus. Edited and designed by Doon Arbus and Marvin Israel. Millerton, N.Y.: Aperture, 1972.

Diane Arbus: Magazine Work. With texts by Arbus and an essay by Thomas W. Southall. Edited by Marvin Israel and Doon Arbus. Designed by Marvin Israel and Wendy Byrne. Millerton, N.Y.: Aperture, 1984.

Diane Arbus: Untitled. With an afterword by Doon Arbus. Edited and designed by Doon Arbus and Yolanda Cuomo. New York: Aperture, 1995.

Diane Arbus Revelations. With texts by Arbus and essays by Sandra S. Phillips, Jeff L. Rosenheim, Neil Selkirk, and Elisabeth Sussman and Doon Arbus. New York: Random House, 2003.

other books

Anthony W. Lee and John Pultz. *Diane Arbus: Family Albums*. New Haven: Yale University Press, 2003.

Diane Arbus: The Libraries. San Francisco: Fraenkel Gallery, 2004. Illustrated record of books in the Diane Arbus Library as featured in the exhibition "Diane Arbus Revelations."

Arbus, Model, Strömholm. Exh. cat. Moderna Museet, Stockholm, 2005–6. Göttingen: Steidl, 2005.

Gregory Gibson. *Hubert's Freaks: The Rare-Book Dealer, the Times Square Talker, and the Lost Photos of Diane Arbus*. Orlando: Harcourt, 2008.

Elisabeth Sussman and Doon Arbus. *Diane Arbus: A Chronology, 1923–1971*. With biographies by Jeff L. Rosenheim. New York: Aperture, 2011. All texts originally appeared in *Diane Arbus Revelations*.

Alexander Nemerov. *Silent Dialogues: Diane Arbus & Howard Nemerov*. San Francisco: Fraenkel Gallery, 2015.

selected magazine articles by Diane Arbus

"The Vertical Journey: Six Movements of a Moment within the Heart of the City." *Esquire* (July 1960), pp. 102–7. Six portraits of New Yorkers with text from notes by Arbus.

"The Full Circle." *Harper's Bazaar* (November 1961), pp. 133–37, 169–73, 179. Five portraits of eccentrics with text by Arbus.

"The Full Circle." *Infinity* (February 1962), pp. 4–13, 19–21. Reprint of *Harper's Bazaar* article with one additional photograph.

"Auguries of Innocence." *Harper's Bazaar* (December 1963), pp. 76–79. Four photographs of children with text excerpts from William Blake, Lewis Carroll, et al.

"Five Photographs by Diane Arbus." *Artforum* 9 (May 1971), pp. 64–69. With text by Arbus.

other artists

BERENICE ABBOTT

Berenice Abbott. *Changing New York*. With text by Elizabeth McCausland. New York: E. P. Dutton, 1939.

———. *A Guide to Better Photography*. New York: Crown Publishers, 1941.

* *Berenice Abbott: Photographs*. New York: Horizon Press, 1970.

Bonnie Yochelson. *Berenice Abbott: Changing New York; The Complete WPA Project*. New York: New Press; Museum of the City of New York, 1997.

ALEXEY BRODOVITCH

Alexey Brodovitch. *Ballet: 104 Photographs by Alexey Brodovitch*. New York: J. J. Augustin, 1945.

Kerry William Purcell. *Alexey Brodovitch*. London: Phaidon, 2002.

WALKER EVANS

Walker Evans. *American Photographs*. Exh. cat. New York: Museum of Modern Art, 1938.

*———. *Many Are Called*. With an introduction by
James Agee. Boston: Houghton Mifflin, 1966.

*———. *Message from the Interior*. New York: Eakins
Press, 1966.

*———. *Walker Evans*. With an introduction by
John Szarkowski. Exh. cat. New York: Museum of
Modern Art, 1971.

*Walker Evans at Work: 745 Photographs Together
with Documents Selected from Letters, Memoranda,
Interviews, Notes*. With an essay by Jerry L.
Thompson. New York: Harper & Row, 1982.

Maria Morris Hambourg, Jeff L. Rosenheim, Douglas
Eklund, and Mia Fineman. *Walker Evans*. Exh. cat.
New York: The Metropolitan Museum of Art in
association with Princeton University Press, 2000.

Jeff L. Rosenheim and Douglas Eklund. *Unclassified:
A Walker Evans Anthology*. Zurich: Scalo Zurich-
Berlin-New York in association with The
Metropolitan Museum of Art, New York, 2000.

LOUIS FAURER

*Louis Faurer, Photographs from Philadelphia and New York,
1937–1973*. With texts by Faurer and Walter Hopps.
Edited by Edith A. Tonelli and John Gossage. College
Park, Md.: University of Maryland Art Gallery, 1981.

Anne Wilkes Tucker with Lisa Hostetler and
Kathleen V. Jameson. *Louis Faurer*. Exh. cat.
London: Merrell in association with the Museum
of Fine Arts, Houston, 2002.

ROBERT FRANK

Robert Frank. *The Americans*. With an introduction
by Jack Kerouac. New York: Grove Press, 1959.

———. *The Lines of My Hand*. Rochester, N.Y.:
Lustrum Press, 1972.

Robert Frank: New York to Nova Scotia. Edited by
Anne Wilkes Tucker and Philip Brookman. Exh. cat.
Houston: Museum of Fine Arts, 1986.

Sarah Greenough. *Looking In: Robert Frank's The
Americans*. With essays by Stuart Alexander, Philip
Brookman, Michel Frizot, Jeff L. Rosenheim, et al.
Exh. cat. Washington, D.C.: National Gallery of
Art, 2009.

LEE FRIEDLANDER

Lee Friedlander. *Self Portrait*. New City, N.Y.:
Haywire Press, 1970.

Saul Anton. *Lee Friedlander: The Little Screens*.
With a foreword by Walker Evans. Exh. cat.
San Francisco: Fraenkel Gallery, 2001.

Peter Galassi. *Friedlander*. With an essay by
Richard Benson. Exh. cat. New York: Museum
of Modern Art, 2005.

WILLIAM KLEIN

* William Klein. *Life Is Good and Good for You in
New York: Trance Witness Revels*. Paris: Editions
du Seuil, 1956. English ed., London: Photography
Magazine, 1956.

*———. *Rome, The City and Its People*. New York·
Viking Press, 1959.

———. *Moscow*. With a preface by Harrison E.
Salisbury. New York: Crown Publishers, 1964.

———. *William Klein: In & Out of Fashion*.
New York: Random House, 1994.

LEON LEVINSTEIN

Bob Shamis. *Leon Levinstein: The Moment
of Exposure*. With an essay by Max Kozloff.
Exh. cat. Ottawa: National Gallery of
Canada, 1995.

Leon Levinstein. Exh. cat., 2001–2. Chicago:
Stephen Daiter Gallery, 2001.

Bob Shamis. *Leon Levinstein*. With an introduction
by Jeff L. Rosenheim and an essay by Carrie
Springer. Göttingen: Steidl; New York: Howard
Greenberg Gallery, 2014.

HELEN LEVITT

* Helen Levitt. *A Way of Seeing: Photographs of
New York*. With an essay by James Agee.
New York: Viking Press, 1965.

Sandra S. Phillips and Maria Morris Hambourg.
Helen Levitt. Exh. cat., 1991–92. San Francisco:
San Francisco Museum of Modern Art, 1991.

Crosstown: Photographs by Helen Levitt. With an
introduction by Francine Prose. New York:
powerHouse Books, 2001.

LISETTE MODEL

Lisette Model. With a preface by Berenice Abbott.
Designed by Marvin Israel. Millerton, N.Y.:
Aperture, 1979.

Ann Thomas. *Lisette Model*. Exh. cat., 1990–91. Ottawa: National Gallery of Canada, 1990.

Lisette Model. Exh. cat., Fundación MAPFRE, Madrid, 2009–10, and Jeu de Paume, Paris, 2010. Paris: Jeu de Paume; Madrid: Fundación MAPFRE, 2009.

AUGUST SANDER

August Sander. *Antlitz der Zeit: sechzig Aufnahmen deutscher Menschen des 20. Jahrhunderts*. Munich: Kurt Wolff Verlag, 1929.

* "August Sander photographiert: Deutsche Menschen." *Du* (Zurich) 19, no. 225 (November 1959), pp. 11–67.

* August Sander and Heinrich Lützeler. *Deutschenspiegel: Menschen des 20. Jahrhunderts*. Gütersloh: Sigbert Mohn Verlag, 1962.

August Sander 1876–1964. With essays by Susanne Lange. Cologne: Taschen, 1999.

PAUL STRAND

Camera Work 49, no. 50 (1917), pp. 7–31. With a portfolio of eleven photographs and an essay by Paul Strand.

Paul Strand: A Retrospective Monograph. 2 vols. With texts by Leo Hurwitz, Helmut Gernsheim, Alfred Stieglitz, Strand, et al. [Millerton, N.Y.]: Aperture, 1971.

Peter Barberie, ed., with Amanda N. Bock. *Paul Strand: Master of Modern Photography*. Exh. cat. Philadelphia Museum of Art, 2014–15, and Fundación MAPFRE, Madrid, 2015. Philadelphia: Philadelphia Museum of Art in collaboration with Fundación MAPFRE, 2014.

GARRY WINOGRAND

Garry Winogrand. *The Animals*. With an afterword by John Szarkowski. New York: Museum of Modern Art, 1969.

John Szarkowski. *Winogrand: Figments from the Real World*. Exh. cat. New York: Museum of Modern Art, 1988.

Leo Rubinfien, ed. *Garry Winogrand*. With essays and texts by Sarah Greenough, Susan Kismaric, Erin O'Toole, Tod Papageorge, et al. San Francisco: San Francisco Museum of Modern Art in association with Yale University Press, New Haven, 2013.

anthologies (by date)

* Edward Steichen. *The Family of Man*. Exh. cat. New York: Maco Magazine Corp. for the Museum of Modern Art, New York, 1955.

* Beaumont Newhall. *Masters of Photography*. Edited and with an introduction by Nancy Newhall. New York: George Braziller, 1958.

* John Szarkowski. *The Photographer's Eye*. Exh. cat., 1964. New York: Museum of Modern Art, 1966.

———. *Looking at Photographs: 100 Pictures from the Collection of the Museum of Modern Art*. New York: Museum of Modern Art, 1973.

———. *Mirrors and Windows: American Photography since 1960*. Exh. cat. New York: Museum of Modern Art, 1978.

Sarah Greenough, Joel Snyder, David Travis, Colin Westerbeck, et al. *On the Art of Fixing a Shadow: One Hundred and Fifty Years of Photography*. Exh. cat. National Gallery of Art, Washington, D.C., 1989; Art Institute of Chicago, 1989; and Los Angeles County Museum of Art, 1989–90. Boston: Bulfinch Press/Little, Brown, 1989.

Mike Weaver, Norman Rosenthal, and Daniel Wolf. *The Art of Photography, 1839–1989*. Exh. cat. Houston: Museum of Fine Arts; Canberra: Australian National Gallery; London: Royal Academy of Arts in association with Yale University Press, New Haven, 1989.

Jane Livingston. *The New York School. Photographs, 1936–1963*. New York: Stewart, Tabori & Chang, 1992.

Colin Westerbeck and Joel Meyerowitz. *Bystander: A History of Street Photography*. Boston: Little, Brown, 1994.

Thomas Weski and Heinz Liesbrock. *How You Look at It: Photographs of the Twentieth Century*. Exh. cat. Sprengel Museum Hannover and Städtisches Kunstinstitut und Städtische Galerie, Frankfurt. New York: D.A.P./Distributed Arts Publishers, 2000.

Max Kozloff. *New York: Capital of Photography*. Exh. cat. New York: Jewish Museum; New Haven: Yale University Press, 2002.

Emma Dexter and Thomas Weski, eds. *Cruel and Tender: Photography and the Real*. Exh. cat. Tate Modern, London, 2003. London: Tate Publishing, 2003.

index

Page numbers in **bold** refer to images.

Abbott, Berenice, 208n3

Andy "Potato Chips" Ratoucheff doing his Maurice Chevalier impersonation, Hubert's Museum, N.Y.C. 1959, **125**, 244

Appointment Book (1959), **84–85**, **225**, 226, 267

Appointment Book (1960), 229, 230, **230**, 231

Appointment Book (1961), **172–73**, 212, 232, **232**, 233, **233**, 234, 235, 235n14, **235**, **236**, 267

Appointment Book (1962), 238, **238**

appointment books, 219, 229, 235

Arbus, Allan, 23, 203, 203n1, 208n4, 208n6

Arbus, Diane
  cameras, 23, 209, 211, 214
  early street photography, 207–13
  film roll numbers, 220n4, 220n6, 222n8
  Guggenheim Foundation applications, 214
  high-school essay on Plato, 203
  marriage, 203n1
  quotations, 1, 203, 212, 271
  self-portrait, **202**, 216
  subjects, 207, 209–11, 212–13, 214
  working method, 211–12

Arbus, Doon, 240

archive, *see* Diane Arbus Archive

Audience with projection booth, N.Y.C. 1958, **103**, 243

Baby Doll, **47**

The Backwards Man in his hotel room, N.Y.C. 1961, **17**, 212, 241

Barbershop interior through a glass door, N.Y.C. 1957, **53**, 242

Bedroom in a store window, N.Y.C. 1957, **61**, 242

Bela Lugosi as Dracula on television 1958, **111**, 244

Benton, Robert, letter to, 228, **228**

Bide a Wee Cemetery, **143**, 245

Big Joe's Happiness Exchange, 211n8

Billboard newspaper, 222

Blonde female impersonator standing by a dressing table, Hempstead, L.I. 1959, **123**, 225–26, 244

Blonde receptionist behind a picture window, N.Y.C. 1962, **191**, 247

Blonde on screen about to be kissed 1958, **11**, 240

Blurry woman gazing up smiling, N.Y.C. 1957–58, **109**, 219–20, 244

Boy above a crowd, N.Y.C. 1957, **77**, 221, **221**, 243

Boy in a cap at a dance, N.Y.C. 1960, **133**, 229–30, 245

Boy at a pool hall, N.Y.C. 1960, **127**, 229, 244

A boy practicing physique posing at the Empire Gym, N.Y.C. 1960, **139**, 245

Boy stepping off the curb, N.Y.C. 1957–58, **87**, 211, 219–20, 243

Brodovitch, Alexey, 208n3

Brooklyn, 223, 224, 231
  Miss Cecilia Lange and Miss Katheryn Lambert with some of their forty dogs, Brooklyn, N.Y. 1960, 231, **231**
  Miss Katheryn Lambert with her dogs in the backyard, Brooklyn, N.Y. 1960, **141**, 231, 245
  Norma and Gallo, members of a Brooklyn teen gang, N.Y.C. 1960, **153**, 224, 245
  see also Coney Island

bus, **55**, **206**, 217, 220, 242

Cabrini, Mother, **147**, 245

cameras, 23, **202**, 203, 205, 207, 209, 211, 214

A castle in Disneyland, Cal. 1962, **193**, 247

Central Park, 221, 222n8
  Boy above a crowd, N.Y.C. 1957, **77**, **211**, 221, 243
  Child with a toy hand grenade in Central Park, N.Y.C. 1962, 212, 247, **257**
  Girl and governess with baby carriage, N.Y.C. 1962, **195**, 247
  Old couple on a park bench, N.Y.C. 1958, **101**, 243
  Woman carrying a child in Central Park, N.Y.C. 1956, **37**, 211, 241

Chevalier, Maurice, **125**, 244

Child teasing another, N.Y.C. 1960, **15**, 240

Child with a toy hand grenade in Central Park, N.Y.C. 1962, 212, 247, **257**

circuses, 221–22

Clouds on screen at a drive-in movie, N.J. 1961, **183**, 211, 232, 246

Clown in a fedora, Palisades Park, N.J. 1957, **79**, 221–22, 243

Club 82, 225

Cocteau, Jean, 212

Coney Island, 222–23, 224
  Coney Island Bather, New York (Model), 208n5, **208**, 217
  Coney Island, New York (Winogrand), **205**, 216
  Couple arguing, Coney Island, N.Y. 1960, **159**, 245
  James Dean in the wax museum, Coney Island, N.Y. 1959, **117**, 244
  Lady in the shower, Coney Island, N.Y. 1959, **121**, 224, **224**, 244
  Man in hat, trunks, socks and shoes, Coney Island, N.Y. 1960, **161**, 213, 246
  Masked boy with friends, Coney Island, N.Y. 1957, **75**, 242–43
  Old woman with hands raised in the ocean, Coney Island, N.Y. 1960, **163**, 246
  Wax museum axe murderer, Coney Island, N.Y. 1959, **119**, 244
  Young man with a paper bag at night, Coney Island, N.Y. 1957, **81**, 222–23, 243

contact sheets, 219, 220n4, 235
  roll 50B, 1956, **210**, 217
  roll 93, 220
  roll 169 #27–29, **222**
  roll 174 #31–32, **221**
  roll 639 #25–27, **236**
  roll 700 #2–19, **229**

Contax D camera, **202**, 214, 216

Contestant in a physique contest, N.Y.C. 1960, **155**, 224, 245

Contortionist Lydia Suarez performing for an audience, Hubert's Museum, N.Y.C. 1958, **95**, 243

Corpse with receding hairline and a toe tag, N.Y.C. 1959, **115**, 244

Couple arguing, Coney Island, N.Y. 1960, **159**, 245

Curse of the Werewolf, 232

Daughters of Jacob, 211, 211n8

Dead pigs hanging, N.Y.C. 1960, **145**, 245

Dean, James, **117**, 244

de Larverie, Stormé, **179**, 246

Deschin, Jacob, 208n3

Diane Arbus, 23, 220n3, 238

Diane Arbus Archive, 23, 208nn5–6, 219

Diane Arbus Revelations, 220, 221, 238

Dickinson, Flora Knapp, **135**, 245

Disneyland, **193**, 247, **269**

A Dominant Picture 1958, 247, **249**

Dostoyevsky, Fyodor, 212

Dracula, **111**, 212, 237, 244

Dracula, Jack, **175**, 213, 235–37, 246

Du magazine, 208n6

Elderly woman whispering to her dinner partner, Grand Opera Ball, N.Y.C. 1959, 226, 247, **253**

Empire Gym, **139**, 245

Empty snack bar, N.Y.C. 1957, **83**, 243

Esquire magazine, 228, 234
  see also "The Vertical Journey"

Estate of Diane Arbus, 219, 240
  hand of, 220, 220nn4–5, 221, 232

Evans, Walker, 203–5
  Subway Passengers, **204**, 216

Father and child at Italian Street Festival, N.Y.C. 1957, **73**, 242

Faurer, Louis, 205
  Times Square, NYC, **204**, 216

Female impersonator holding long gloves, Hempstead, L.I. 1959, **13**, 212, 225–26, 240

Female impersonator putting on lipstick, Hempstead, L.I. 1959, 225–26, 247, **251**

female impersonators, **13**, **123**, **129**, **171**, 211n8, 212, 225–26, 240, 244, 246, 247, **251**

film sleeves, 219, 220, 220nn4–5, **220**, 221, 226, **226**, 233

Fire Eater at a carnival, Palisades Park, N.J. 1957, **67**, 221, 242

Five members of The Monster Fan Club, N.Y.C. 1961, **181**, 246

Flora Knapp Dickinson, Honorary Regent of the Washington Heights Chapter of the Daughters of the American Revolution, N.Y.C. 1960, **135**, 245

42nd Street movie theater audience, N.Y.C. 1958, **107**, 244

Frank, Robert, 205
  Parade, Hoboken, New Jersey, **205**, 216

Friedlander, Lee, 205
  Shadow, New York City, **205**, 216

Ginsberg, Allen, 212
Girl and governess with baby carriage, N.Y.C. 1962, **195**, 247
Girl in her circus costume backstage, Palisades Park, N.J. 1960 **156**, 222, 245
Girl with a pointy hood and white schoolbag at the curb, N.Y.C. 1957, **56**, 242
Girl in profile looking up, N.Y.C. 1956, **29**, 241
Girl with schoolbooks stepping onto the curb, N.Y.C. 1957, **9**, 240
Girl with a white handbag, N.Y.C. 1960, 247, **255**
Grand Opera Ball, **131**, 226–28, 244, 247, **253**
Guggenheim Foundation, 214

Hagerstown, Md., *The Man Who Swallows Razor Blades, Hagerstown, Md. 1960*, **165**, 246
Hamid-Morton Circus, 222
Harrison, Ronald C., **186**, 233, 246
Headless woman, Palisades Park, N.J. 1961, **187**, 222, 247
Headstone for "Killer" at Bide a Wee Cemetery, Wantagh, N.Y. 1960, **143**, 245
Helping Hand Haven, 231
Hempstead, Long Island
Blonde female impersonator standing by a dressing table, Hempstead, L.I. 1959, **123**, 225–26, 244
Female impersonator holding long gloves, Hempstead, L.I. 1959, **13**, 212, 225–26, 240
Female impersonator putting on lipstick, Hempstead, L.I. 1959, 225–26, 247, **251**
Seated female impersonator in an open kimono, Hempstead, L.I. 1959, **129**, 225–26, 244
Hempstead Theater, 225–26
Hezekiah Trambles, "The Jungle Creep," on stage at Hubert's Museum, N.Y.C. 1960, **157**, 245
horror
Dracula, **111**, 212, 237, 244
Headless woman, Palisades Park, N.J. 1961, **187**, 222, 247
Monster Fan Club, **181**, 246
movies, **105**, **111**, **189**, 232, 234, 244

Screaming woman with blood on her hands 1961, **189**, 234, 247
subjects, 211, 234, **234**, **235**
Wax museum axe murderer, Coney Island, N.Y. 1959, **119**, 244
Horrors of the Black Museum, 234
Hubert's Museum, **95**, **125**, **157**, 235, 243, 244, 245
The Human Pincushion, Ronald C. Harrison, N.J. 1961, **186**, 233, 246
Hunt Bros. Circus, 222

I Am an American Day, 221, 221n7
Israel, Marvin, 208n6

Jack Dracula at a bar, New London, Conn. 1961, **175**, 213, 235–37, 246
James Dean in the wax museum, Coney Island, N.Y. 1959, **117**, 244
Jet magazine, 228
Jewel Box Revue, 211, 211n8, 225–26

Kid in black face, N.Y.C. 1957, **69**, 242
Kid in a hooded jacket aiming a gun, N.Y.C. 1957, **51**, 242
Kiss from "Baby Doll," N.Y.C. 1956, **47**, 241
Klein, William, 205
Christmas Shopping, Macy's, New York, **205**, 216

Lady on a bus, N.Y.C. 1957, **55**, **206**, 217, 220–21, 242
Lady in front of a portrait, N.Y.C. 1956, **7**, 240
Lady in the shower, Coney Island, N.Y. 1959, **121**, 224, **224**, 244
Lambert, Katheryn, **141**, 231, **231**, 245
Lange, Cecilia, 231, **231**
Lao Tzu, 212
Levinstein, Leon, 205
New York, **204**, 216
Levitt, Helen, 205
New York, **204**, 216
Levittown, **199**, 238, 247
Life magazine, 228
Little Italy, **73**, **99**, 242
Little man biting woman's breast, N.Y.C. 1958, **99**, 243
Loew's State Theater, 226
Long Island, 226n11, 238

Headstone for "Killer" at Bide a Wee Cemetery, Wantagh, N.Y. 1960, **143**, 245
Xmas tree in a living room in Levittown, L.I. 1962, **199**, 238, 247
see also Hempstead
Lugosi, Bela, **111**, 244

The Madman from Massachusetts in an empty bar, N.Y.C. 1960, **149**, 245
Makrina, Miss, **126**, 244
Man with a curious baby on the subway, N.Y.C. 1956, **43**, 241
Man in hat, trunks, socks and shoes, Coney Island, N.Y. 1960, **161**, 213, 246
Man holding a sleeping child, N.Y.C. 1957, **57**, 242
Man at the Municipal Shelter, holding up a dollar bill, N.Y.C. 1960, **137**, 245
Mannequin in evening gown, N.Y.C. 1956, **31**, 241
Man on screen being choked 1958, **105**, 244
The Man Who Swallows Razor Blades, Hagerstown, Md. 1960, **165**, 246
Man yelling in Times Square, N.Y.C. 1958, **88**, 243
Masked boy with friends, Coney Island, N.Y. 1957, **75**, 242–43
Mighty Mouse western cartoon 1958, **104**, 243
Miss Cecilia Lange and Miss Katheryn Lambert with some of their forty dogs, Brooklyn, N.Y. 1960, 231, **231**
Miss Katheryn Lambert with her dogs in the backyard, Brooklyn, N.Y. 1960, **141**, 231, 245
Miss Makrina, a Russian midget, in her kitchen, N.Y.C. 1959, **126**, 244
Miss Marian Seymour dancing with Baron Theo Von Roth at the Grand Opera Ball, N.Y.C. 1959, **131**, 226–28, 244
Miss Stormé de Larverie, the Lady Who Appears to be a Gentleman, N.Y.C. 1961, **179**, 246
Model, Lisette
Coney Island Bather, New York, 208n5, **208**, 217
photography class, 208, 208n3
Monster Fan Club, **181**, 246
Mood meter machine, N.Y.C. 1957, **65**, 242
morgue, 211, 226

Corpse with receding hairline and a toe tag, N.Y.C. 1959, **115**, 244
Mother Cabrini, a disinterred saint in her glass and gold casket, N.Y.C. 1960, **147**, 245
Mother contemplating her toddler, N.Y.C. 1956, **207**, 217
movies
Audience with projection booth, N.Y.C. 1958, **103**, 243
Bela Lugosi as Dracula on television 1958, **111**, 244
Blonde on screen about to be kissed 1958, **11**, 240
Clouds on screen at a drive-in movie, N.J. 1961, **183**, 211, 232, 246
A Dominant Picture 1958, 247, **249**
42nd Street movie theater audience, N.Y.C. 1958, **107**, 244
horror, **105**, **111**, **189**, 232, 234, 244
Kiss from "Baby Doll," N.Y.C. 1956, **47**, 241
Man on screen being choked 1958, **105**, 244
Mighty Mouse western cartoon 1958, **104**, 243
Movie theater usher standing by the box office, N.Y.C. 1956, **39**, 241
Mrs. Dagmar Patino at the Grand Opera Ball, N.Y.C. 1959, 226
Mulberry Street, **93**, 243
municipal shelter, **137**, 245
Museum of Modern Art (MoMA), 23, 208n6, 220, 220n3
Myers, C. Kilmer, 230n13

Newark Drive-In, 232
New Holland Hotel, **151**, 245
New Jersey
Clouds on screen at a drive-in movie, N.J. 1961, **183**, 211
The Human Pincushion, Ronald C. Harrison, N.J. 1961, **186**, 233, 246
Parade, Hoboken, New Jersey (Frank), **205**, 216
Siamese twins in a carnival tent, N.J. 1960, **167**, 246
Stripper with bare breasts sitting in her dressing room, Atlantic City, N.J. 1961, **185**, 213, 233, 246
see also Palisades Park

New London, Conn., *Jack Dracula at a bar, New London, Conn. 1961*, **175**, 213, 235–37, 246
New School for Social Research, 208n3
New York City
Central Park, **37**, **77**, 211, **211**, 212, 221, 222, 222n8, 241, 243, 247, **257**
Empire Gym, **139**, 245
42nd Street, **107**, 244
Grand Opera Ball, **131**, 226–28, 244, 247, **253**
Hubert's Museum, **95**, **125**, **157**, 243, 244, 245
Little Italy, **73**, 242
morgue, 211, 226
Mulberry Street, **93**, 243
municipal shelter, **137**, 245
New Holland Hotel, **151**, 245
"N.Y.C." in photograph titles, 223
photographs made in, 3, 7, 9, 15, 17, **27**, **29**, **31**, **33**, **34**, **35**, **39**, **41**, **43**, **45**, **47**, **49**, **51**, **53**, **55**, **56**, **57**, **59**, **61**, **63**, **65**, **69**, **83**, **87**, **89**, **91**, **97**, **99**, **101**, **103**, **107**, **109**, **113**, **115**, **126**, **127**, **133**, **135**, **145**, **147**, **149**, **153**, **155**, **169**, **171**, **177**, **179**, **181**, **191**, **195**, **197**, **204**, **205**, **206**, **207**, **209**, 211, 212, 213, 214, **215**, 217, 219–21, **221**, 224, 229–30, 240, 241, 242, 243, 244, 245, 246, 247, **255**
Times Square, **88**, 226, 243
New York Times, 222, 228
Nikon F camera, 214
Nikon S3 camera, 214
Norma and Gallo, members of a Brooklyn teen gang, N.Y.C. 1960, **153**, 224, 245
Notebook 1 (1958–59), **200–201**, 212, 267
Notebook 2 (1959), **24–25**, 267
Notebook 3 (1960), 231
Notebook 6 (1961), 237, **237**
Notebook 7 (1961), **234**
Notebook 9 (1962), 213, **213**, 217
notebooks, 211–12, 219, 226, 235

Old couple on a park bench, N.Y.C. 1958, **101**, 243
Old woman with hands raised in the ocean, Coney Island, N.Y. 1960, **163**, 246
Old woman in a hospital bed, N.Y.C. 1958, **113**, 244

Palisades Park, N.J., 221–22, 222n8
Clown in a fedora, Palisades Park, N.J. 1957, **79**, 221–22, 243
Fire Eater at a carnival, Palisades Park, N.J. 1957, **67**, 221, 242
Girl in her circus costume backstage, Palisades Park, N.J. 1960, **156**, 222, 245
Headless woman, Palisades Park, N.J. 1961, **187**, 222, 247
Sunny South Syncopaters and other sideshow banners at night, Palisades Park, N.J. 1957, **71**, 221–22, 242
Patino, Dagmar, 226
Patti, a resident of the New Holland Hotel seated on her bed, N.Y.C. 1960, **151**, 245
physique
A boy practicing physique posing at the Empire Gym, N.Y.C. 1960, **139**, 245
Contestant in a physique contest, N.Y.C. 1960, **155**, 224, 245
Picasso, Pablo, 212
Plato, 203, 212
print sleeves, **218**, 219, 219n2, 223, **223**, **224**, 238, **239**
Puddle on the sidewalk, N.Y.C. 1957, **49**, 242

Ratoucheff, Andy "Potato Chips," **125**, 244
Revelations, see *Diane Arbus Revelations*
Ringling Bros. and Barnum & Bailey Circus, 222
Rocks on wheels, Disneyland, Cal. 1962, 247, **269**
Rolleiflex camera, *see* Wide-Angle Rolleiflex

Sander, August, 208–9, 208n6
The Painter Anton Räderscheidt, **209**, 217
Santa Claus on the street with a lady passing, N.Y.C. 1956, **34**, 241
Screaming woman with blood on her hands 1961, **189**, 234, 247
Seated female impersonator with arms crossed on her bare chest, N.Y.C. 1960, **171**, 246
Seated female impersonator in an open kimono, Hempstead, L.I. 1959, **129**, 225–26, 244

Self-portrait with 35mm Contax D camera, 1959, **202**, 216
Seymour, Marian, **131**, 226–28, 244
Sheraton-East Hotel, 226
Show magazine, 234
Siamese twins in a carnival tent, N.J. 1960, **167**, 246
St. Augustine's Chapel, 230n13
Steichen, Edward, 208n6
Stoker, Bram, 212
Strand, Paul, 203–5
Portrait—New York, **204**, 216
Stripper with bare breasts sitting in her dressing room, Atlantic City, N.J. 1961, **185**, 213, 233, 246
Suarez, Lydia, **95**, 243
subway, **43**, **204**, 205, 216, 241
Sunny South Syncopaters and other sideshow banners at night, Palisades Park, N.J. 1957, **71**, 221–22, 242

Talese, Gay, 235n14
Tall partygoer in a taffeta dress, N.Y.C. 1962, **197**, 214, 247
Taxicab driver at the wheel with two passengers, N.Y.C. 1956, **45**, 241
Times Square, 88, **204**, 226, 243
Trambles, Hezekiah, **157**, 245
Trapeze act, N.Y.C. 1957, **59**, 242
Two Cha-Cha dancers performing for an audience, N.Y.C. 1958, **91**, 243
Two girls by a brick wall, N.Y.C. 1961, **177**, 246

Uncle Sam leaning on a cot at home, N.Y.C. 1960, **169**, 246

"The Vertical Journey" expense list, 226, **227**, 230
Von Roth, Theo, Baron, **131**, 226–28, 244

Wantagh, N.Y., *Headstone for "Killer" at Bide a Wee Cemetery, Wantagh, N.Y. 1960*, **143**, 245
Wax museum axe murderer, Coney Island, N.Y. 1959, **119**, 244
Wide-Angle Rolleiflex camera, 214
Wilde, Oscar, 212
Windblown headline on a dark pavement, N.Y.C. 1956, **3**, 211, 240

Winogrand, Garry, 205
Coney Island, New York, **205**, 216
Woman in a black hat with a pearl choker, N.Y.C. 1956, **33**, 241
Woman carrying a child in Central Park, N.Y.C. 1956, **37**, 211, 241
Woman with a change purse at a pastry counter, N.Y.C. 1958, **97**, 243
Woman with a crescent rhinestone brooch, N.Y.C. 1957, **63**, 242
Woman in a mink stole and bow shoes, N.Y.C. 1956, **35**, 213, 241
Woman on the street with her eyes closed, N.Y.C. 1956, **27**, 241
Woman on the street with parcels, N.Y.C. 1957, **209**, 217
Woman in white fur with a cigarette, Mulberry Street, N.Y.C. 1958, **93**, 243
Woman with white gloves and a pocket book, N.Y.C. 1956, **41**, 214, 241
Wrestlers in the ring, N.Y.C. 1958, **89**, 243

Xmas tree in a living room in Levittown, L.I. 1962, **199**, 238, 247

Young man with a paper bag at night, Coney Island, N.Y. 1957, **81**, 222–23, 243
Young man in a plaid coat with a toothpick, N.Y.C. 1961, **215**, 217

credits

photograph credits

204 Walker Evans: © Walker Evans Archive, The Metropolitan Museum of Art

Louis Faurer: © The Estate of Louis Faurer. Courtesy Howard Greenberg Gallery, New York

Leon Levinstein: © Howard Greenberg Gallery, New York

Helen Levitt: © Film Document LLC. Courtesy Galerie Thomas Zander, Cologne

Paul Strand: © Aperture Foundation Inc., Paul Strand Archive

205 Robert Frank: © 2016 Robert Frank from *The Americans*. Courtesy Pace/MacGill Gallery, New York

Lee Friedlander: © Lee Friedlander. Courtesy Fraenkel Gallery, San Francisco

William Klein: © William Klein. Courtesy Howard Greenberg Gallery, New York

Garry Winogrand: © The Estate of Garry Winogrand. Courtesy Fraenkel Gallery, San Francisco. © The Museum of Modern Art/Licensed by SCALA / Art Resource, NY

208 Lisette Model: © The Lisette Model Foundation, Inc. (1983). Used by permission. Courtesy baudoin lebon, Paris

209 August Sander: © 2016 Die Photographische Sammlung/SK Stiftung Kultur - August Sander Archiv, Cologne/ARS, NY

two-page spreads

24 Diane Arbus, Notebook 2 (1959), pp. [264–65]. L.2008.77.2.2

84 Diane Arbus, 1959 Appointment Book, September 13–14. L.2008.77.1.1

172 Diane Arbus, 1961 Appointment Book, July 5–6. L.2008.77.1.3

200 Diane Arbus, Notebook 1 (1958–59), pp. [238–39]. L.2008.77.2.1.

epigraphs

1 Diane Arbus to Bob and Lyn Meservey, letter, July 1957, quoted in *Diane Arbus Revelations* (New York: Random House, 2003), p. 141.

271 Diane Arbus, master class, March 1971, quoted in *Diane Arbus* (Millerton, N.Y.: Aperture, 1972), p. 14.

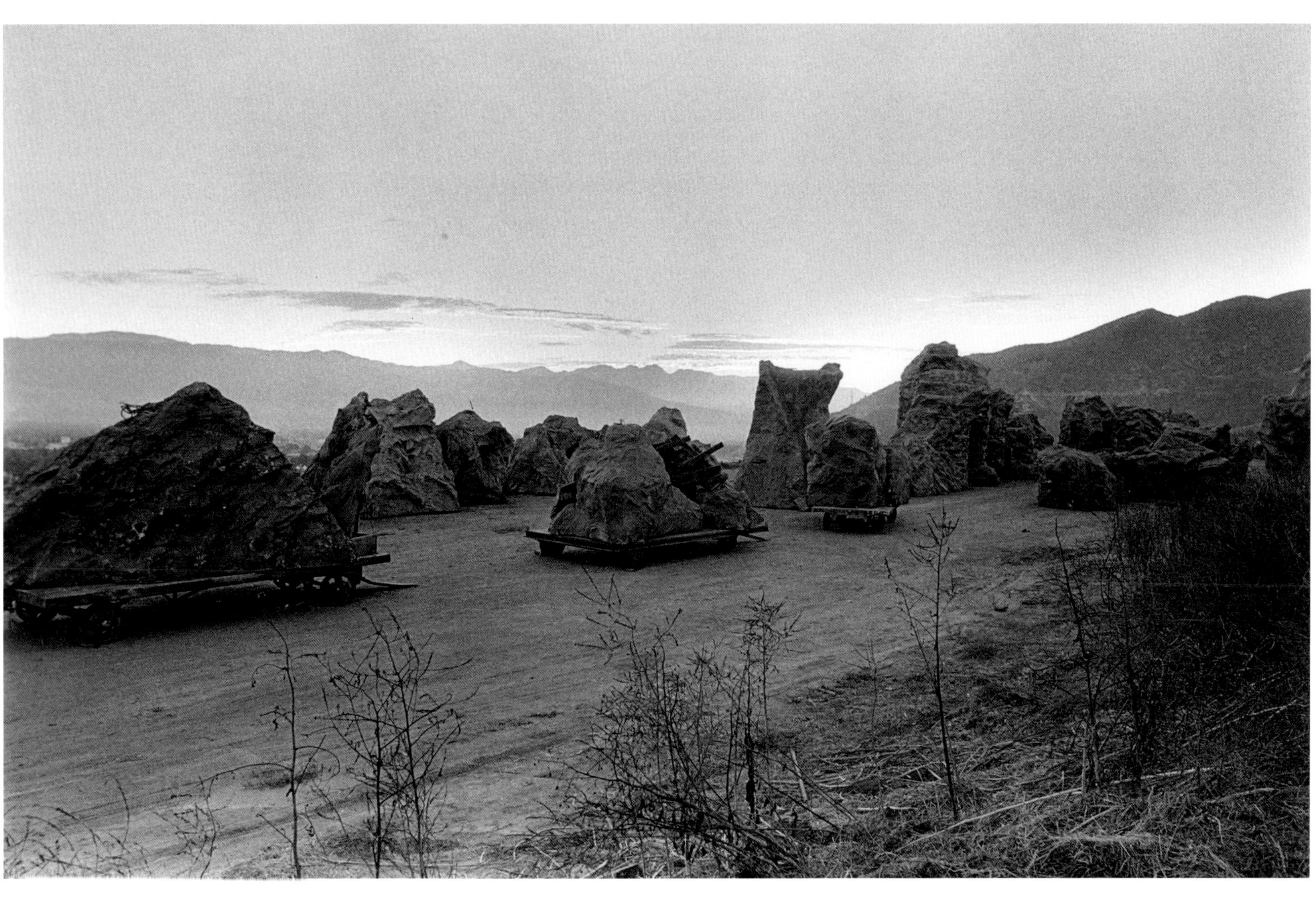

Rocks on wheels, Disneyland, Cal. 1962

The thing that's important to know is that you never know.
You're always sort of feeling your way.

This catalogue is published in conjunction with
"diane arbus: in the beginning," on view at
The Metropolitan Museum of Art, New York,
from July 12 through November 27, 2016,
and the San Francisco Museum of Modern Art,
from January 21 to April 30, 2017.

The exhibition is made possible in part by the
Alfred Stieglitz Society.

Additional support is provided by the
Art Mentor Foundation Lucerne.

Published by The Metropolitan Museum of Art, New York
Mark Polizzotti, Publisher and Editor in Chief
Gwen Roginsky, Associate Publisher and
    General Manager of Publications
Peter Antony, Chief Production Manager
Michael Sittenfeld, Senior Managing Editor

Edited by Kamilah Foreman
Designed by Daphne Geismar
Production by Peter Antony and Lauren Knighton
Image acquisitions and permissions by Elizabeth De Mase

Digital image files by Eileen Travell, The Photograph
Studio, The Metropolitan Museum of Art, unless
otherwise noted on p. 267.

Typeset in Elzevir
Printed on 150 gsm Tatami
Tritone separations by Martin Senn
Printed and bound by Brizzolis/El Viso, Madrid

Cover photograph: *The Backwards Man in his hotel room,
N.Y.C. 1961*. Copyright © The Estate of Diane Arbus

The Metropolitan Museum of Art endeavors to respect
copyright in a manner consistent with its nonprofit
educational mission. If you believe any material has been
included in this publication improperly, please contact
the Publications and Editorial Department.

The Metropolitan Museum of Art
1000 Fifth Avenue
New York, New York 10028
metmuseum.org

Distributed by
Yale University Press, New Haven
yalebooks.com/art

Cataloguing-in-Publication Data is available from the
Library of Congress.
ISBN 978-1-58839-595-5